**TIME**
**LIFE** ®
**BOOKS**

*Other Publications:*

*This volume is one of a series that explains and demonstrates
how to prepare various types of food, and that offers in each
book an international anthology of great recipes.*

# Sauces

BY
THE EDITORS OF TIME-LIFE BOOKS

TIME-LIFE BOOKS/ALEXANDRIA, VIRGINIA

*Cover: A serving ladle is lifted from a sauceboat of melted butter sauce (page 20). Made by gradually whisking cubes of cold butter into hot water, this smooth, light sauce is excellent with boiled or steamed vegetables.*

Time-Life Books Inc.
is a wholly owned subsidary of
**TIME INCORPORATED**

*Founder:* Henry R. Luce 1898-1967

*Editor-in-Chief:* Henry Anatole Grunwald
*President:* J. Richard Munro
*Chairman of the Board:* Ralph P. Davidson
*Executive Vice President:* Clifford J. Grum
*Editorial Director:* Ralph Graves
*Group Vice President, Books:* Joan D. Manley
*Vice Chairman:* Arthur Temple

**TIME-LIFE BOOKS INC.**

*Editor:* George Constable. *Executive Editor:* George Daniels. *Director of Design:* Louis Klein. *Board of Editors:* Dale M. Brown, Thomas A. Lewis, Martin Mann, Robert G. Mason, John Paul Porter, Gerry Schremp, Gerald Simons, Rosalind Stubenberg, Kit van Tulleken. *Director of Administration:* David L. Harrison. *Director of Research:* Carolyn L. Sackett. *Director of Photography:* John Conrad Weiser. *Design:* Arnold C. Holeywell (assistant director), Anne B. Landry (art coordinator), James J. Cox (quality control). *Research:* Jane Edwin (assistant director), Louise D. Forstall. *Copy Room:* Susan Galloway Goldberg (director), Celia Beattie. *Production:* Feliciano Madrid (director), Gordon E. Buck, Peter Inchauteguiz

*President:* Reginald K. Brack Jr. *Executive Vice Presidents:* John Steven Maxwell, David J. Walsh. *Vice Presidents:* George Artandi, Stephen L. Bair, Peter G. Barnes, Nicholas Benton, John L. Canova, Beatrice T. Dobie, James L. Mercer, Paul R. Stewart

**THE GOOD COOK**
The original version of this book was created in London for Time-Life Books B.V.
*European Editor:* John Paul Porter. *Photography Director:* Pamela Marke. *Planning Director:* Alan Lothian. *Chief of Research:* Jackie Matthews. *Chief Sub-Editor:* Ilse Gray. *Chief of Editorial Production:* Ellen Brush. *Quality Control:* Douglas Whitworth

Staff for *Sauces:* *Editor:* Ellen Galford. *Series Coordinator:* Deborah Litton. *Text Editor:* Jane Havell. *Anthology Editor:* Anne Jackson. *Staff Writers:* Alexandra Carlier, Sally Crawford, Thom Henvey. *Researchers:* Margaret Hall (principal), Stephanie Lee, Debra Raad. *Designer:* Cherry Doyle. *Sub-Editors:* Charles Boyle, Kate Cann, Frances Dixon, Sally Rowland. *Editorial Department:* Judith Heaton, Aquila Kegan, Lesley Kinahan, Debra Lelliot, Jane Lillicrap, Linda Mallett, Janet Matthew, Sylvia Osborne, Ros Smith, Molly Sutherland

U.S. Staff for *Sauces:* *Editor:* Gerry Schremp. *Designer:* Ellen Robling. *Chief Researcher:* Barbara Levitt. *Associate Editors:* Ellen B. Phillips (text), Marion F. Briggs (pictures). *Writer:* Rita Mullin. *Researchers:* Ann Ready (techniques), Patricia N. McKinney (anthology). *Assistant Designer:* Peg Schreiber. *Copy Coordinators:* Tonna Gibert, Nancy Lendved. *Art Assistant:* Mary L. Orr. *Picture Coordinator:* Nancy C. Scott. *Editorial Assistants:* Andrea Reynolds, Patricia Whiteford. *Special Contributor:* Christine B. Dove

CHIEF SERIES CONSULTANT

*Richard Olney,* an American, has lived and worked for some three decades in France, where he is highly regarded as an authority on food and wine. Author of *The French Menu Cookbook* and of the award-winning *Simple French Food,* he has also contributed to numerous gastronomic magazines in France and the United States, including the influential journals *Cuisine et Vins de France* and *La Revue du Vin de France.* He has directed cooking courses in France and the United States and is a member of several distinguished gastronomic and oenological societies, including L'Académie Internationale du Vin, La Confrérie des Chevaliers du Tastevin and La Commanderie du Bontemps de Médoc et des Graves. Working in London with the series editorial staff, he has been basically responsible for the planning of this volume, and has supervised the final selection of recipes submitted by other consultants. The United States edition of The Good Cook has been revised by the Editors of Time-Life Books to bring it into complete accord with American customs and usage.

CHIEF AMERICAN CONSULTANT
*Carol Cutler* is the author of a number of cookbooks, including the award-winning *The Six-Minute Soufflé and Other Culinary Delights* (republished as *Cuisine Rapide*). During the 12 years she lived in France, she studied at the Cordon Bleu and the École des Trois Gourmandes, and with private chefs. She is a member of the Cercle des Gourmettes, a long-established French food society limited to just 50 members, and a charter member of Les Dames d'Escoffier, Washington Chapter.

SPECIAL CONSULTANTS
*David Schwartz,* who was born in North Carolina, has run restaurants both in Boston and in London, and is the author of a book about chocolate. He prepared many of the dishes for the photographs in this volume.
*Jolene Worthington* received degrees from the Culinary Institute of America in Hyde Park, New York, and worked as a restaurant chef for many years. Formerly the Test Kitchen Chef in recipe development at *Cuisine* magazine, she contributes articles to food magazines and conducts cooking classes in Chicago. She has been responsible for demonstrating several of the step-by-step photographic sequences in this volume.

PHOTOGRAPHER
*Tom Belshaw* was born near London and started his working career in films. He now has his own studio in London. He specializes in food and still-life photography, undertaking both editorial and advertising assignments.

INTERNATIONAL CONSULTANTS
GREAT BRITAIN: *Jane Grigson* has written a number of books about food and has been a cookery correspondent for the London *Observer* since 1968. *Alan Davidson* is the author of several cookbooks and the founder of Prospect Books, which specializes in scholarly publications about food and cookery. FRANCE: *Michel Lemonnier,* the cofounder and vice president of Les Amitiés Gastronomiques Internationales, is a frequent lecturer on wine and vineyards. GERMANY: *Jochen Kuchenbecker* trained as a chef, but worked for 10 years as a food photographer in several European countries before opening his own restaurant in Hamburg. *Anne Brakemeier* the co-author of a number of cookbooks. ITALY: *Massimo Alberini* is a well-known food writer and journalist with a special interest in culinary history. His many books include *La Tavola all'Italiana, 4000 Anni a Tavola* and *100 Ricette Storiche.* THE NETHERLANDS: *Hugh Jans* has published cookbooks and recipes appear in several Dutch magazines.

Correspondents: Elisabeth Kraemer (Bonn); Margot Hapgood, Dorothy Bacon (London); Miriam Hsia, Lucy Voulgaris (New York); Maria Vincenza Aloisi, Josephine Brusle (Paris); Ann Natanson (Rome)
Valuable assistance was also provided by: Janny Hovinga (Amsterdam); Berta Julia (Barcelona); Bona Schmid (Milan); Mimi Murphy (Rome)

For information about any Time-Life book, please write:
Reader Information, Time-Life Books
541 North Fairbanks Court, Chicago, Illinois 60611

Library of Congress CIP data, page 176.

# CONTENTS

# Finishing Touches

n the kitchens of fine restaurants, the saucemaker, or *saucier,* as an honored place, second in importance only to the executive chef. The *saucier* functions with an adroitness and finesse worthy of a magician. Yet the art of sauce making, like the magician's sleight-of-hand, owes its diverse effects to the intelligent application of just a few basic skills.

There is nothing mysterious about good sauces. Some are simple and speedy, consisting of little more than a few spoonfuls of melted butter or the juices from a roast. Others are ambitious, demanding many ingredients and long simmering, but repaying these investments with a remarkable concentration of flavors. Whatever its elements or method, a sauce's purpose is always to enhance the food it accompanies, contributing the sum of its own flavor, color and texture to the whole.

Today the word "sauce" encompasses savory concoctions and sweet ones, and raw as well as cooked mixtures. Most sauces are liquid or, at the least, fluid enough to pour easily—but some are so thick they must be served with a spoon. The word derives from the Latin *salsus,* meaning "flavored with salt." Roman sauces certainly deserved the appellation: They were almost invariably seasoned with the potent condiment known as liquamen, produced from heavily salted and fermented fish.

Strong-flavored sauces that lent savor to almost every kind of food—and disguised the taste of bad meat—were to remain typical of Western cooking until the very end of the Middle Ages. The marinades used to tenderize meat, for instance, were necessarily based on acidic liquids—wine, vinegar or verjuice, the juice of unripe grapes or other sour fruit—that broke down tough meat fibers. Then, as now, resourceful cooks transformed marinades into sauces to accompany the cooked meat.

The art of cooking made great gains in sophistication as the modern era began. In 17th and 18th Century France, master cooks were courted and coveted by prospective employers; nobles and even kings dabbled in the kitchen. Sauces were not neglected. François Pierre La Varenne, sometimes called the father of classical French cuisine, published his magisterial *Le Cuisinier François* in 1651 and introduced the invaluable fat-and-flour sauce thickener known as a roux. Talented cooks named their creations for their patrons. Thus the Marquis de Béchamel achieved immortality through a white sauce *(pages 22-23),* and the memory of the Prince de Soubise lives on by virtue of an onion purée *(pages 38-39).*

Perhaps the most important legacy of this gastronomic golden age was a small group of basic formulations from which hundreds of variations spring. Sometimes called the "mother sauces," they comprise stock-based velouté or brown sauce; milk-based white sauce; hollandaise and other preparations derived from egg yolks. Another basic sauce came somewhat later: It took a century or two after the tomato's arrival from the New World before cooks shed the belief that its scarlet flesh was poison and realized how easily it broke down to a piquant purée.

Sauce cookery has had its fads and fashions: Types of thickening and specific ingredients fall into and out of favor, are taken up with the fervor of a religious conversion, then abandoned for new sensations (although rarely so eccentric as that proposed in 1920 by the Italian Futurist writer Marinetti, who suggested saucing meat with eau de Cologne). But the principles behind the making of honest sauces have changed relatively little, even if the equipment and ingredients available to the modern cook are beyond the wildest dreams of La Varenne.

Although every cuisine has its characteristic sauces, the French influence has been paramount in European cookery, and that predominance is reflected in the contents of this volume. The introductory pages include a guide to some useful herbs and spices, and a compendium of flavorings and garnishes—including a versatile chopped mushroom mixture that La Varenne himself invented for the Marquis D'Uxelles.

The sauces demonstrated in Chapter 1 are simple mixtures of harmonious ingredients: olive oil and wine vinegar stirred into a vinaigrette; melted butter sharpened into a creamy *beurre blanc* by the addition of a little reduced wine and vinegar; classic white sauce; and dessert sauces based on sugar and chocolate. Chapter 2 teaches the techniques for puréeing and cooking produce to form sauces ranging from fragrant, basil-scented *pesto* to fresh tomato and fruit sauces. The art of making stocks and stock-based sauces of consummate flavor and perfect clarity is the subject of the third chapter, while Chapter 4 demonstrates techniques for preparing egg-based sauces: gleaming mayonnaise; delicate hollandaise and its colorful derivatives, maltaise, béarnaise and Choron; savory and sweet sabayons; and the ingenious *sauce bâtarde,* swiftly prepared by beating egg yolks into water thickened with a roux.

The final chapter explores meat, fish and vegetable preparations that virtually create their own integral sauces while they cook. The principle of wasting none of the food's flavor is applied to a range of sautéed, roasted, poached and braised dishes, including an elaborate meat stew complete with garnishes *(pages 84-85).* These illustrated techniques are followed by an anthology of 220 sauce recipes, ancient and modern, putting into practice the principles presented in the first half of the book.

# A Panoply of Flavorings

### Fragrances from the Herb Garden

Among the array of herbs that serve a good cook, the dozen shown below are most useful for sauce making. With only a few exceptions, the herbs should be fresh. The intensity of flavor they impart will be determined by the stage of cooking at which they are introduced.

The usual function for assertive herbs is to lend background fragrance to a sauce's dominant flavor. Lengthy cooking, which draws the essence from such herbs, yields this effect. A classic combination of herbs scents long-simmered stocks that form sauce bases. Known as

a bouquet garni, the mixture is bundled for easy removal after the herbs render their flavors *(opposite, bottom)*.

When the object is to reveal the particular characters of fresh herbs, the leaves must go in at the very end of cooking so that none of their perfume is lost. For the traditional blend called fines herbes—chives, chervil, parsley and tarragon—the leaves are simply chopped to release oils, then whisked into a finished sauce. Or the leaves may be added to a compound butter *(page 12)* used to enrich a sauce.

Fresh herbs can also be used alone, to give a sauce a single scent. Basil, for instance, is essential to *pesto;* tarragon gives béarnaise its character; and mint is excellent for salad dressings. Spicy rosemary will enhance simple deglazing sauces for poultry or lamb.

Certain herbs—oregano, thyme and savory among them—are more flavorful when dried. The three together—augmented, perhaps, with marjoram or rosemary—compose a blend for use in a mirepoix *(page 8)*, or wherever mixed dried herbs are called for.

Flat-leafed parsley

Tarragon

Rosemary

Bay leaves

Chives

Chervil

Basil

Oregano

Spearmint

Winter savory

Marjoram

Thyme

## A Sampler of Spices

For most sauces, spices are as essential as salt. Peppercorns *(top row)* are the most familiar; black peppercorns retain their skins and are more assertive than white ones. Either should go into a sauce toward the end of cooking; long simmering makes them bitter. A mix of 10 parts peppercorns to one part aromatic allspice berries forms an unusual blend for grinding in a pepper mill.

Saffron *(center row)* lends color and a slightly bitter flavor to fish or poultry sauces. Juniper berries, with their piney taste, are traditionally used in game sauces. Fiery cayenne pepper is a natural partner for pungent sauces, especially those accompanying fish.

Sweet, aromatic nutmeg, more delicate mace—nutmeg's outer covering— and the spicy buds of the clove tree *(bottom row)* are surprisingly versatile. Used alone or in combination, they add flavor to concoctions as diverse as vegetable, bread and meat sauces.

Black peppercorns

White peppercorns

Allspice berries

Powdered saffron

Juniper berries

Cayenne pepper

Mace blades

Nutmegs

Cloves

## Assembling a Bouquet Garni

The most convenient flavoring for all stocks, and for sauces created as part of a braised or poached dish, is the bouquet garni: Herbs and aromatic vegetables bound into a neat package with string so that they can be conveniently added to and removed from the pot.

The vegetables—celery ribs and leek leaves in most cases—function as a wrapping, preventing the herbs from falling apart and dispersing in the liquid during lengthy cooking.

The herbal mainstays of a bouquet garni are bay leaf, thyme and parsley. The bay leaf and thyme can be either fresh or dried. Parsley, however, should always be fresh; for the strongest flavor, choose flat-leafed rather than curly parsley. Include the plant's aromatic stems and, if possible, the washed root. For variety, include other fresh or dried herbs—most notably rosemary, tarragon or savory—or even a small piece of orange or lemon peel.

1 **Preparing ingredients.** Cut the green leaves from a washed leek. Assemble flat-leafed parsley, a bay leaf, thyme sprigs, a celery rib, and some kitchen string or twine for tying.

2 **Tying the bundle.** Bunch the herbs together and wrap the leek greens and celery around them. Wind string tightly around the bundle from top to bottom, and knot the string firmly. Make a loop with the loose end of the string to make the bundle easy to handle.

# Subtle Effects from Diverse Additions

Specially prepared sauce enhancements are of two kinds. First are the liquid flavorings that are added early in the cooking and blend in completely. Second—and more diverse and versatile—are the garnishes: Added at the end of cooking, these are solid—or nearly so—and retain their individual characters while adding textural interest.

Among the simplest liquid flavorings are the juices of roasted meat *(right)*. Cleansed of fat, these form a rich essence for intensifying any sauce based on meat stock. Another and more assertive liquid flavoring is red wine that has simmered with aromatic vegetables *(page 10, bottom)* until the alcohol evaporates and the wine reduces to a scented concentrate for enriching fish, meat or game sauces.

Vegetables complement a broad range of sauces, but they must be softened for easy incorporation. Tomatoes should be peeled and seeded *(opposite, left);* brief cooking will turn them into a coarse purée, longer cooking into a denser, more velvety one. Red peppers must be peeled, too, but then the sweet flesh need simply be pounded to a paste or sieved *(opposite, right)*. Both tomato and pepper purées will combine smoothly with a vinaigrette or suffuse a white sauce or velouté with flavor and color.

Vegetables that lend aromatic support without becoming a part of the finished sauce need not be puréed. For example, mirepoix *(below)* is a blend of onions, carrots, celery and herbs, chopped and softened so that they render their flavors quickly when added to a stock. After cooking, the solids are strained out and the stock used as a sauce base. By contrast, the chopped mushroom mixture known as *duxelles (opposite, bottom)* acts as both a flavoring and a garnish. Cooked in butter, it makes an ideal supplement to any mild sauce—fish velouté, for instance *(page 53)*.

Foods that serve primarily for garnishing should be prepared as small pieces that provide a pleasing contrast to a smooth sauce. Tiny mushrooms can be blanched whole to whiten them—and, incidentally, to produce a flavoring liquid *(page 11, top right)*. Shellfish also provide both garnish and a flavoring liquid when they are cooked in a court bouillon *(page 10, top and center)*. Marrow *(page 11, bottom)* need only be diced and poached before use as a rich garnish for meat-based sauces.

The ultimate in sauce garnishes is, of course, fresh truffles, available during the winter months at specialty markets in large cities. Tough truffle skins should be peeled, but not wasted. Pounded to a paste, they provide a flavoring. The truffle flesh may be softened by simmering in butter and brandy *(page 11, left)*.

## Pan Juices from a Roast

1 **Pouring off juices.** Remove meat from its roasting pan. Using a towel to protect your hands, pour the juices into a small bowl.

2 **Removing surface fat.** Cool the juices, then refrigerate them until the fat rises to the surface and solidifies. Use a spoon to scrape off the fat; discard it.

## Mirepoix: Finely Diced Vegetables

1 **Dicing.** Chop onions fine. Slice carrots lengthwise into strips, then cut the strips into small cubes. Dice ribs of celery in the same way.

2 **Cooking.** Melt butter in a pan. Add the diced vegetables, mixed dried herbs (page 6) and salt. Then cook the mixture over low heat for about 30 minutes, stirring occasionally.

3 **Storing.** Transfer the mirepoix to a bowl, packing it down well. When it is cool, cover it with plastic wrap, pressing the wrap against the surface. Refrigerate the mixture until needed.

## Preliminary Treatment for Tomatoes

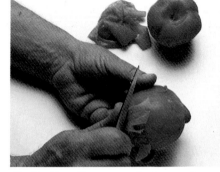

1 **Loosening skins.** Cut out the cores of tomatoes. Cut a cross in the base of each tomato and plunge the tomato into boiling water. After 10 seconds transfer it to cold water.

2 **Peeling.** Starting at the base where you have cut the cross, grip a section of skin between your thumb and the blade of a knife and strip it off. Repeat to strip off the rest of the skin.

3 **Seeding.** Halve each tomato crosswise to expose the seeds. Use your finger tips to dislodge the seed clusters, then shake each tomato half to rid it of any remaining seeds.

4 **Chopping.** Pile up the tomato halves together on a cutting board. Use a large, heavy knife to chop them into coarse pieces.

## Puréeing Sweet Peppers

1 **Peeling.** Broil peppers—turning them frequently—for four to 10 minutes, or until charred. Cool them under a damp towel. Pull out the stems and seeds; strip off the skins.

2 **Puréeing the flesh.** Remove stray seeds from the pepper flesh. Then use a pestle to purée the flesh through a sieve set over a bowl.

## Duxelles: A Marriage of Mushrooms and Onions

1 **Chopping mushrooms.** Using a heavy knife, slice whole mushrooms—and any mushroom stems left over from other preparations. Pile the slices together and chop them fine.

2 **Cooking duxelles.** Chop onions fine. Sauté them in butter until soft—about five minutes. Add the mushrooms; increase the heat and stir for 10 minutes, until the mushrooms look almost dry.

3 **Adding herbs.** Chop parsley fine and add it to the mixture in the pan. Add lemon juice and salt, grind in pepper, and continue cooking for two minutes, until the juices evaporate.

## Poaching and Peeling Shrimp

1 **Poaching.** Drop fresh shrimp into simmering white-wine court bouillon *(recipe, page 164)*. Poach them for one to three minutes, until firm and opaque. Drain the shrimp in a colander.

2 **Peeling.** Beginning at the head end, peel the shell and attached legs from each shrimp. Pinch off the tail, if you like. Reserve the shell, legs and tail for making compound butter *(page 13)*.

3 **Deveining.** Using a small, sharp knife, slit each shrimp along the center of the back to expose the dark intestinal vein. Pull out and discard the vein.

## Steaming Mussels in White Wine

1 **Preparing.** Scrub mussels, scrape them and discard the fibrous "beards." Put them in a pot with chopped onions, garlic, thyme, parsley and a bay leaf. Add a splash of white wine.

2 **Steaming.** Cover the pot and cook the mussels over high heat for five minutes, until the shells open. Drain in a colander over a bowl. Pluck the flesh from opened shells; discard unopened ones.

3 **Straining.** Strain the cooking liquid into another bowl through a sieve lined with dampened cheesecloth. Use some of the liquid to moisten the mussels; reserve the rest as a flavoring.

## Reducing Red Wine to Intensify Flavor

1 **Flavoring red wine.** Pour red wine into a nonreactive pan. Spoon in cooked mirepoix *(page 8)*—here, two heaping spoonfuls of mirepoix are added to one bottle of wine.

2 **Skimming.** Bring the wine to a boil; reduce the heat, set the pan half off the burner, then simmer until the wine reduces by two thirds. Remove scum as it rises on the cooler side of the liquid.

3 **Straining.** Strain the reduced wine into a bowl through a nylon or stainless-steel sieve lined with dampened cheesecloth. Squeeze out the liquid, then discard the solids.

## Capturing the Essence of Truffles

1 **Peeling truffles.** Using a small brush, scrub truffles under cold water. Peel the truffles with a vegetable peeler, dropping the peel into a mortar.

2 **Pounding peelings.** With a pestle, pound the truffle peelings to a paste. Refrigerate the paste in a covered container to add to sauce when truffles are used as a garnish.

3 **Cutting shapes.** Use a sharp knife to cut the truffles into thin slices. Leave the slices whole or cut them into whatever shape you like. Here, they are diced.

4 **Cooking.** Rub a heavy pan with garlic, and butter it heavily. Add the diced truffles and moisten them with brandy. Cover, and warm the truffles over very low heat for 10 to 15 minutes.

## Keeping Mushrooms White

1 **Adding lemon juice.** Slice off the stems of small button mushrooms. Put the caps in a nonreactive pan with salt, butter, a little water and a splash of lemon juice.

2 **Simmering.** Bring the liquid to a boil, then reduce the heat, cover, and simmer the mushrooms for three minutes. Cool and drain them, reserving the juices for flavoring.

## Extracting the Goodness of a Marrowbone

1 **Simmering the bones.** Add sections of beef marrowbone to a pan of boiling salted water. Bring the water back to a boil, reduce the heat and simmer, uncovered, for 10 minutes.

2 **Extracting the marrow.** Drain the bones. When cool enough to handle, lift each bone at its narrow end and give the bone a sharp shake—the marrow will slide out in a single piece.

3 **Dicing and cooking.** Chill the marrow to firm it, then cut it into small cubes. Poach the cubes in salted water for one or two minutes, until they are transparent; then drain them.

# Flavored Butters to Give Gloss

A simple way to lend body and sheen to hot sauces is to whisk in pieces of cold butter at the last minute. Plain butter will do, but a compound, or flavored, butter *(recipe, page 157)* will add a bonus of extra taste and color to the sauce.

As a base for compound butter, you will need unsalted butter soft enough to blend with flavorings. Do not warm the butter to soften it: Warming will make it oily. Instead, pound chilled butter with a rolling pin until it is malleable, then beat it with a spoon to force in air and lighten the butter—a process called creaming.

Almost any ingredient can be used to flavor the creamed butter, if the ingredient has been reduced to a paste fine enough for even amalgamation. Herbs for a green butter should be blanched to intensify their color before being pounded in a mortar *(right)* or puréed in a food mill or processor. Salt anchovies must be soaked to remove excess salt and to soften them so that they can be easily turned to paste *(below)*. The trimmings from shrimp, lobster or the crayfish shown on the opposite page must be pounded or puréed, then sieved to refine their texture, but the flavor of the resulting butter fully justifies the work involved.

All of these butters, once blended, may be kept in tightly covered containers in the refrigerator for two or three days or in the freezer for up to two weeks.

## Nuances of Flavor from Herbs and Shallots

1 **Blanching herbs.** Plunge parsley, chervil and tarragon leaves and chives into boiling salted water. Boil the herbs for about a minute, drain them, rinse in cold water and squeeze them dry.

2 **Adding shallots.** Put the blanched herbs in a mortar. Chop shallots fine. Cook them in boiling water for two minutes; drain them well and squeeze them dry. Add them to the herbs.

3 **Pounding ingredients.** Sprinkle a little coarse salt into the mortar, then pound the herbs and shallots until they form a paste. Add creamed butter and pound again to blend all the ingredients thoroughly.

4 **Sieving.** Using a plastic scraper, press a spoonful of the butter at a time through a fine-meshed sieve set over a plate. Scrape the mixture from the underside of the mesh onto the plate. Discard any fibers caught in the mesh.

## Piquancy from Pounded Anchovies

1 **Filleting.** Soak salt anchovies in cold water for 30 minutes. Split each anchovy lengthwise, remove the backbone and separate the fillets. Drain the fillets on paper towels.

2 **Pounding.** Place the anchovy fillets in a mortar and pound them to a paste. Add creamed butter and pound the mixture again until the ingredients are smoothly blended.

3 **Sieving.** Using a plastic scraper, press the butter mixture through a fine-meshed sieve. Scrape the mixture from the underside of the mesh. Put the flavored butter in a bowl; cover and chill it.

# The Delicacy of Crayfish

1 **Shelling crayfish.** Poach live crayfish in a white-wine court bouillon *(recipe, page 164)* until they are firm and opaque—about five minutes. Drain and cool. Twist the tail of each crayfish to snap it from the head. Put the heads in a mortar. Shell the tails, reserving the meat; add the shells to the mortar.

2 **Pounding.** Use a pestle to pound the shells and heads together. Continue to pound until the solids are reduced to a creamy paste containing fragments of shell—a process that will take up to 30 minutes. Alternatively, purée the shells and heads in a food processor, operating it in short bursts.

3 **Grinding the paste.** Fit a food mill with a coarse disk and set the mill over a large bowl. To remove pieces of shell from the paste, pass the mixture through the food mill, discarding any fragments that are left behind.

4 **Sieving the paste.** Set a drum sieve over a large plate. To eliminate all traces of debris and shell from the paste, and to ensure that it is smooth, press a little of the paste at a time through the drum sieve, using a plastic scraper. Scrape the paste from the underside of the mesh onto the plate.

5 **Blending the paste with butter.** Put butter that has been pounded to pliability into a large mixing bowl and beat it with a wooden spoon until it is fluffy. Add the crayfish paste and beat it into the butter *(above, left)* until the two elements are uniformly blended *(right)*. Cover the mixture and chill it well before using it.

# 1
# Simple Sauces
## Exploiting Elemental Ingredients

The legerdemain of sauce making is nowhere more remarkable, or easier to explain, than in the simple concoctions that turn kitchen staples into delicious accompaniments to salads, main courses, even desserts. A few ingredients—as ordinary as oil and butter, flour and sugar—are all that the *saucier* requires. An understanding of the chemical properties of such ingredients makes it possible to handle them artfully.

Some simple sauces, for example, owe their character to the ways fatty and watery ingredients emulsify, or become suspended in one another. The oil and vinegar that compose a vinaigrette unite when agitated, but soon separate when left to stand *(pages 16-17)*. By contrast, the acid of lemon juice acts on the protein of heavy cream within minutes to produce an emulsified dressing that stays firm for several hours *(pages 18-19)*. In tart cream, buttermilk replaces the lemon juice: The action is similar, but proceeds at an extremely slow pace, yielding an emulsion that keeps for days. Still another tactic for producing emulsified sauce is utilized in *beurre blanc,* where heat is applied as butter and liquid are whisked together *(pages 20-21)*.

Creating emulsions is not the only trick in the *saucier's* repertoire. When flour is heated in butter, the granules expand and soften so that they will absorb liquid readily. This basic flour mixture, or roux, is the foundation for white, or béchamel, sauces liquefied with milk and cream *(pages 22-23),* and also for velouté sauces liquefied with stock *(page 53)*. As with emulsified sauces, an inherent virtue of white sauce is that its basic flavor is mild and consequently it can be embellished in myriad ways: with grated cheese, chopped herbs, ground spices, puréed vegetables or compound butter.

Savory sauces are not the only kind a knowing cook can put together simply. Sugar, when cooked alone or in combination with water, dissolves and melts into a rich caramel *(page 25)*. When melted with butter and water, then enriched with cream, sugar turns into luxurious butterscotch. Like sugar, sweet or semisweet chocolate need only be melted to become saucelike. Adding a little cream makes it possible to melt chocolate over direct heat. Otherwise the chocolate burns easily and should be melted in a pan or bowl set above hot water; adding butter to the chocolate yields a sauce elegant enough to amply reward any extra effort.

elvety lemon cream sauce is
ivished onto a platter of peeled fresh
gs that were cut from top to stem into
uarters so that each fruit could be
pened up like a flower. The sauce is
ased on heavy cream, thickened as well
s flavored by lemon juice in which
esh mint leaves were crushed and
acerated *(pages 18-19)*.

# Vinaigrette and Its Variants

Vinaigrette is no more than vinegar, oil and seasonings, stirred briskly until the ingredients blend and the drops of vinegar are trapped within the oil. In its most pristine form *(top demonstration; recipe, page 158)*, vinaigrette is the classic dressing for green salads and cold vegetables such as asparagus or artichokes. Combined with extra flavorings *(bottom demonstrations)*, it becomes the basis for a family of sauces that complement meat, poultry, fish and shellfish.

Any vinaigrette is only as good as its ingredients. For a robust taste, choose wine vinegar—preferably an Orleans-process vinegar, produced by fermenting wine in wood barrels, which endow it with a nutty undertone. The red wine version is more assertive than the white.

To vary the sauce, you can experiment with sherry vinegar, which is rich and sweet, or Asian rice vinegars: The Chinese type has an acidic sharpness; the Japanese is mild and sweet.

Oils differ as much as vinegars do. Olive oil has an inimitable fruity flavor, at its best in oils labeled "first pressing virgin" or *"extra vierge."* Walnut and hazelnut oils lend a nutty quality, whereas peanut oil, like corn and safflower oils, is so mild as to be almost flavorless.

Stir the vinegar and oil together just before serving the vinaigrette: Left to stand, the emulsion soon separates. The usual proportions for vinaigrette are one part vinegar to four parts oil, but the ratio can be varied to suit the food the sauce accompanies or the other flavorings in the dressing. Slightly bitter salad greens, such as chicory, endive and rocket, call for more vinegar than does Bibb or Boston lettuce. Less vinegar is needed if you add acidic flavorings—puréed raw tomatoes or peppers, for example.

Flavorings for a vinaigrette can be as simple as a dash of prepared mustard, a few spoonfuls of chopped fresh herbs or a bit of pounded garlic, or as complex as the herb-and-spinach blend in green vinaigrette, known in Italy as *salsa verde.*

As well as improvising flavorings, you can replace the basic ingredients. Lemon juice can substitute for vinegar, for example, and a favorite dressing for a salad of pungent dandelion leaves calls for hot bacon fat rather than oil.

## Oil and Vinegar: The Classic Combination

1 **Blending ingredients.** Put salt and freshly ground pepper in a bowl. Stir in red wine vinegar *(above, left)* and continue stirring until the salt dissolves. Stirring vigorously, pour in olive oil *(right)*: Use about four parts of oil to one part of vinegar. To give the salad greens a thin coating of dressing, allow about ½ cup [125 ml.] of vinaigrette for each quart [1 liter] of greens. If you are not using the vinaigrette immediately, stir it again just before serving.

## Intensity of Hue from Ripe Tomatoes

1 **Flavoring.** Dissolve salt in wine vinegar. Peel and seed tomatoes and cut them into chunks *(page 9)*. Press them through a fine-meshed sieve set over a bowl. Add the tomato purée to the vinegar and stir. Pour in oil gradually, stirring the mixture until it is blended.

2 **Serving the sauce.** Just before serving, stir the sauce thoroughly again. Here, it is spooned over veal brains that have been soaked in several cleansing changes of cold water, peeled, poached in a white-wine court bouillon *(recipe, page 164)* for 25 minutes, then weighted, cooled and sliced.

2 **Dressing a salad.** Pour the vinaigrette over a salad—in this case, composed of chicory, corn salad, oakleaf lettuce, watercress, chervil and chopped herbs. Using your hands, toss the salad thoroughly until the leaves are evenly coated (*inset*).

## A Pungent Green Dressing

**Pounding.** Soak, fillet, rinse and dry salt anchovies (*page 12*). In a large mortar, pound the anchovies with peeled garlic cloves and coarse salt until the mixture forms a smooth paste.

2 **Adding herbs.** With the pestle, stir in vinegar and then oil. Add chopped herbs—parsley, chives, tarragon, basil and chervil. Finally, stir in chopped capers and spinach that has been parboiled for 30 seconds, drained, squeezed dry and chopped.

3 **Serving.** Present the vinaigrette in the mortar or a bowl. In this instance, the sauce is served with a dish of mixed poached meats—beef shank, corned beef tongue, pork sausage and chicken.

# Capitalizing on Cream

Like the vinaigrettes shown on pages 16-17, thickened cream sauces combine fat—in this case, from the cream—with an acid. However, unlike vinaigrettes, cream sauces can be prepared well in advance of serving.

The most basic of these sauces—lemon cream—mixes heavy cream with mint-infused lemon juice *(top demonstration; recipe, page 158)*. The cream is whisked into the strained lemon juice gradually to prevent curdling. As they blend, the acidic lemon thickens the mixture until, after about 10 minutes, it falls from a raised whisk in ribbons—a consistency ideal for dressing a tossed green salad or, as here, embellishing figs. The sauce can be served immediately or refrigerated for up to three hours.

Instead of being tinged with mint, lemon cream can be spiced with dry mustard, ground ginger or cayenne pepper. A lighter-textured, sharper-tasting variation can be made by flavoring the lemon juice with red-pepper purée and whisking in light cream *(right, bottom)*.

An American version of the classic thickened French cream known as *crème fraîche* is tart cream *(opposite, bottom)*. It consists of heavy cream that is fermented slightly by a mildly acidic cultured dairy product such as buttermilk, yogurt or commercial sour cream. Heated to 85° F. [30° C.] and left to stand at room temperature for 24 hours, tart cream becomes thick enough to hold its shape in a spoon. If covered and refrigerated, tart cream can be kept for up to a week before being used to sauce salads, main courses or desserts.

## A Rich Alliance with Lemon

**1 Infusing with mint.** Squeeze a lemon and strain the juice into a bowl. Add fresh mint leaves and crush them lightly with a pestle. Let the bruised mint macerate in the juice for at least 15 minutes to release its flavor, then strain the liquid and discard the mint leaves.

**2 Pouring in cream.** Allowing about 1 cup [¼ liter] of heavy cream for each lemon used, pour cream into the lemon juice in a thin stream. Stir the mixture constantly with a whisk to incorporate the cream and thicken the mixture.

## Tinting Cream with Pepper Purée

**1 Adding red-pepper purée.** Put salt and pepper in a bowl and add lemon juice, stirring until all of the salt is dissolved. Stir in a red-pepper purée (page 9). Stir light cream into the red-pepper mixture as for lemon cream (above). Continue adding cream until the sauce has reached the color and consistency desired.

**2 Serving.** Serve the red-pepper and cream sauce with salads, poached fish or—as here—fresh shrimp that have been poached in a court bouillon (page 10, top), cooled and peeled.

**Testing consistency.** Continue stirring until the sauce holds firm peaks when the spoon is lifted. Use the finished sauce at once or cover and refrigerate it for up to three hours. Here, it is served with fresh figs that were peeled, slit and opened into quarters, then garnished with strips of prosciutto and whole fresh mint leaves.

## Crème Fraîche, American-Style

**Warming the cream.** In an enameled pan, stir buttermilk and cream over low heat until they reach 85° F. [30° C.] as measured on a meat-and-yeast thermometer. Pour the mixture into a jar or crock, cover and let stand at room temperature (60° to 85° F. [15° to 30° C.]) for up to 24 hours.

2 **Checking the consistency.** When a spoonful of the mixture poured back onto the surface forms soft peaks, the cream is ready to be served. Serve immediately, or cover and store in the refrigerator for up to a week.

3 **Spooning crème fraîche.** Spoon the mixture over a hot baked apple glazed with brown sugar. The sauce's slightly biting flavor will provide a complement to the apple's sweetness.

# Melted Butter, Whisked with Vinegar

When cubes of cold butter are whisked gradually into a small amount of liquid over heat, the mixture will expand—or mount—to form a smooth, creamy sauce. For the whipped butter sauce known in France as *beurre blanc* and classically served with poached fish, the liquid is a piquant reduction of wine, vinegar and chopped shallots *(right; recipe, page 157)*. For a mild sauce, lighter in texture and flavored by just the fresh butter itself, the only added ingredient is water *(box)*. Such a sauce is suitable for serving with hot, plainly cooked vegetables.

The liquid reduction for *beurre blanc* should be prepared from good dry white wine and high-quality white wine vinegar so that the mixture will be rich tasting but colorless. You can alter the intensity of the sauce's flavor by using anywhere from ½ to 1 pound of butter [¼ to ½ kg.] for each cup [¼ liter] of liquid.

The secret of perfectly smooth mounted butter sauce is to blend the butter and liquid in such a way that the butter softens and thickens without melting and thus becoming oily. Before you begin to whisk in the butter, the heat must be adjusted to keep the liquid warm, rather than hot. A heat-diffusing pad is an invaluable aid in maintaining the liquid at an even, low temperature. The butter itself must be cold: Take it from the refrigerator just before cutting it into cubes, and add the cubes to the liquid right away. To keep the sauce temperature constant, the butter should be incorporated in small batches and each batch whisked until it is almost completely absorbed before more cubes are added.

Butter sauces should be served without delay since they solidify as they cool. If any sauce remains, it can be refrigerated for use later. Cooled and set, *beurre blanc* can be used—like a compound butter *(pages 20-21)*—as a finish for other sauces. Both leftover *beurre blanc* and plain butter sauce can also be cut into cubes and allowed to melt over grilled fish or meat, or hot vegetables.

1 **Chopping shallots.** Pour dry white wine and white wine vinegar into a heavy, nonreactive pan. Peel shallots and halve them lengthwise. Set each half with its cut side down on a work surface and slice it horizontally; then cut lengthwise across the slices to make strips, and across the strips to produce fine dice.

2 **Reducing the liquid.** Add the shallots to the pan. Cook the mixture over medium heat. When it boils, lower the heat to maintain a simmer, and continue to cook until the liquid becomes syrupy and is reduced to 1 to 2 tablespoons [15 to 30 ml.].

## A Variation Made with Water

1 **Adding butter.** Cut cold butter into cubes. In a heavy pan, bring water almost to a boil, allowing 2 tablespoons [30 ml.] for each ½ pound [¼ kg.] of butter; add seasoning. Over very low heat—using, if you like, a heat-diffusing pad—add butter, a few cubes at a time, whisking well before adding more. The mixture will become light and creamy.

2 **Serving the sauce.** Transfer the sauce to a warmed sauceboat or serve it directly from the pan. Immediately pour the butter sauce over the main dish—in this case, spears of boiled broccoli.

3 **Adding butter.** Remove the pan from the heat; season the mixture with salt and white pepper and let it cool for a few seconds. Meanwhile, cut cold butter into cubes. Put the pan on a heat-diffusing pad set over low heat and add the butter a few cubes at a time. Whisk until each addition has almost disappeared before adding more butter.

4 **Whisking.** Continue to add the butter by small amounts, whisking constantly. As more butter is added, the sauce will thicken slightly until finally it has the consistency of light cream.

5 **Serving the sauce.** Transfer the sauce immediately to a warmed sauceboat *(left)*: Take care that the vessel is not too hot, lest it make the sauce oily. Alternatively, you can serve the sauce from the pan. Ladle the sauce over fish—here, a piece of poached halibut *(below)*.

# White Sauce: A Versatile Foundation

One of the most useful thickening agents in the whole repertoire of sauce making is a roux—butter and flour blended to a smooth paste over gentle heat. The white sauce shown at right *(recipe, page 156)* is perhaps the most fundamental roux-based sauce, consisting simply of the paste itself, milk and a little cream.

To make the roux, the butter is first melted so that the flour will combine with it smoothly and evenly. After the flour has been stirred in, the resulting paste is cooked for only a minute or two—until it begins to bubble—before milk is added. Longer cooking at this stage would not only lessen the flour's thickening power but discolor the roux and hence the finished sauce.

Once the milk has been added, the mixture should be brought to a boil while being whisked to prevent lumps, and then simmered gently for at least 45 minutes. This long cooking improves both the texture and the flavor of the sauce: The liquid reduces and thickens, and any taste of raw flour disappears. After sieving, the sauce is seasoned with salt and white pepper, then thinned with cream until it has the consistency desired.

The blandness of a plain white sauce is an invitation to flavorings and colorings, which are easily incorporated at this stage. With the pan removed from the heat, the sauce can be enlivened with any of the compound butters shown on pages 12-13, or grated cheese, finely chopped herbs or capers, or a spoonful of prepared mustard. Here, for example, white sauce is turned into a Nantua sauce with the addition of crayfish butter *(right, bottom)* and into a Mornay with the addition of cheese *(opposite, bottom)*.

The versatility of a white sauce does not end with the variety of flavorings it can accept. The sauce itself can be used as a cooking medium: Thinned with extra cream to allow for further reduction in the oven, the sauce can be poured over prepared fish or vegetables, and this dish cooked to make a golden gratin.

## A Basic Blend Enriched with Cream

1 **Adding milk.** Melt butter in a heavy pan. When the butter foams, shake an approximately equal amount of flour evenly over its surface. With a whisk, stir the flour rapidly into the butter. Cook the resulting paste for a minute or so, then slowly pour in cold milk, whisking the mixture continuously.

2 **Cooking the sauce.** Increase the heat and bring the sauce to a boil—sti whisking constantly to prevent the formation of lumps. Season with a little salt. Reduce the heat to very low and simmer the sauce gently for at lea 45 minutes. To keep the sauce from sticking to the pan, stir it from time to tim with a wooden spoon or a whisk.

## Nantua: Finishing with Crayfish Butter

1 **Adding flavored butter.** Prepare and chill crayfish butter *(page 13)*. Break the butter into rough pieces. Make a white sauce *(Steps 1 to 4, top)*; remove the pan from the heat and place it on a trivet. Add the crayfish butter, a handful at a time, stirring continuously.

2 **Serving.** When the mixture is evenly blended, pour the sauce into a warme sauceboat. Serve this sauce with any poached, delicately flavored fish such turbot, flounder, sole or—as here—monkfish. You can also use it to make gratin of crayfish tails.

**3** **Straining the sauce.** Place a sieve over a mixing bowl or a second saucepan. Pour the sauce into the sieve and let it drain through without pressing the mixture. Return the strained sauce to the heat.

**4** **Finishing with cream.** To enrich the sauce and thin it to the right consistency, whisk in heavy cream. Add white pepper to taste, and, if you like, a little freshly grated nutmeg. Serve at once over vegetables, or finish the sauce with additional flavoring.

## Mornay: Sharpening with Cheese

**Adding grated cheese.** Grate firm cheese fine—in this case, equal amounts of Gruyère and Parmesan. Make a white sauce (Steps 1 to 4, top), using extra cream to give it a thin consistency. Off the heat, add the grated cheese to the sauce and stir until it is melted.

**2** **Pouring on the sauce.** Arrange prepared vegetables—here, boiled celery—in a gratin dish. Ladle the Mornay sauce over the vegetables, then sprinkle more grated cheese on top.

**3** **Serving the gratin.** Put the gratin dish in an oven preheated to 375° F. [190° C.]. After 15 to 20 minutes, when the sauce is slightly reduced and thickened and the surface is pale golden, remove the vegetable from the oven. Serve the gratin straight from the dish.

# A Melding of Bread and Milk

A rustic relation of the roux shown on page 22—perhaps, in fact, its ancestor—is crumbled bread, which has been used from time immemorial to turn hot liquids into sauces. The bread is merely broken or torn into small pieces and simmered in the liquid until these disintegrate. Whisking then smooths the sauce.

The paradigm of bread sauces is the blend of white bread and milk demonstrated here *(recipe, page 158)* and traditionally served in England as a complement to roasted fowl. The bread gives the sauce a slight sweetness that, in this case, is balanced by infusing the sauce with onion, clove, bay leaf and mace. The aromatics are added in their whole forms so that they can be conveniently lifted out of the bread sauce after they have released their flavors.

To vary the flavor, the onion might be replaced by whole shallots or garlic cloves or by chunks of celery or such roots as parsnips or turnips. Whole peppercorns or allspice may be included in the seasoning; so might sprigs of such herbs as thyme, tarragon or rosemary.

The consistency of the sauce will depend primarily on the ratio of bread to milk. As a general rule, allow two 1-inch [2½-cm.] slices of firm, homemade-style white bread for each cup [¼ liter] of milk to yield a sauce thick enough to hold its shape in a spoon.

Here, a dollop of heavy cream is stirred in at the last minute to enrich the sauce; whisking in cold butter pieces gives the sauce a silky finish. For piquancy, fresh horseradish could be grated into the mixture just before it is served.

**1 Adding bread.** Remove the crusts from stale, firm-textured white bread and tear the bread into pieces. In a pan, combine milk, an onion stuck with one or two whole cloves, a blade of mace, a bay leaf and salt. Bring the milk to a boil, then lower the heat and add the bread.

**2 Removing flavorings.** Over low heat, simmer the bread, milk and flavorings for about 20 minutes, or until the bread has disintegrated. Remove the onion, mace blade and bay leaf and discard them.

**3 Finishing the sauce.** Whisk the sauce to give it a smooth texture. If it is not thick enough, stir in fresh white bread crumbs and cook it for a few minutes longer. If additional richness is desired, whisk in heavy cream, then remove the pan from the heat. To finish the sauce, whisk in pieces of cold butter, a few at a time.

**4 Serving the sauce.** Transfer the sauce to a warmed bowl or sauceboat. Serve the hot bread sauce with roasted poultry such as chicken or turkey or with game birds—roast partridge is shown.

# Caramel: A Gleaming Pool of Molten Sugar

Caramel sauce—a golden crown for everything from simple puddings and ice cream to glamorous cream puffs—consists only of sugar syrup that is boiled to the caramel stage and diluted with water, as shown here *(recipe, page 167)*. The syrup is a dense solution of granulated sugar and water, combined in a ratio of only 1 cup [¼ liter] of water for each 2 cups [½ liter] of sugar. In this concentration the water evaporates relatively fast, thus speeding the transformation of the sugar into caramel.

Before the boiling can begin, the solution must be stirred gently over low heat until the sugar has dissolved completely. If even a few granules are left intact, they will regroup into crystals when the mixture is boiled, and the crystals will increase in size and number to eventually turn the syrup into a solid mass.

As soon as the solution is smooth, the sides of the pan should be wiped down with a moistened pastry brush to dissolve sugar granules that might have splashed up despite careful stirring. Or the pan may be covered briefly so that stray granules will be washed down from the sides by steam condensing on the lid.

When the syrup is absolutely clear, all stirring should stop. Agitation may trigger crystallization. The heat under the pan is then increased to high and, when the syrup comes to a boil, the burner adjusted to keep the syrup at a bubble.

After the sugar has been caramelized and thinned with water *(Step 2)*, the sauce can be served immediately. Alternatively, it can be cooled, transferred to a tightly covered container and kept refrigerated indefinitely; the sauce will not crystallize or harden when cold and, if desired, can be easily rewarmed over gentle direct heat for serving.

1 **Dissolving sugar.** Combine cold water and granulated sugar in a heavy pan. Over low heat, stir gently until the sugar dissolves completely. If the mixture begins to boil before all of the sugar has dissolved, remove it from the heat but continue to stir it. After a few seconds return the syrup to the heat.

2 **Diluting caramel.** Wipe down the syrup with a pastry brush that has been dipped in hot water. Then bring the syrup to a boil without stirring it, and boil it undisturbed until it turns reddish amber—about 20 minutes. To arrest further cooking, dip the pan briefly in ice water. Set the pan on a trivet and pour in cold water.

3 **Dissolving the caramel.** Return the pan to low heat. Stir the water and caramel until the caramel is smoothly dissolved—three or four minutes.

4 **Serving caramel sauce.** Pour the sauce into a pitcher and serve it hot or cold, with a hot or cold dessert. Here, hot caramel sauce is poured over a portion of just-baked bread pudding.

# A Trio of Dessert Sauces

Sugar and chocolate, melted and combined with butter, cream or both, form sumptuous, candy-like sauces that can turn the end of any meal into a celebration. The techniques for cooking these sauces vary with the ingredients, but none requires more than patience and a steady hand.

Melting sugar is the first step in preparing the creamy butterscotch shown at right (recipe, page 153). Like the caramel sauce on page 25, butterscotch starts as a sugar-syrup solution—in this case, based on brown sugar. Besides water, the solution contains corn syrup as an additional liquid, and butter for enrichment. As the syrup cooks, it becomes increasingly concentrated and its temperature rises. To achieve a perfectly thickened but pourable syrup, its temperature should be watched with a candy thermometer and its consistency should be checked with the soft-ball test demonstrated in Step 2. When the syrup forms an easily flattened ball, the syrup is ready for mixing with vanilla extract and

heavy cream, which helps give butterscotch a taste as lush as its texture.

Chocolate sauces also require cooking and—because chocolate scorches easily—careful monitoring of temperature. When pieces of chocolate are combined with a generous amount of heavy cream, the liquid surrounds and insulates the chocolate so that the sauce can be safely prepared in a heavy pan over direct heat.

For a slightly thicker chocolate sauce, the chocolate pieces are moistened with a little water and melted in a bowl or pot suspended over hot water (opposite, bottom). Bits of butter are then stirred into the melted chocolate to create an elegant, silky sauce.

Chocolate sauces have to be served warm; if allowed to cool they will solidify. Butterscotch can be served at room temperature, but if chilled, it too will become impossible to pour. All of these sauces will keep, covered and refrigerated, for up to two weeks. To return them to a pouring consistency, reheat them by the method you used to cook them originally.

## Lush Butterscotch

1 **Dissolving sugar.** Put brown sugar, light corn syrup, water and butter in a heavy pan. Stir over medium heat until the butter melts and the sugar dissolves. Stop stirring, insert a candy thermometer, and boil the syrup until it reaches 234° to 240° F. [112° to 116° C.]. Dip the pan in ice water to arrest the cooking.

## Delicate Chocolate Cream

1 **Heating the ingredients.** Pour heavy cream into a saucepan. Add pieces of chocolate—semisweet chocolate is used here—and set the pan over low heat. Stir the ingredients with a wooden spoon until the chocolate melts and the cream comes to a boil.

2 **Blending the chocolate.** Continue stirring until the chocolate mixture becomes smooth and thickly coats the spoon. Allow the sauce to cool slightly, then use it immediately. If cooled completely it will harden.

3 **Serving the sauce.** Transfer the hot sauce to a warmed pitcher or serve it directly from the pan. It can accompany cold desserts or hot ones, such as this crepe filled with orange soufflé.

2 **Testing the consistency.** Place a spoonful of syrup in ice water. Mold the cooled syrup into a ball, then lift it out of the water. Squeeze the ball gently between your finger and thumb. If it holds its shape under the water but rapidly flattens when taken out, the syrup has reached the soft-ball stage.

3 **Stirring in cream.** If the sugar syrup is too liquid, return it to the heat and test it again when the temperature has risen by a few degrees. Once the syrup has reached the soft-ball stage, let it cool slightly. Pour in heavy cream, add vanilla extract and stir until the syrup and cream are blended.

4 **Serving the sauce.** Serve the sauce warm or cool. If you are serving it over ice cream, as shown above, the sauce should not be meltingly hot. If you refrigerate the sauce to store it, remove the sauce from the refrigerator an hour or so before serving, so that it will pour easily.

## An Amalgam of Chocolate and Butter

1 **Melting chocolate.** Break semisweet or sweet chocolate into pieces and put them in a heatproof bowl with a little cold water. Suspend the bowl on the rim of a pan partially filled with hot—not boiling—water and set over medium heat. Stir the chocolate until all of the pieces have melted smoothly.

2 **Incorporating butter.** Cut cold butter into cubes—allowing about 4 tablespoons [60 ml.] of butter for every ½ pound [¼ kg.] of chocolate. Remove the pan from the heat and stir a few butter cubes into the chocolate. When the butter is blended in, add more. Continue until all of the butter is incorporated and the mixture is smooth.

3 **Serving the sauce.** Serve the chocolate sauce immediately, while it is still hot: The sauce sets as it cools. Here, the sauce is poured over puffs of chou pastry filled with ice cream.

# 2
# Vegetable and Fruit Sauces
## Matching Methods to Materials

Binding purées with oil
Cream and butter enrichments
White sauce used as a thickener
Sieving raw and cooked fruits
How to handle cornstarch

A golden-hued carrot sauce is poured into a warmed sauceboat. Cooked gently with butter, sugar and a little water, the carrots were glazed over high heat, then puréed in a food processor. Reheated to serving temperature, the purée was mixed with cream and finished with butter (pages 36-37).

Indispensable for grace notes of flavor and color in such concoctions as vinaigrette or lemon cream *(pages 16-19)*, vegetables and fruits may also play a dominant role in sauces. Produce of every sort has potential—predictable types such as fresh tomatoes, and unexpected ones such as dried beans. The ranks of vegetable and fruit candidates for the sauce pot are further swelled by mild-mannered herbs that can be used as leafy greens—basil and parsley among them—and by nuts, which botanists classify as dry fruits.

To achieve a saucelike consistency, vegetables and most fruits must first be reduced to purées. Cooking alone will break down peeled tomatoes *(pages 34-35)* or apples *(pages 40-41)*, turning their flesh into relatively smooth sauces. But most ingredients need to be pounded, mashed, sieved, milled or processed—either at the raw stage or after they have been cooked to tenderize them or to drive off excess liquid. The choice of puréeing methods depends on the ingredients and the texture desired.

Crushing raw or cooked ingredients by pounding them with a mortar and pestle, for example, is the time-honored way to produce rustic sauces such as *pesto*—fresh basil spiked with raw garlic and enriched with pine nuts, grated cheese and olive oil *(pages 30-31)*. Although pounding takes a lot of time, its very slowness is an advantage: The cook has complete control of the texture of the sauce.

A quicker method for puréeing a vegetable or fruit is to force it through a food mill or sieve. Every particle will be of uniform size, and its delicacy or coarseness can be determined by the choice of the disk for the mill or of a sieve with appropriately fine mesh. A food processor is even more speedy, reducing vegetables or fruits to pulp in seconds. For a smooth purée, the machine should be operated in short bursts, and the bowl scraped down often with a rubber spatula—precautions that also help prevent nuts from disintegrating into oily paste and keep starches such as boiled potatoes from becoming gluey.

Once puréed, most vegetable and fruit sauces benefit from the addition of cream, which adds flavor and serves to dilute the sauces slightly. The notable exceptions are sauces based on the juices of fresh fruits, rather than on purées; these require thickening, not thinning, and cornstarch or jelly will supply the jelling action essential *(pages 42-43)*.

# Pastes Pounded in a Mortar

The most rudimentary way to turn the garden's bounty into sauces is to pound ingredients to a purée with a mortar and pestle. Everything from tender greens to crisp nuts and starchy potatoes can be pounded—singly or in combinations. Flavorings and thickeners can be incorporated as the purée is formed, and oil can be worked into the mixture to bind it.

Old-fashioned as mortars and pestles certainly are, they give the cook control over the contents at all stages. The purée may be made satiny smooth or left coarse and chunky. Modern food processors, although easier to use, often produce uneven pieces from hard ingredients and, because of their speed, the blades may liquefy soft ingredients or reduce fatty ones such as nuts to a greasy mass.

For pounding, advance preparation of ingredients need only be minimal. Elements that are woody or fibrous—stems, seeds, skins and the strings of such vegetables as fennel or celery—should be removed. The foods may be raw or cooked. Boiling or steaming will soften dense-textured ones; sautéing or simmering will drive off excess moisture.

To achieve a perfectly blended sauce, crush the most resistant ingredients first to form a fairly smooth base for the softer or more liquid ingredients. For classic Italian *pesto (right; recipe, page 102)*, garlic and pine nuts are ground to a purée to which fresh basil can be added. To finish the sauce, olive oil and grated cheese are pounded in gradually. *Pesto* can then be served or—when partnered with pasta, as shown here—further diluted with the pasta's cooking liquid.

The pounded flesh of boiled potatoes is the base for the garlic-flavored sauce known in Greece as *skordalia (pages 32-33, top; recipe, page 103)*. The purée becomes a thick sauce when oil is gradually stirred in. For extra smoothness, you can add an egg yolk to the sauce.

Bread cubes and almonds, sautéed in oil to enrich their flavor, give Spanish *romesco (pages 32-33; recipe, page 107)* a coarser texture than that of either *pesto* or *skordalia*. The bread and nuts are pounded together with sautéed tomatoes and garlic, and the paste bound with more oil to create a sauce that is as pungent as it is colorful.

## Pesto: The Powerful Presence of Fresh Basil

**1 Pounding garlic.** Rinse basil leaves; measure pine nuts. Grate hard cheese fine—in this case, a mixture of pecorino and Parmesan. In a mortar, pound garlic cloves together with coarse salt—the salt will act as an abrasive to help grind the garlic to a purée.

**2 Adding pine nuts.** Drop the pine nuts, a few at a time, into the mortar. Use the pestle to crush the nuts before adding more. Then pound the crushed nuts to a coarse purée. Continue to pound, stirring occasionally with the pestle, until the pine nuts are smoothly blended with the garlic.

**5 Testing consistency.** Continue to add cheese and oil alternately—pounding the mixture well after each addition—until the purée is cohesive and thick enough to hold its shape. Stir the sauce to make sure the ingredients are blended thoroughly.

**6 Thinning the purée.** Cook pasta—egg noodles are used in this demonstration—and drain it, reserving the cooking liquid. Transfer the pasta to a warmed serving bowl. Stir into the purée enough of the reserved cooking liquid to make the sauce thin enough to pour easily.

3 **Adding basil.** Remove the stems from the basil leaves and discard them. Add the leaves to the mortar. Use the pestle to pound the leaves to a pulp and stir them into the rest of the mixture.

4 **Adding grated cheese and oil.** To enable you to control the flow of olive oil, cut a lengthwise groove down one side of the bottle's cork. Sprinkle a spoonful of the grated cheese (above, left) into the basil mixture and pound to incorporate it. Then trickle in a little oil (right) and pound the mixture again.

7 **Serving the sauce.** Ladle the sauce over the pasta in the serving bowl (above). Then toss the pasta until the sauce coats each strand evenly, and serve immediately on warmed plates.

## Skordalia: A Creamy Fusion of Potatoes and Garlic

1 **Pounding potatoes.** Boil whole potatoes until they are tender; drain and peel them. In a large mortar, pound garlic cloves together with coarse salt to make a paste. Add the potatoes to the mortar while they are still warm. Mash them with the garlic and coarse salt until they form a smooth purée.

2 **Stirring in oil.** Squeeze half a lemon and set the juice aside. Add olive oil to the mortar in a thin stream, stirring the purée continuously with the pestle. If the mixture becomes unmanageably thick, stir in a little lemon juice or tepid water to thin it.

3 **Finishing the sauce.** Continue to add oil until the mixture becomes glossy and is almost too thick to stir. For piquancy, pour in the lemon juice.

## Romesco: Flavor and Substance from Sautéed Nuts

1 **Sautéing.** Peel, seed and chop tomatoes coarse (page 9). Remove the crusts from thick slices of stale white bread; cube the bread. Blanch and peel almonds. Heat oil in a skillet and sauté the bread cubes on all sides until golden. Put these croutons in a mortar. Sauté the almonds with whole garlic cloves and add them to the mortar.

2 **Pounding.** Sauté the tomatoes rapidly over high heat for a few minutes until they are reduced to a coarse pulp. Add the tomatoes to the mortar. Pound the mixture vigorously to break down the croutons, almonds and garlic until they become a fairly smooth, even-colored paste.

3 **Adding flavorings.** To give the paste more flavor and to thin it a little, pour in dry sherry in a thin stream, stirring with the pestle. Then stir in cayenne pepper, salt and black pepper.

4 **Serving.** Stir the sauce *(left)*, taste it and, if necessary, add more lemon juice. Season the sauce and serve it from the mortar, spooning it to the side of the main dish *(above)*. Here, the *skordalia* accompanies poached salt cod, steamed periwinkles, and boiled green beans, new potatoes, young carrots and a small artichoke.

4 **Blending in oil.** Add olive oil in a thin stream, stirring all the time with the pestle to incorporate it. As you stir in the oil, the mixture will lighten in color.

5 **Finishing the sauce.** Continue to add oil until the mixture is glossy. The finished sauce should be soft enough to retain an impression when the pestle is drawn through it *(above)*. Taste and adjust the seasoning if necessary.

6 **Serving the sauce.** Spoon the sauce directly from the mortar to the side of the main dish. In this case, the sauce accompanies pieces of poached squid, its pouch cut crosswise into rings and its tentacles left whole.

# Vibrant Color from Sun-ripened Tomatoes

Ripe tomatoes simmered with aromatics and herbs form delicious coarse-textured or velvety purées that can be served as sauces in their own right or used to color and flavor other sauces.

The textural differences between the purées are largely the result of their different cooking times. Peeled, seeded and chopped, then cooked rapidly to evaporate excess liquid, tomatoes are quickly reduced to a rough pulp that retains their fresh savor *(top demonstration)*. Longer, slower cooking, followed by sieving and reduction, produces a dense, smooth purée with a more concentrated flavor *(bottom demonstration; recipe, page 159)*.

Since part of the attraction of any tomato sauce lies in its dramatic color, choose fresh tomatoes that have ripened to a deep red. Both standard tomatoes such as those shown here and the somewhat pulpier, pear-shaped plum tomatoes are suitable.

Locally grown and vine-ripened specimens will yield sauce of the best color and flavor, but out of season you can substitute fresh hothouse tomatoes. When these alternatives are unavailable or too expensive, the wisest course is to prepare the sauce with canned tomatoes.

Many herbs and aromatics combine well with tomatoes, and it is worth experimenting to find the ones you like best. Try thyme, oregano, tarragon or a last-minute addition of fresh basil. Onions, garlic, shallots or celery will add extra piquancy to a sauce: Chop them fine and sauté them until they are soft before you add the tomatoes.

## Brief Cooking to Retain Freshness

1 **Peeling tomatoes.** Using a small, sharp knife, cut around the core of each tomato. Lift out the core and stem together. Peel and seed the tomatoes and chop the flesh into coarse chunks.

2 **Adding flavorings.** Pour a little olive oil into a nonreactive pan to prevent the ingredients from sticking. Put the tomatoes in the pan with flavorings; in this instance, a sprig of thyme and two lightly crushed but unpeeled garlic cloves are used. Season with salt and pepper.

## Slow Simmering to Concentrate Flavor

1 **Preparing ingredients.** Chop onions and garlic cloves. Sauté them in olive oil in a heavy, nonreactive pan over low heat until the onions are soft but not colored—about five minutes. Chop large tomatoes into chunks, or quarter small ones. Add the tomato pieces to the pan with a bay leaf and a few sprigs of thyme.

2 **Cooking.** Cook the tomato mixture, uncovered, over medium heat, stirring and crushing it occasionally with a wooden spoon. After about 30 minutes most of the moisture released by the tomatoes will have evaporated.

3 **Judging the consistency.** Stirring frequently with a wooden spoon, sauté the tomatoes over high heat until most of the liquid has evaporated and the pulp is fairly smooth—about 10 minutes. The sauce should be thick enough to hold its shape: When the spoon is drawn across the bottom of the pan, it should leave a clean trail.

4 **Serving the sauce.** Remove and discard the garlic and thyme; taste the sauce for seasoning, and add more salt and pepper if required. Above, the sauce is served with boiled rice and garnished with finely chopped parsley.

3 **Making a purée.** Remove the mixture from the heat and discard the thyme and bay leaf. Place a sieve over a deep bowl. Using a wooden pestle, press the mixture through the sieve a little at a time. Discard the skins and seeds that remain in the sieve. Return the purée to the pan and cook it over low heat, stirring frequently.

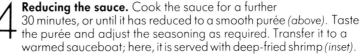

4 **Reducing the sauce.** Cook the sauce for a further 30 minutes, or until it has reduced to a smooth purée *(above)*. Taste the purée and adjust the seasoning as required. Transfer it to a warmed sauceboat; here, it is served with deep-fried shrimp *(inset)*.

# Vegetable Purées: The Garden's Delights

Puréed root and leaf vegetables diluted with cream, wine or stock furnish a range of light sauces to complement roasted, grilled or broiled meats of any kind.

All root vegetables, from salsify to carrots, need lengthy cooking. In the demonstration at right, for example, carrots simmer for about 45 minutes in water and butter, with sugar added to underscore their sweetness *(recipe, page 159)*. When tender, the vegetables can be puréed in a food processor as shown, or pressed through a sieve or food mill.

By contrast, leaf vegetables—spinach or sorrel, for example—need only brief boiling to make them soft enough to purée. Or, to best preserve their green color, leaf vegetables can be shredded and stewed in butter *(below)*. Tender young leaves literally may melt down to a purée; older leaves need to be sieved.

Whatever liquid you choose to convert a vegetable purée into a sauce, you can enrich the end product with cold butter. Whisk it in, a few pieces at a time, after removing the sauce from the heat.

## Glazed Carrots Transformed in a Processor

**1 Preparing carrots.** Peel and trim carrots. Leave young carrots whole. Halve older ones lengthwise and cut out their tough cores; cut the carrots into pieces. Put the carrots in a pan; for every pound [ ½ kg.], add 2 tablespoons [30 ml.] of butter and 1 tablespoon [15 ml.] of brown or white sugar. Add salt; half-cover with water.

**2 Puréeing.** Bring the water to a boil, then partially cover the pan and simmer the carrots gently for up to 45 minutes, or until they are tender. Remove the lid and increase the heat to high. Shaking the pan constantly, boil the carrots until they are coated with a syrupy glaze. Transfer the carrots and glaze to a food processor and purée them.

## Sorrel Sieved for Extra Smoothness

**1 Shredding sorrel.** Pick over sorrel leaves, discarding any that are blemished. Wash and drain the sorrel, then fold each leaf in half and tear out the central stem. Roll a few leaves at a time into a tight cylinder and, with a sharp knife, slice across the cylinder to cut the sorrel into shreds.

**2 Cooking sorrel.** Melt a little butter in a pan over low heat and toss in the shredded sorrel. Stew the sorrel gently, stirring occasionally to prevent it from sticking to the bottom of the pan. When the sorrel has broken down almost to a purée—after 10 to 20 minutes, depending on the age of the leaves—remove it from the heat.

**3 Sieving the sorrel.** A little at a time, spoon the purée into a fine-meshed drum sieve set over a plate. With a flexible plastic scraper, force the sorrel purée through the sieve. Discard any fibers that remain in the sieve.

3 **Thinning the purée.** Return the carrot purée to the pan and stir it continuously over medium heat until it is heated through. Then whisk in enough heavy cream to give the sauce a pouring consistency.

4 **Serving the sauce.** Remove the purée from the heat and whisk in cold butter pieces a few at a time *(above)*. Pour the sauce into a warmed sauceboat and serve it immediately; in this instance, the sauce accompanies slices of roast veal *(inset)*.

4 **Adding cream.** Transfer the sieved purée to a clean pan and return it to low heat. Pour in heavy cream, stirring with a wooden spoon until the cream blends smoothly into the purée.

5 **Serving.** Continue adding cream until the purée has a pouring consistency; in this case, about 1 cup [¼ liter] of cream was added for every pound [½ kg.] of sorrel. Pour the sauce into a warmed sauceboat; here, it is served with broiled veal sweetbreads.

# Harmonious Partnerships

Although most vegetables require little more than cooking and puréeing to reach a saucelike consistency, there are some classic choices that require additional treatment. Onions, for example, yield the rich and tangy sauce known in France as *soubise*. However, onion purée lacks body, and must be thickened with an approximately equal volume of white sauce *(right; recipe, page 156)* or with puréed cooked rice or potatoes—added in a ratio of about 1 cup [¼ liter] of thickener to each 2 cups [½ liter] of onion purée.

Dried beans, on the other hand, create such stiff purées that considerable thinning is required to transform them into sauces. For a white bean sauce *(below)*, presoaked beans are cooked with aromatic vegetables, puréed, and thinned a little with their cooking liquid. The mixture is then diluted to pouring consistency—and colored and flavored—with a tomato purée or a red-pepper purée *(page 9)*. For a *flageolet* sauce, the green hue of the beans might be intensified with a spinach or basil purée.

## An Onion Purée Bound with White Sauce

1 **Peeling baked onions.** In a preheated 375° F. [190° C.] oven, bake large unpeeled onions until they feel soft when lightly squeezed—after one to two hours, depending on size. When the onions are cool enough to handle, use a small, sharp knife to remove the skins and any discolored parts.

2 **Puréeing the onions.** Place the peeled onions in a sieve set over a bowl. Using a wooden pestle and a circular motion, press the onion pulp through the sieve into the bowl. Discard any membrane left in the sieve.

## A Mellow Mixture of Beans and Tomatoes

1 **Adding aromatics.** Soak dried beans—here, navy beans—in cold water overnight. Drain them and pour in fresh water to cover them by about 1 inch [2½ cm.]. Add an onion stuck with whole cloves, unpeeled garlic cloves, carrots and a bouquet garni *(page 7)*.

2 **Puréeing the beans.** Boil the beans for 10 minutes, then cover and simmer them for two hours, or until a bean crushes easily when squeezed. Discard the aromatics and drain the beans, reserving their cooking liquid. A few ladlefuls at a time, transfer the beans to a sieve set over a bowl and use a pestle to press the pulp through.

3 **Moistening the beans.** As you purée the beans, moisten them with a little of the reserved cooking liquid so that they can pass through the sieve easily. Discard the bean skins that remain in the sieve after each batch.

**3** **Thickening the purée.** Make a white sauce (pages 22-23). Transfer the onion purée to a saucepan. Using a wooden spoon, stir in a little of the white sauce. As each batch is absorbed, continue stirring in more sauce until the mixture is evenly blended and its consistency is to your liking.

**4** **Finishing the sauce.** Place the pan over low heat and warm the sauce through, stirring continuously. To finish and enrich the sauce, stir in a little heavy cream or pieces of cold butter.

**5** **Serving the sauce.** Transfer the finished sauce to a warmed sauceboat. Serve the sauce with grilled, broiled or roasted meat. Here, it accompanies a serving of roast saddle of lamb.

**4** **Adding tomato purée.** Prepare a tomato purée (pages 34-35). Whisk it into the bean purée a little at a time, until the sauce has attained the color and consistency that you desire.

**5** **Finishing the sauce.** Put the sauce in a pan. Over high heat, bring the sauce to a boil, stirring continuously. Remove the pan from the heat and whisk in a few pieces of cold butter.

**6** **Serving.** Transfer the bean-and-tomato sauce to a warmed sauceboat. In this case, the sauce is ladled onto a dinner plate, as an accompaniment to grilled pork loin chops.

# Capturing the Sweetness of Seasonal Fruits

Fruit sauces generally begin as purées. If liquid enough to pour, the purées need no additions. If stiff, they can be diluted easily—and tastily—with a little sugar syrup, wine or cream.

Different fruits require different techniques of puréeing. Sweet, soft berries —raspberries *(below),* strawberries or blueberries, for instance—can be converted into pourable purées simply by sieving out seeds or skins. Firm, tart berries such as cranberries or gooseberries need to be softened by poaching before sieving. In either case, aluminum may react with fruit acid to taint flavor, so the sieve must be nylon or stainless steel.

Apples *(right),* pears and quinces have fine-textured flesh and require only peeling, coring and simmering in a little water to break them down into smooth purées. Apricots *(opposite, bottom),* plums, peaches and cherries have more fibrous flesh. They should be halved, pitted and poached, then pressed through a sieve.

Very hard or fibrous fruits such as pineapple or rhubarb need to be cut up and poached, then puréed in a food processor.

The flavors of fruit sauces can easily be modified. Vinegar, onion or freshly ground pepper will lend a sharp edge to a sauce to be served with a savory dish. Dessert sauces usually include an additional sweetening of sugar or honey, perhaps mixed with a liqueur or spirit. Rum, for example, makes an excellent flavoring for a hot apricot sauce. Grated citrus peel and such spices as cloves and nutmeg will add piquancy to any fruit sauce, savory or sweet.

Fruit sauces with a touch of tartness— a purée of gooseberries or cranberries, for example—are traditional accompaniments for meat and game dishes. But sweeter sauces need not be restricted to desserts. Applesauce is a traditional accompaniment to pork, duck and goose— rich meats that have a slightly sweet flavor of their own.

## Apples Stewed to a Sauce

1 **Preparing apples.** Acidulate a bowl of cold water with the juice of a lemon. Cut apples into quarters. Peel and core each quarter and drop it immediately into the acidulated water to prevent discoloring.

## Berries Sieved and Sweetened

1 **Puréeing berries.** Pick over ripe, soft berries—raspberries are shown— removing any leaves or stems. Place a fine-meshed nylon sieve over a deep bowl. With a pestle, press the berries through the sieve to make a liquid purée.

2 **Sweetening the purée.** Sprinkle a little sugar over the purée—superfine sugar will dissolve faster and more evenly. Stir in the sugar and taste the purée for sweetness. If necessary, stir in a little more sugar.

3 **Serving.** Pour the sauce into a pitcher. If you plan to serve the sauce with a cold dessert, refrigerate it for an hour o so. In this instance, chilled raspberry sauce is poured over vanilla ice cream and cold poached peaches, forming the concoction known as Peach Melba

2 **Cooking the apples.** Transfer the apple quarters to a nonreactive pan. Add a little fresh water or apple cider and, if you like, some sugar. Cook the apples over low heat, stirring them from time to time, until they are reduced to a purée—about 20 minutes. Remove the pan from the heat.

3 **Enriching the sauce.** Cut cold butter into small pieces— allowing about ½ tablespoon [7 ml.] of butter for each apple. Stir the butter pieces, a few at a time, into the hot apple purée. Serve the sauce with meat—in this case, with roast pork loin *(inset)*.

## Apricots Poached and Puréed

1 **Poaching apricots.** Make a light sugar syrup *(recipe, page 167)*. Halve ripe apricots and remove the pits. Poach the fruit in the syrup until it is soft— about five minutes. Place a nylon sieve over a deep bowl. Transfer the apricots to the sieve, reserving the syrup. With a pestle, press the apricot flesh through the sieve; discard the skins.

2 **Thinning the purée.** Stir enough of the poaching liquid into the purée to give it a pouring consistency. Transfer this sauce to a pitcher. Reserve the remaining poaching liquid to use for other preparations.

3 **Serving the sauce.** Serve the sauce with roast pork or with a dessert. The sauce can be used hot or cold; here, it is poured cold over a molded tapioca pudding *(recipe, page 151)*.

# Preserving the Clarity of Fruit Juices

The jewel colors of fruits shine through clearest in sauces based on their strained juices. Some fruits—cranberries and apples among them—are high in both the jelling agent called pectin, which makes juices thicken when cooked with sugar, and in the acids that activate pectin. But most fruits lack adequate amounts of these components, and their juices need supplementing either with a cornstarch solution (right) or with jelly (below) to thicken into sauces.

The juices can be produced in whatever way is most convenient for that fruit. Lemons and oranges are easily squeezed in a juicer. Hard fruits such as rhubarb can be simmered in water until tender, then drained in a fine-meshed sieve. Soft fruits such as cherries or peaches can be crushed, wrapped in cloth and squeezed.

Whatever extraction method is used for the juice, a cornstarch solution will thicken it without altering its flavor. Because hot liquid makes cornstarch jell, or set, almost instantly, the solution will be lumpy unless the cornstarch is moistened with cold liquid and warmed gently. Other dry granular ingredients such as salt or sugar should be mixed with the cornstarch before the liquid is added.

The solution should be cooked only until it thickens and clears. At this stage, the juice and other final flavorings—here, lemon juice, lemon peel and butter (recipe, page 154)—can be added. Once heated through, the sauce must be served immediately. The fragile cornstarch cannot survive long keeping or reheating.

Jellies flavor a fruit-juice sauce as well as thicken it. However, in comparison to cornstarch, jelly (jam sieved to remove its solid ingredients) is simplicity itself to use: Just warm the desired amount of jelly over boiling water. When the jelly melts, it is ready to be combined with the juice and other flavorings. In the Cumberland sauce below (recipe, page 106), currant jelly forms the base; to it are added orange and lemon juices and peels, vinegar, port and shallots.

## A Shiny Lemon Topping

1 **Cooking the solution.** Mix sugar, cornstarch and salt in a nonreactive saucepan. Stir in cold water. Place the saucepan over low heat and stir until the solution becomes translucent and will fall from the spoon like honey—after approximately five minutes.

## Cumberland: The Meeting of Sweet and Sour

1 **Blanching peels.** Using a sharp knife, pare the colorful peels from an orange and a lemon, leaving the bitter white pith on the fruits. Cut the peels into julienne. To remove any bitterness, parboil the peels for a minute or two, then drain them. Chop the shallots fine and parboil them in the same way.

2 **Assembling the ingredients.** Melt red currant jelly in a bowl set over a pan of boiling water; remove the pan and bowl from the heat. Add the peels and shallots to the jelly. Squeeze the orange and lemon and measure port and white wine vinegar.

2 **Finishing the sauce.** Stirring constantly, pour freshly squeezed and strained lemon juice into the thickened solution. Stir in grated lemon peel. Then add pieces of cold butter and continue stirring until the butter melts completely.

3 **Serving the sauce.** As soon as the sauce is smooth, transfer it from the pan to a warmed pitcher. Serve the sauce—while still warm—over hot or cold puddings or cakes. In this case, the sauce is poured over a square of gingerbread.

3 **Finishing the sauce.** Stir in the juices of the orange and lemon, the port and the vinegar *(above)*. Transfer the finished mixture to a warmed sauceboat and serve the sauce over slices of cold meat or game *(inset)*—in this instance, roast venison.

# 3
# Sauces from Stocks
## Coaxing Flavors from a Simmering Pot

Stock is one of the principal elements of all good cooking and the foundation for a wide repertoire of superb sauces. Although it is invested with a certain mystique, stock making is simplicity itself: The appropriate ingredients—meat, poultry or fish combined with aromatic vegetables— are given gentle simmering in liquid, and the resulting broth is carefully cleansed to produce a clear, richly flavored essence.

Since an important purpose of a stock-based sauce is to complement the flavors of a finished dish, the stock ingredients may be supplemented or even wholly supplied by trimmings from the meat that the sauce will accompany. Most kinds of meat, poultry and game are suitable elements in a stock, provided that they contain enough gelatin to give body to the liquid. Often, however, a sauce has to be prepared quite independently of the main dish, and in these cases a basic veal stock *(opposite)* will supply an excellent foundation. Full-bodied yet unassertive in flavor, veal stock marries well with other meats. The counterpart of veal stock for fish and shellfish dishes is *fumet de poisson*, or fish stock, which is made with fish carcasses *(page 46)*.

In sauce making, stocks are points of departure rather than ends in themselves. With sufficient reduction by boiling, a meat stock yields a meat glaze, or *glace de viande*—a concentrated essence that can be introduced into any meat sauce to give it added depth of flavor and color *(pages 48-49, top)*. Another savory concentrate, *coulis (pages 48-49, bottom)*, is a kind of double stock: Meats are browned, then simmered in previously made veal stock, and the resulting savory liquid is concentrated by reduction.

Thickening with a roux of flour and butter is the usual means by which a basic stock is turned into a sauce. A very dark roux yields brown sauce *(pages 50-51)*; a light-colored roux yields the classic velouté *(page 53)*. Brown sauce is profitably combined with garnishes, flavorings and thickeners. A basic velouté can also be varied with enrichments such as cream or butter and with flavorings ranging from puréed tomatoes to pieces of poached marrow. And enriched velouté can be reduced by simmering, then chilled to form *chaud-froid*— literally, "hot-cold"—an aspic cream that provides a decorative coat for cold foods *(pages 56-57)*.

veal stock *(pages 46-47)*—ready for use in any one of hundreds of sauces—is ladled into a pan. To make the stock, meat and bones were simmered in water for several hours to release their flavors; the liquid was then strained and cooled so that fat could rise to the surface and be removed.

# Extracting the Essence of Meat and Fish

The stocks that serve as sauce foundations may be based on almost any meats or fish, but the techniques for forming them vary little: The ingredients must provide the maximum flavor and body to the liquid, and steps must be taken to ensure that the stock is clear.

Delicious, full-flavored stocks can be made from any meat, but a stock made primarily from veal *(right; recipe, page 159)*, with its unassertive taste and light color, is the most versatile. Meat trimmings may be used—they should be rich in natural gelatin, which lends body and smoothness. Bony and cartilaginous cuts such as veal and beef shanks are good choices; other gelatinous meats include pork rinds and calf's and pig's feet.

Simmering in water draws the flavor from the meat and bones and also draws out proteins, which form a scum on the water's surface during the early stages of cooking. To obtain a clear stock, this scum must be skimmed *(Step 2, right)*. Once the stock is clear you can add herbs and vegetables. For maximum flavor, the stock must be simmered for at least five hours. Fat is drawn from the meats in the process but is easily removed *(Step 5)*.

A basic meat stock can be used as is or turned into either of two more emphatically flavored sauce bases. If the stock is simmered long enough, it reduces to a concentrated meat glaze *(pages 48-49, top)*. Known in France as *glace de viande*, the glaze adds body as well as flavor to stock-based sauces. Or the stock can be transformed into the enriched veal stock called *coulis*, a luxurious meat essence *(pages 48-49, bottom; recipe, page 160)*. *Coulis* is a double stock: Basic meat stock is used as a braising liquid for veal and ham, then it is strained, reduced and cleansed for a voluptuous sauce base.

Delicately scented fish stocks, or *fumets de poisson (below; recipe, page 164)*, are rarely reduced, but the basic stocks are made the same way as meat stock, although the cooking time is shorter. For flavor, choose whole, mild-tasting white fish such as flounder. For body, add cod, one of the few fish rich in gelatin.

## Basic Steps to a Veal Stock

**1** **Preparing the meats.** Place meat and bones—here, sections of veal and beef shank, a veal knuckle, chicken necks and wings—on a rack in a large pot: The rack prevents the meats from sticking. Add enough water to cover the meats by about 2 inches [5 cm.].

## A Delicate Distillation from Fish

**1** **Assembling ingredients.** Peel and slice carrots, onions, leeks and celery and put them in a large, nonreactive pan together with thyme, parsley and bay leaves. Rinse whole, gutted fish free of blood and pull off the gills. Then cut up the fish. Flounder and sole are used here, with a salmon head for extra flavor.

**2** **Adding water.** To prevent the pieces of fish from sticking, place them on the bed of aromatics. Add red or white wine and enough water to cover the fish. Set the pan on low heat and bring the liquid to a boil, skimming off any scum that rises to the surface. Simmer the stock for about 30 minutes.

**3** **Completing the stock.** Strain the fish stock through a colander lined with dampened cheesecloth. Use the stock at once, or refrigerate it for as long as one week, bringing it to a boil and straining it every two days in the same way as meat stock *(Step 7, opposite)*. The stock will keep in the freezer for up to three months.

2 **Removing scum.** Set the pot on low heat. With a spoon, skim off the scum that surfaces as the temperature rises. To retard boiling, add a little cold water from time to time: If the liquid comes to a boil too quickly, the scum disperses. Skim until no more scum rises.

3 **Seasoning.** Add carrots, onions—one stuck with cloves—a garlic bulb and a bouquet garni *(page 7)*. Do not add salt: As the stock reduces during sauce making later, it would become too salty. Bring the stock slowly to a boil, then reduce the heat until it barely simmers.

4 **Straining.** Partly cover the pot to keep the stock from reducing too quickly yet let steam escape. Simmer for five hours, skimming off fat. Strain the stock into a bowl; discard the solids. Strain the liquid through a colander lined with dampened cheesecloth.

5 **Cleansing the stock.** Let the stock cool, then cover and refrigerate it until it has set to a jelly—eight hours or overnight. As the stock cools, the fat rises to the surface and sets in a solid layer. Scrape off the fat from the surface with a spoon and discard it.

6 **Removing traces of fat.** Press paper towels gently onto the surface of the jellied stock: The paper will absorb any small specks of fat that remain.

7 **Using the stock.** To melt the jellied stock, spoon it into a small pan and set it on low heat. Stir the jelly until it liquefies. Leftover stock can be kept for up to two weeks in the refrigerator; every two days it must be brought to a boil, then simmered for 15 minutes and strained. The stock can be stored for up to six months in the freezer.

## Meat Glaze: A Syrupy Reduction

1 **Skimming the stock.** Put cleansed veal stock (pages 46-47) in a pan, filling the pan almost to the top. Bring the stock to a boil; then set the pan half off the heat and let the stock boil gently. Impurities will repeatedly form a skin on the cooler side of the pan. Pull the skin to the side with a spoon and remove it.

2 **Reducing the stock.** Let the stock simmer, skimming off the skin every time it thickens, for about one hour, or until the stock has reduced by about a third. Pour the reduced liquid through a fine-meshed sieve into a smaller pan where it will be easier to skim.

3 **Removing impurities.** Return the stock to the heat, setting the pan half off the burner as before. Continue to simmer the stock and to skim off any impurities that form a skin.

## Coulis: A Doubling of Flavor

1 **Browning ingredients.** Heat olive oil in a large pot. Add veal and ham—in this case, veal shank with a meaty ham knucklebone—and coarsely chopped carrots and onions. Cover the pan and cook the ingredients over low heat, turning them occasionally, for about 45 minutes, until they have browned.

2 **Deglazing.** Add a little white wine, then scrape the bottom of the pot vigorously with a wooden spoon or spatula, loosening all the caramelized deposits so that they dissolve in the wine. Turn up the heat and boil the wine until it evaporates. When the juices begin to brown again, add more wine, and scrape and reduce as before.

3 **Removing scum.** Pour in enough veal stock (pages 46-47) to cover the coulis ingredients. Bring the stock to a simmer and skim off the scum that rises t the surface. When no more scum appears, add a bouquet garni (page 7 and partly cover the pot. Simmer the coulis for about four hours.

4 **Straining the stock.** When the stock has again reduced by about a third, remove the pan from the heat. Pour the reduced stock through a fine-meshed sieve into a smaller pan. Set the pan half off the heat and continue to simmer and skim the stock as before.

5 **Completing the reduction.** When the stock has again reduced by a third and is thick and syrupy *(above)*—after about three hours in all—pour it into a bowl. Cool the liquid, then chill it. It will set to a rubbery jelly *(inset)* that will keep indefinitely; the jelly does not require the periodic boiling used for veal stock because it contains so little liquid that bacterial growth is not a danger.

4 **Sieving vegetables.** Take the meats out of the pan and discard them. Transfer the bouquet garni to a sieve set over a pan just large enough to hold the liquid; press the juices from the bouquet garni through the sieve and discard it. Pour the *coulis* into the sieve; press the juices from the carrots and onions and discard them.

5 **Straining the coulis.** Set the pan of liquid half off the heat and simmer gently, skimming off the skin that forms on the cooler side of the pan. When the liquid has reduced by about half, remove the pan from the heat. Pour the liquid through a very-fine-meshed sieve—here, a *chinois*—into a bowl.

6 **Cooling the coulis.** Set the pan of *coulis* in a bowl of ice water and stir it continuously until it cools. Refrigerate the *coulis* until it sets to a firm jelly—eight hours or overnight. It will keep indefinitely, provided it is brought to a boil and strained every few days in the same way as veal stock *(pages 46-47)*.

# Brown Sauce: A Savory Concentrate from Deglazed Meats

Concentrated brown sauce, or *demi-glace* *(right; recipe, page 160)*, the classic foundation for a broad range of meat and game sauces, acquires its rich flavor and deep color from meticulous cooking and cleansing. The making of this famous "mother sauce" is a lengthy process, but the steps are no more difficult than those for making basic stock, and the sumptuous results are well worth the effort.

Meats or game and vegetables that are browned in oil in a hot oven give the sauce its character: The browning intensifies the flavors of the ingredients and deepens the color of the sauce. To thicken it, flour is added to the browning ingredients. The flour darkens and blends with the oil and the fat released by the heat, thus forming a brown roux that both colors the sauce and gives it body.

During this preliminary cooking, the juices drawn from the meats collect on the bottom of the browning pan as savory deposits, and these, too, enrich the sauce. The deposits are dissolved by deglazing the pan with white wine so that they will form part of the liquid.

To draw out their flavors and gelatin, the browned ingredients are simmered in liquid for hours, then strained, cleansed and reduced in a manner similar to that used in making veal stock *(pages 46-47)*. The liquid for simmering can be water, but for greater depth of flavor, veal stock can be used, as in this demonstration. If the brown sauce is based on game, the liquid can be either game or veal stock.

A finished concentrated brown sauce may be used at once or stored in the same way as veal stock. In any case, the sauce always is combined with garnishes and flavorings that complement the dish the sauce is intended for. Among the many ingredients that enhance a concentrated brown sauce are ham, stewed mushrooms or tiny onions, or tomato purée.

More lavish additions can be used for special sauces: To complement the game pâté on page 52, for example, a game-based brown sauce is garnished with truffles warmed in brandy. To enhance grilled steaks, a bordelaise is chosen—a basic brown sauce combined with a reduction of red wine and aromatics, then flavored with meat glaze *(pages 48-49, top)* and garnished with diced marrow.

## Oven Roasting to Deepen Color

1 **Coating with oil.** Blanch pork rind for two to three minutes, rinse it and chop it coarse. Put the rind in a roasting pan with cubed veal shoulder, pieces of veal knuckle, cut-up beef shanks and chicken wings. Add chopped carrot, onion, leek and celery, crushed garlic cloves, thyme and bay leaves. Toss the ingredients with oil.

2 **Adding flour.** Put the pan in a preheated 450° F. [230° C.] oven. After about 15 minutes, turn the ingredients with a spatula so that they will brown evenly. Bake the ingredients for 15 minutes more, or until they all are well browned. Sprinkle on flour and stir it into the mixture with the spatula.

5 **Removing the meat and bones.** Take the pan off the heat. Set a sieve over a large bowl and put a few ladlefuls of the cooked meat into the sieve *(above, left)*. Pick out any bones and discard them. To extract the meat juices, press the meat with a wooden pestle *(right)*. Discard the pressed meat and extract the juices from the rest of the meat in the same way. Strain the cooking liquid from the pan into the bowl; let the liquid cool slightly, then skim off any fat on the surface.

**3 Deglazing.** Bake the mixture for about 10 minutes, until the flour has browned. Then set the pan on medium heat. Add enough wine to moisten all the ingredients and dissolve the concentrated meat juices *(above, left)*. Using the spatula, scrape free the deposits on the bottom of the pan *(right)*. Increase the heat, bring the liquid to a boil and cook rapidly for about 10 minutes, or until almost all of the liquid has evaporated.

**4 Adding stock.** Melt veal stock *(pages 46-47)*. Transfer the contents of the roasting pan to a large saucepan. Add enough stock to cover all the ingredients generously. Bring the liquid to a boil; reduce the heat and set a lid slightly ajar on the pan. Simmer very gently for at least three hours, preferably for five or six hours.

**6 Straining the sauce.** Strain the liquid, a ladleful at a time, through a fine-meshed sieve—here, a *chinois*—into a pan. Move a small ladle up and down, very gently, in the liquid to help it pass through the mesh, but take care not to press any solids through the mesh. Discard the solids left in the sieve.

**7 Cleansing the sauce.** Place the pan on medium heat. Bring the liquid to a boil; set the pan half off the heat and let the sauce reduce. Repeatedly pull to one side and discard the skin of impurities that collects on the cooler side of the pan. When the sauce has reduced to the consistency of heavy cream, remove the pan from the heat and adjust the seasoning.

## A Game-based Sauce with Truffles

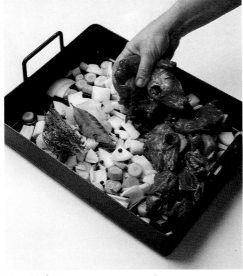

1 **Making a game sauce.** Prepare a brown sauce *(pages 50-51)*, using game carcasses and trimmings instead of beef and veal. Here, rabbit and partridge carcasses are used and the ingredients are simmered in game stock. When the cleansed sauce has reduced to the desired consistency, remove the pan from the heat.

2 **Garnishing the sauce.** Scrub and peel truffles; pound the peelings to a paste. Dice the truffles fine and warm them with brandy and butter *(page 11)*. Add the truffles and puréed peelings to the brown sauce.

3 **Serving the sauce.** Stir the truffles and peelings into the sauce, and immediately transfer it to a warmed sauceboat for serving. Here, the sauce i spooned over slices of hot game pâté.

## Brown Sauce Enhanced with Red Wine

1 **Adding wine flavoring.** Make a basic brown sauce *(pages 50-51)*. Put the reduced and cleansed sauce in a large pan. Prepare a reduction of red wine and aromatics *(page 10)*, then put the pan containing the sauce over medium heat and pour in an equal quantity of the reduced red wine.

2 **Enriching the sauce.** Bring the sauce to a boil, reduce the heat and set the pan half off the heat. Let the sauce boil gently until it has reduced to just over a third of its original volume, skimming off any skin that forms on the cooler side of the pan. Add a spoonful of meat glaze *(pages 48-49)* and stir it into the sauce with a little lemon juice.

3 **Serving the sauce.** To avoid clouding the sauce's clear color, do nc add any garnish that has been sautéed in fat. Here, poached and dice bone marrow *(page 11)* is added. Transfer the sauce to a warmed sauceboat and serve it at once. In this case, the sauce is ladled over boneless top-loin steaks.

# Velouté: A Base to Build On

Any basic meat or fish stock thickened with a roux becomes a light, smooth sauce known as a velouté—a velvety sauce. The sauce is made in the same way as a white sauce *(pages 22-23):* A flour-and-butter roux is formed, flavored liquid—at right, fish stock—is whisked in, and the mixture is simmered and cleansed for at least 45 minutes to eliminate any taste of flour. And, like white sauce, velouté serves as a base for myriad delicious variations.

Because veloutés lack the body that is characteristic of milk-enhanced white sauces, the first addition to the finished sauce is inevitably an enrichment, which may be butter, cream or egg yolks. If you choose egg yolks, you must take precautions against overcooking: Yolks that are heated too quickly or too much will begin to coagulate, making the sauce lumpy. To prevent this mishap, beat the yolks, then whisk in a little warm velouté to heat and thin them. After this, you can whisk the mixture into the pan of velouté and cook the sauce over very low heat—the liquid must never approach a boil—until the sauce thickens to the consistency of heavy cream.

Once it is enriched, a velouté can easily be turned into vividly colored, complex-tasting sauces. If the enrichment for the sauce is to be butter, for instance, you can whisk in a flavored butter *(pages 12-13).* Alternatively, a purée of red peppers *(page 9)*, spinach or tomatoes, or a little saffron dissolved in hot water will add color as well as flavor. Garnishes *(pages 9-11)* should be chosen to complement the sauce's basic flavor. Poached shrimp and mussels, for example, make good partners for a fish velouté. Poached bone marrow goes well with a game velouté, and mushrooms or truffles with all veloutés—fish, meat and game.

A velouté is usually served as an accompaniment to a dish, but it also can be an integral part. On page 54, for instance, strips of poached sole are served with a butter-enriched velouté *(top);* on page 55, a sauce flavored with mushrooms and onions provides a protective coating for a gratin of fish *(bottom).*

## Merging Roux with Stock

1 **Whisking in fish stock.** In a pan set over medium heat, blend butter and flour to make a roux *(page 22).* After a minute or two, when the roux begins to foam, ladle fish stock *(page 46)* into the pan, whisking continuously. When all the stock has been added, whisk until the mixture comes to a boil, then reduce the heat so that the liquid simmers.

2 **Cleansing the sauce.** Set the pan half off the heat and simmer the sauce for at least 45 minutes, repeatedly skimming off the skin of fatty impurities that forms on the surface at the cooler side of the pan. When the sauce has reduced by half and only a thin skin forms, put the pan fully back on the heat.

3 **Enriching with cream.** Pour in heavy cream *(inset)* and stir it into the velouté with a wooden spoon *(above).* The finished sauce should have a light, creamy consistency and be just thick enough to coat the spoon. Remove the sauce from the heat. Before finishing the sauce with the flavoring or garnish of your choice, taste it and adjust the seasoning if necessary.

## A Satin-smooth Coating for Fragments of Fish

1 **Whisking in butter.** Make a velouté with fish stock and enrich it with cream *(page 53)*. Remove the pan from the heat. Whisk small cubes of chilled butter, a handful at a time, into the sauce.

2 **Adding fish fillets.** Cut sole fillets into strips about ½ inch [1 cm.] wide. Put the strips in a buttered pan and simmer them for two to four minutes in a little fish stock *(page 46)*. Drain the fillets in a sieve, then add them to the pan of sauce.

3 **Serving the sauced fish.** Gently stir the fillets into the sauce, taking care not to break the fish. If necessary, return the pan briefly to the heat to warm the sauce through before serving.

## Enrichment and Color from an Herb Butter

1 **Adding herb butter.** Prepare and chill herb butter *(page 12)*; break it into chunks. Make fish velouté; add cream *(page 53)*. Remove the pan from the heat. Whisk in the herb butter, a little at a time. Here, 2 tablespoons [30 ml.] are added for every cup [¼ liter] of sauce.

2 **Serving the finished sauce.** When all the herb butter has been incorporated and the sauce is evenly colored, pour it into a warmed sauceboat *(above)*. Serve the sauce immediately. In this instance, the sauce provides a colorful accompaniment for a fillet of flounder poached in fish stock *(inset)*.

## A Golden Tint from Saffron

1 **Coloring with saffron.** Prepare a garnish of shrimp and mussels *(page 10)* and dissolve powdered saffron in a little hot water. Make a fish velouté and stir in cream *(page 53)*. Remove the pan from the heat. Stir the saffron liquid into the sauce.

2 **Ladling the sauce over the fish.** Stir the garnish of shrimp and mussels into the saffron-colored velouté sauce. Transfer the sauce to a warmed sauceboat and ladle it over the fish you are serving—in this case, poached fillet of flounder.

## Texture and Flavor from Duxelles

1 **Adding mushrooms.** Prepare *duxelles (page 9)*. Make a fish velouté and stir in cream *(page 53)*. Remove the pan from the heat. Stir the *duxelles* into the sauce, adding about ½ cup [125 ml.] to every cup [¼ liter] of sauce.

2 **Coating fish.** Sauté white bread crumbs in butter. Spread half the sauce in the bottom of a shallow ovenproof dish. Place a trimmed fish—here, sole—on the sauce. Cut along the fish's backbone, partially separating the fillets from the bones, and insert butter beneath the fillets. Ladle the rest of the sauce over the fish; sprinkle the bread crumbs on top.

3 **Serving the gratin.** Bake the fish in a preheated 375° F. [190° C.] oven for about 20 minutes, until the fish is cooked and the surface of the gratin is golden and crisp. To serve, lift portions of fish off the bone and accompany them with a little sauce spooned out from under the fish.

# Chaud-froid: A Creamy Sheathing of Aspic

Stocks and the sauces derived from them offer a special opportunity to the ambitious cook: When a gelatinous stock or sauce cools, it sets into a firm, light jelly that can be turned into a delicious coating for cold food. If the liquid is stock, the jelly will be a clear aspic that gives dishes a glittering, translucent finish. If the liquid is velouté, it becomes the basis for a luxurious aspic cream (recipe, page 163).

Any stock-based velouté can become an aspic cream. Fish or shellfish, for instance, requires a sauce based on fish velouté. (The stock for the velouté must be reinforced with powdered gelatin since fish does not contain enough gelatin to make a fish stock jell.) For cooked rabbit or pheasant, you could choose a game-stock velouté. And a velouté made from veal stock is suited to all kinds of meats and is especially versatile.

To form the aspic cream, you can simply enrich the velouté with cream and reduce the mixture to concentrate it. But for a matchless complexity of taste, you can follow the more elaborate procedure shown here: Veal velouté is fortified with meat glaze, which provides extra body, then flavored in two ways before the reduction takes place. Half the velouté receives a game-based brown sauce (page 52), which produces a mahogany-colored aspic cream suitable for coating dark game meats. For light-colored meats, the rest of the fortified velouté is enriched with heavy cream to make a white coating. For further variety of color and flavor, you could add tomato or pepper purée (page 9) to white aspic cream.

In all of these variations, the order of battle is the same. The foods to be coated and any garnishes are prepared in advance and chilled so that they are ready when the sauce is. The aspic cream, once formed, must be cooled over ice until it is syrupy—it should be partly set but still liquid enough to coat the meat evenly. When the meat pieces have been coated and garnished, they are chilled to set the aspic cream; the cream will hold the garnishes—which can range from sprigs of blanched herbs to chopped truffles—in place. For a shining finish, the assembled dish may be given a final coating of clear aspic, flavored, if you like, with a dash of fortified wine such as Madeira or sherry.

**1** **Making velouté.** Prepare a roux and, over low heat, whisk in veal stock. Increase the heat, and keep whisking continuously until the mixture boils, then reduce the heat so that the liquid is simmering (page 53).

**2** **Adding meat glaze.** Set the pan half off the heat and simmer the sauce until it is reduced by about one half—45 minutes or so—skimming off skin as it forms on the cooler side of the pan. Add a couple of spoonfuls of meat glaze (pages 48-49) and continue to cook the velouté, stirring, until the glaze is evenly incorporated.

**6** **Making white aspic cream.** Place the pan of reserved velouté (Step 3) over low heat and bring it to a simmer. Add heavy cream—in this case, ½ cup [125 ml.] was added to 1 cup [¼ liter] of velouté. Skimming from time to time, cook the sauce until it has reduced by half. Transfer the aspic cream to a metal bowl and cool it (Step 4).

**7** **Coating chicken breasts.** One at a time, dip a piece of meat—here, roasted, skinned, chilled chicken breasts—in the sauce. Place the piece on a rack set over a tray and garnish it. In this case, the garnish is finely chopped pickled tongue and hard-boiled egg white. When all the pieces are coated and garnished, refrigerate them.

3 **Making brown aspic cream.** Pour half the velouté into a small pan; stir to cool it and prevent a skin from forming, then set it aside. Pour the rest of the velouté into another pan and set it over low heat. Add a few spoonfuls of brown sauce (page 52), then simmer the sauce until it has reduced by about a third. Transfer the sauce to a metal bowl.

4 **Cooling the sauce.** Set the metal bowl in a bowl filled with ice. Stir the sauce with a figure-8 motion until it has cooled and coats the spoon. Remove the bowl from the ice. If the sauce becomes too thick for coating, set it over warm water and stir until it liquefies, then stir it over ice until the correct consistency is achieved.

5 **Dipping.** One at a time, dip chilled meat pieces—here, roasted partridges, halved and skinned—in the sauce. Let excess sauce drip off, then drain each piece on a rack set over a tray. Apply a garnish—finely chopped truffles are used here. Chill the meat to set the aspic cream; this will take five to 10 minutes.

8 **Preparing aspic.** Melt veal stock (pages 46-47) over low heat. Allow it to cool to nearly room temperature; stir in Madeira. Pour a little of the stock into a metal bowl set in a bowl of ice. Stir the stock until it thickens and is on the point of setting (above); remove it from the ice. Take the meats from the refrigerator; trim them of any excess aspic cream.

9 **Glazing with aspic.** Transfer the meats to clean racks set over trays. Spoon the aspic over each piece of meat, preparing more aspic as necessary. Return the meats to the refrigerator to set the glaze. After about 10 minutes, apply another coat of aspic and let it set. Continue the process until the meats are smoothly glazed.

10 **Serving.** Arrange all the partridge halves and the chicken breasts on a platter—in this instance, they are laid on a bed of chicken mousse. Cover the entire surface of the dish with more aspic; refrigerate it to set the glaze. Set the platter on crushed ice for serving, to keep the aspic from melting.

# 4

# Egg-based Sauces
## Elegant Emulsions

**Achieving perfect mayonnaise**
**Incorporating hard-boiled egg yolks**
**The many guises of hollandaise**
**Foamy sabayons**
**Pouring custard, plain and flavored**

The prime importance of the egg in sauce making lies in the yolk's ability to form emulsions with different liquids. Vigorous beating of egg yolks with oil, butter or stock causes the liquid to become evenly suspended in the egg, so the elements are bound together. The resulting rich, smooth sauces, cold and hot, are among the most impressive in all cookery.

Careful control of temperature and timing are the keys to success for each of these sauces, as illustrated by the rules for making mayonnaise. The ingredients for this uncooked sauce—egg yolks and oil, sharpened by a dash of vinegar or lemon juice—should all be at room temperature before mixing begins: Chilled ingredients are too viscous to blend properly. Even so, the egg yolks can absorb oil only gradually. The oil, which may be olive oil, milder-tasting vegetable oil or a blend of the two, must always be added to the yolks slowly—literally drop by drop at first—while the yolks are beaten vigorously. The result is a voluptuously thick emulsion that lends itself to emphatic flavorings: Garlic, anchovies, tomatoes and herbs are just a few of the possibilities.

For cooked sauces, regulation of temperature is paramount. Gentle cooking heats the eggs enough so that they thicken, adding body to the sauces; but if the temperature gets too high, the emulsion will break—the yolks will separate from the liquid. To prevent the sauces from curdling in this way, the best technique is to use a water bath so that the heat remains indirect and therefore low.

Among cooked egg sauces, hollandaise is the archetype and the foundation for a family of related sauces *(pages 62-65)*. Flavored with tarragon and vinegar, a basic hollandaise becomes a béarnaise; tomato purée creates a Choron sauce and the juice of blood oranges a maltaise *(opposite)*. A simple-to-make mock hollandaise, or *sauce bâtarde (pages 66-67),* is a similarly versatile vehicle for a range of flavorings.

Besides oil and butter, egg yolks can be emulsified with stock, wine, milk or cream to produce sauces of quite different characters *(pages 68-71)*. Whisked with fish or meat stock over gentle heat, for instance, the yolks become savory, fluffy sabayon; if the liquid is wine, and sugar is included, the same technique produces a classic dessert sauce. If the liquid is milk or cream, the result is custard sauce, rich, satiny, and—like other egg-based sauces—the basis for delicious variations.

*Maltaise sauce (page 65)—a variation on a basic hollandaise—completes a serving of boiled asparagus spears. The sauce, made by combining butter with egg yolks and lemon juice over gentle heat, gets its dramatic color from its flavoring: the freshly squeezed juice of a blood orange.*

# Mayonnaise: An Archetypal Suspension

Classic mayonnaise *(right; recipe, page 165)* consists merely of egg yolks, olive or vegetable oil and seasonings, and is simplicity itself to make, provided a few rules are observed. For a properly rich yet light sauce, the ingredients must be combined in just the right proportions. Eggs are such efficient emulsifiers that one yolk can absorb as much as 2 cups [½ liter] of oil, but this mayonnaise would be heavy and stiff. For a soft, smooth consistency, use about 1 cup [¼ liter] of oil per yolk. So that they will be fluid enough to emulsify, the ingredients should be at room temperature.

The sauce is formed by whisking the yolks to liquefy them, then whisking in the oil. The yolks can emulsify oil only gradually: It is essential that the oil be added slowly—drop by drop at first, then, as the mixture thickens, in a controlled trickle. Too much oil added at once will cause the sauce to separate or "break"; if this happens, you can restore it by beating a fresh yolk separately, then slowly whisking the broken mayonnaise into it. A sauce that becomes too thick can be thinned by whisking in a little lemon juice, vinegar or water.

The only equipment you need to make mayonnaise is a whisk and a mixing bowl, but you can speed the operation considerably by using a blender or food processor instead. However, mayonnaise made by these machines must include egg white—which keeps the sauce from thickening too much—and thus will not be as rich as yolk-based mayonnaise.

Different ingredients may be added to either type of mayonnaise to vary its color, flavor and texture. Almost any cooked vegetable, diced or puréed, can be incorporated. Green mayonnaise *(below)* is created by stirring in chopped herbs and spinach; for a spicy pink mayonnaise, use puréed red peppers and tomatoes. Aioli *(recipe, page 132)* is a mayonnaise flavored with puréed garlic. And gribiche, or tangy mayonnaise *(opposite, below; recipe, page 165)*, gains body from hard-boiled yolks and pungency from mustard, capers and sour gherkins.

## A Smooth Blend with Oil

1 **Adding lemon juice.** Separate eggs, reserve the whites for another use and put the yolks in a mixing bowl. Season with salt and pepper. Whisk the yolks until they are smooth in texture and pale in color. Still whisking, pour freshly squeezed lemon juice into the bowl in a thin, slow stream.

## An Herb-flecked Dressing

1 **Adding herbs and spinach.** Make mayonnaise *(Steps 1 and 2, top)*. Wash, stem and parboil spinach; then drain it, squeeze it dry and chop it. Chop fresh parsley, chives, tarragon and chervil to make fines herbes; sprinkle them on the mayonnaise, then add the spinach.

2 **Mixing the ingredients.** Stir the herbs and spinach into the mayonnaise until they are evenly incorporated and the sauce is pale green with darker flecks. If you wish, add other flavorings; in this case, the puréed coral of a poached lobster was used.

3 **Serving green mayonnaise.** Serve this colored and flavored sauce with any fish or shellfish dish—here, it garnishes a cold lobster arranged on a bed of lettuce leaves. Or serve the green mayonnaise—without the addition of the lobster coral—with dishes such as cold roast chicken, poached brains or steamed vegetables

2 **Incorporating oil.** Whisking continuously, add olive oil drop by drop *(above, left)*. For maximum control, place the measured oil in a bottle and regulate the flow by inserting your thumb in the bottle's neck. When the mixture begins to thicken and acquire a gloss, dribble the oil in a thin stream *(center)*, continuing to whisk. As the sauce thickens, increase the flow of oil *(right)*. When almost all of the oil has been added, lift out some sauce and drop it into the bowl; if the drop just holds its shape, the sauce is ready. If it is stiff, whisk in a few drops of lemon juice, vinegar or water.

3 **Serving mayonnaise.** The sauce is best served at once with a salad or simple cold dish, such as roast chicken garnished with sour gherkins *(above)*. To store mayonnaise, cover it and put it in the refrigerator. It will keep for up to three days. Stir or whisk briefly before using.

## Gribiche: Piquancy from Capers and Gherkins

1 **Mashing yolks.** Place hard-boiled egg yolks in a bowl, reserving the whites. Add a raw egg yolk and prepared mustard. With a pestle, mash the yolks to a paste. Add lemon juice. Incorporate the oil, as for mayonnaise *(Steps 1 and 2, top)* to form a creamy sauce.

2 **Adding flavorings.** Cut the egg whites into julienne. Rinse, drain and chop capers and sour gherkins. Prepare fines herbes. Add all these ingredients to the mayonnaise and stir until the gribiche is thoroughly blended.

3 **Serving.** Gribiche provides a complement to hot or cold fish or shellfish dishes. In this instance, the sauce garnishes chilled poached sea scallops arranged on a bed of chiffonade—lettuce leaves cut into julienne.

# Hollandaise: Theme and Variations

Among the most luxurious of hot sauces are hollandaise and its variations, demonstrated at right and on the following pages *(recipes, page 166)*. All of these sauces are merely flavored emulsions of egg yolks and butter, and while there are minor differences among the techniques for making them, the preparations all are governed by the same principles.

A classic hollandaise usually is made by beating cold butter cubes into warmed egg yolks *(right)*, but for a more satiny, translucent version, you can use clarified butter—butter whose milky solids have been removed, leaving only pure fat *(box, opposite)*. In either case, the hollandaise is flavored with lemon juice. When the same basic emulsion is mixed with the juice of blood oranges—available during the winter and spring at specialty markets—it becomes the bittersweet pink sauce called maltaise. Béarnaise sauce is made the same way as hollandaise, except that before the butter is added, the yolks are combined with a reduction of wine and vinegar made fragrant with tarragon, chervil and shallots. (A Provençal version of béarnaise, demonstrated on pages 64-65, includes olive oil rather than butter.) For Choron sauce, a coarse-textured tomato purée is stirred into a completed béarnaise.

In making all of these sauces, you must ensure that the egg yolks absorb the butter without separating or curdling: The yolks must remain fluid, they must never be overheated, and they must be given time to emulsify the fat. To keep the yolks fluid, mix them with water or another liquid before heating them. To prevent them from overheating and solidifying, set the saucepan in a water bath—a pan half-filled with almost-simmering water, which diffuses heat and keeps it low. To let the eggs emulsify the butter gradually, whisk the butter in a little at a time, making sure each portion is almost absorbed before adding the next.

Each of these sauces is best served immediately. As soon as the desired consistency is reached, remove the pan from the water bath to prevent the sauce from thickening further. If necessary, you can hold the sauce for a short time before serving by setting the pan in a warm—but not hot—water bath.

## An Emulsion Based on Cold Butter

1 **Heating egg yolks and water.** Cut chilled butter into small cubes. Squeeze the juice from a lemon, remove the seeds and reserve the juice. Set a trivet in a large pan, and pour in water until the trivet is just covered. Heat the water to just below the simmering point. Combine egg yolks with a little water, salt and white pepper in a saucepan, and set the pan on the trivet *(above, left)*. Beat the yolks with a whisk *(right)* for about two minutes, until the mixture begins to thicken slightly.

2 **Thickening the sauce.** Whisking continuously, add the butter cubes, a handful at a time. Allow each batch of butter to melt almost completely before adding more *(above, left)*. Whisk until all of the butter is blended in and the sauce begins to thicken *(right)*. Turn off the heat but continue to whisk the sauce.

## Clarified Butter for a Silken Finish

**1** **Clarifying butter.** Melt butter gently in a heavy pan set over low heat. Remove the pan from the heat and let the butter cool for about 20 minutes so that the white milk solids can settle. Spoon away the froth that rises to the surface. Carefully pour the clarified liquid butter into another pan, leaving the milky residue. Discard the residue.

**2** **Adding the clarified butter.** In a saucepan set in a water bath, whisk egg yolks, water and seasoning together until the yolks thicken slightly (*Step 1, opposite*). Add the cooled clarified butter, a ladleful at a time, whisking the mixture continuously as you pour. When the hollandaise begins to thicken, whisk in strained lemon juice.

**3** **Completing the sauce.** Continue to whisk for three to five minutes, until the hollandaise is thick and creamy; then remove the pan from the heat. If the sauce becomes too thick to pour, whisk in a little warm water or a few more drops of lemon juice.

**3** **Adding lemon juice.** Still whisking, pour the lemon juice into the sauce and blend it thoroughly into the mixture. Remove the pan from the water bath and whisk the sauce briefly. It should have a firm, velvety consistency but still be pourable; if not, whisk in more lemon juice or water.

**4** **Serving hollandaise.** Serve the sauce warm—with poached fish, vegetables or egg dishes. Here, it is ladled over poached eggs resting on a bed of spinach that was parboiled, squeezed, and sautéed in butter, then molded in small ramekins.

## Béarnaise: The Tang of Tarragon

1 **Reducing the flavorings.** Chop shallots, tarragon and chervil fine and place them in a pan. Add white wine and white wine vinegar. Bring the mixture to a boil, reduce the heat, and let the mixture simmer for 10 to 15 minutes, stirring occasionally. When only a couple of spoonfuls of liquid remain, remove the pan from the heat.

2 **Straining.** Pour the contents of the pan through a sieve into a bowl; press the herbs and shallots to extract all the juices, then discard them. Pour the liquid into a small saucepan. Add egg yolks; set the saucepan in a water bath heated to just below the simmering point. Whisk the yolks and liquid together.

3 **Adding oil.** When the egg mixture pales in color and thickens slightly, add butter or, as here, olive oil in a thin, steady stream, whisking continuously. (The oil was measured into a bottle whose cork contains V-shaped cuts that allow a controlled flow of oil.) The sauce will thicken and become lighter in color as the oil is whisked into it.

## Choron: A Rosy Tint from Tomatoes

1 **Adding tomato.** Make a coarse tomato purée (pages 34-35). Prepare a béarnaise (Steps 1 to 5, top); if you wish, omit the final addition of herbs. Stir the tomato purée into the sauce.

2 **Serving the sauce.** Transfer the sauce to a warmed sauceboat (above). In this case, the sauce is served with grilled kidneys (inset); it can be served with other grilled meats, poultry or such robustly flavored fish as salmon, tuna or sturgeon.

4 **Adding water.** If the sauce becomes too thick, stop adding oil and whisk in warm water or a little lemon juice. When the sauce is thick but pourable, translucent and shiny, remove the pan from the water bath.

5 **Adding herbs.** Stir finely chopped tarragon and chervil into the sauce. Immediately transfer the finished béarnaise sauce from the pan to a warmed sauceboat.

6 **Serving the sauce.** Béarnaise is traditionally served with grilled poultry or meat. Here, it is spooned over a grilled boneless top-loin steak. Alternatively, the sauce could garnish poached or grilled fish or vegetables.

## Maltaise: Brilliant Color from Blood Oranges

**Whisking.** Squeeze the juice from blood oranges, strain it and set it aside. Whisk egg yolks with water and salt until they are smooth; put the yolks into a pan set in a water bath, and whisk in chilled butter cubes (page 62, Step 2) to make a thick, smooth hollandaise.

2 **Adding orange juice.** Pour the orange juice in a steady stream into the sauce, whisking all the time. As more juice is added, the sauce will take on a deep raspberry color. Whisk in a little lemon juice to give the sauce extra tartness, if you like. Remove the pan from the heat, continuing to whisk.

3 **Serving.** Pour the finished sauce into a warmed sauceboat. Maltaise most often accompanies boiled asparagus spears, served hot or tepid (above); alternative vegetables include broccoli, cauliflower and small leeks.

# Bâtarde: A Velvety Sauce Made in Minutes

Mock hollandaise, or *sauce bâtarde,* is made by cooking a flour-and-butter roux *(page 22),* then whisking in eggs, water and butter to form an emulsion, a technique that has several advantages for the busy cook. A sauce made this way has much of the richness and lightness of true hollandaise *(pages 62-63)* but few of the worries: Mock hollandaise is quickly and easily prepared, and is far less fragile than its classic counterpart.

The strength of the sauce derives from the flour in the roux: Starch in the flour binds the proteins and fats in the eggs and butter, stabilizing the emulsion and eliminating the danger of separation. Because of this, a mock hollandaise can be cooked over direct heat—gentle heat, to keep the yolks from scrambling—instead of in a water bath, and it can be made as much as a day in advance of serving. (If the sauce is made in advance, it should be covered, refrigerated and then reheated slowly in a water bath before serving.)

Of course, the basic rules for forming an egg-yolk-and-butter emulsion still apply; that is, the yolks must not be overheated and the butter must be added very gradually to the sauce to give the yolks time to absorb it. However, the lengthy cooking required to eliminate the floury taste from other roux-thickened sauces is not needed for mock hollandaise, because the yolks will mask any flavor of flour.

A mock hollandaise may be augmented in a variety of ways *(recipes, page 166).* The sauce may be enriched with cream, for instance. And it may be flavored with capers, herbs such as parsley, chervil, tarragon or fennel, curry powder or prepared mustard. Depending on the seasoning, the sauce is suitable for baked or broiled fish or poultry, or boiled or steamed vegetables.

1 **Preparing ingredients.** Squeeze the juice from a lemon; remove the seeds and reserve the juice. Separate eggs, dropping the yolks into a bowl and saving the whites for another use. Add cold water to the yolks and beat the mixture until it is smooth.

2 **Adding water.** Melt butter in a heavy pan set over low heat. Add flou and stir the roux until it begins to foam Then pour in lightly salted warm water, whisking the mixture rapidly.

5 **Thickening the sauce.** Return the pan to low heat and continue whisking until the sauce thickens to the consistency of heavy cream. Do not let the mixture approach a boil.

6 **Finishing the sauce.** When the sauce thickens, remove the pan from th heat. Add the reserved lemon juice, then add finely chopped parsley, whisking until it is evenly distributed in the sauce. Whisk in handfuls of cold butter cubes, blending in each handful before adding the next.

3 **Thickening the roux.** Continue to whisk the mixture as it heats, so that all the ingredients are smoothly blended. As soon as the mixture reaches a boil, remove the pan from the heat.

4 **Whisking in egg yolks.** Let the roux stand for a minute or two so that it cools slightly. Then whisk in the reserved mixture of egg yolks and water.

7 **Serving the sauce.** The mock hollandaise is ready when all the butter is incorporated and the mixture has a smooth and velvety consistency (left). Season it to taste, transfer it to a warmed sauceboat and serve immediately; here, it is poured over steamed cauliflower (above).

# Sweet and Savory Sabayons

Thinned with liquid and whisked over gentle heat, egg yolks develop into sabayons. These sauces have the velvety texture of hollandaise, to which they are closely related, and a special frothy consistency all their own. Vigorous whisking forces air into the yolks—so much that they more than double in volume—while the liquid keeps them from thickening too much as they cook. The technique is a simple one, and can be used to make either sweet or savory sauces.

A savory sabayon *(recipe, page 167)* is made by whisking the yolks with fish stock—as in demonstration at right—or chicken stock or veal stock, the choice depending on the nature of the dish the sauce will garnish. In any case, the stock must be reduced to concentrate its flavor before sauce making begins. Once the stock and yolks have emulsified, the savory sabayon is enriched by cold butter, in the same way as hollandaise.

Sweet sabayons *(recipe, page 167)* are made by essentially the same technique as savory ones, the difference being the flavorings involved. For a sweet sabayon, egg yolks are mixed with sugar and lightened with wine. To ensure that the granules dissolve completely, use superfine sugar and whisk it into the yolks at the very start of cooking. The wine—usually white—may be sparkling or still, sweet or dry. A fortified wine such as Madeira, sherry or Marsala will give the sauce a more assertive flavor.

A classic sweet sabayon sauce is not enriched, as the savory version is, but two fine sauces based on sabayon can be made by adding ingredients after the basic sauce is formed. For an incomparably airy hot sabayon, you can fold stiffly beaten egg whites into the sauce just at the end of cooking. For a creamy cold sauce, chill a finished sabayon by setting the pan in a bowl of ice and whisking the sauce, then fold in whipped cream.

## Eggs and Fish Stock Whisked to a Froth

1 **Forming an emulsion.** Put fish stock *(page 46)* in a pan and boil it until it is reduced by two thirds. Remove the pan from the heat and let the stock cool until it is lukewarm, then add egg yolks. Place the pan in a water bath containing water that has been heated to just below a simmer. Whisk the yolks into the stock *(above, left)* until they are thoroughly blended. Continue whisking until the mixture begins to thicken *(right)*.

## Wine and Sugar Lightly Whipped

1 **Mixing yolks and sugar.** Pour superfine sugar into a large pan—here, a copper pan designed for making sabayon—and add egg yolks. Place the pan in a water bath containing water that has been heated to just below a simmer. Whisk the yolks and sugar.

2 **Adding wine.** Continue to whisk until the sugar has thoroughly dissolved in the yolks and the mixture becomes creamy and pale. Begin to pour in white wine, whisking all the time.

2 **Enriching with butter.** A handful at a time, drop chilled butter cubes into the egg-and-fish-stock mixture, whisking continuously. As each handful of cubes almost disappears into the liquid, add another, until all the cubes have been incorporated.

3 **Serving.** Remove the pan from the heat and continue whisking for a few moments, until the sauce is thick and frothy and coats the side of the pan. Immediately transfer the sauce to a warmed sauceboat. Here, the sabayon accompanies a fish terrine; it may also garnish any poached white fish dish.

3 **Completing the sweet sabayon.** Continue to whisk the wine into the eggs and sugar; the mixture will slowly become whiter and frothier and will double in volume after about five minutes (above, left). Whisk for a further five to 10 minutes to finish the sauce: It should be thick, light and foamy (right).

4 **Serving the sauce.** Transfer the sauce to a warmed sauceboat and serve it with cooked fruit such as the poached pears shown. Or set the pan in a bowl of ice, whisk the sauce until it is cold, and serve it with fresh fruit, cake, pies, sweet soufflés or puddings.

# The Opulence of a Classic Custard

Mild, sweet and rich, custard sauce—like sweet sabayon *(pages 68-69)*—is a mixture of egg yolks, sugar and liquid. However, for a custard, the liquid is milk or cream and it is used in much greater proportion than wine is in a sabayon. As a result, the sauce is somewhat less demanding to make than sabayon, and the finished custard is creamily smooth rather than frothy.

The richness and thickness of a custard sauce can be varied as you like by using all milk, part milk and part cream, or all cream for the liquid, and by varying the proportion of liquid to egg yolks. The ratio of two egg yolks to 1 cup [¼ liter] of milk is usual, but you can make a thinner sauce by increasing the volume of milk to as much as 2 cups [½ liter]. For a thicker, richer custard, add an extra yolk to the basic mixture.

Like other egg-based sauces, custard must be cooked gently to keep the yolks from curdling. But the high volume of liquid dilutes the yolks and shields them against the heat: The sauce may safely be cooked in a heavy pan set directly on a burner rather than over water. To speed cooking, heat the milk, then whisk it into the yolks and sugar off of the heat. During cooking, stir the sauce constantly, alternating figure-8 with circular motions, to distribute the heat evenly throughout.

The sauce lends itself to many flavorings. For a vanilla custard, steep a vanilla bean in the hot milk, removing the bean before whisking the milk into the yolks, or add vanilla extract to the sauce at the end of cooking; alternatively you could add rum, brandy or extra-strength coffee to the custard. For the caramel custard at right, stir caramel sauce *(page 25)* into the yolks with the hot milk, or, as in the box at right, whisk the sauce into the finished custard.

Custard and its variations are equally good served hot, warm or cold. For cold custard, stir the sauce over ice *(Step 4, opposite)* until it is chilled; or stir the custard until it cools, then place plastic wrap directly on its surface to prevent a skin from forming, and refrigerate the custard for as long as three days before serving. If the chilled sauce becomes too thick to pour, whisk it thoroughly, or stir in a little cream.

1 **Combining egg yolks with sugar.** Place egg yolks in a mixing bowl and add superfine sugar. With a whisk, break up the yolks *(above, left)*, then whisk the ingredients together until the sugar is completely absorbed and the mixture is smooth *(center)*. As you whisk, the beaten yolks will become paler and will increase in volume. After about 10 minutes, when the mixture is thick and almost white, test the consistency by lifting out a little on the whisk and dribbling it across the surface of the bowl. It should form a ribbon-like trail *(right)*.

## A Last-Minute Addition of Caramel

1 **Incorporating flavoring.** Boil a sugar syrup to the caramel stage and stir a little water into it to make a caramel sauce. Prepare a custard *(Steps 1 to 5, top)* and whisk the caramel into it.

2 **Serving the custard.** When the caramel is evenly incorporated, pour the sauce into a warmed pitcher. Serve at once with a hot or cold dessert; or stir over ice until cool, then cover it carefully and refrigerate.

2 **Scalding milk.** Heat milk until bubbles appear at its edges, stirring to prevent a skin from forming. Remove the pan from the heat and let the milk cool slightly; then pour it into the yolk-and-sugar mixture, whisking slowly but continuously. When the mixture is blended, transfer it to a saucepan.

3 **Cooking the custard.** Place the saucepan over very low heat. With a wooden spoon, stir the custard continuously as it heats, making sure you include the entire contents of the pan. After seven to 10 minutes the custard should be smooth and should coat the back of the spoon evenly.

4 **Arresting the cooking.** Remove the pan from the heat and dip it at once into a bowl of ice to stop the sauce from thickening further. Stir the sauce so that it does not form a skin.

5 **Straining.** If the sauce is to be used hot, immediately strain it into a warmed bowl *(left)* and serve it with a dessert—in this case, chocolate pudding *(inset)*. Or cover the pan and set it off the heat in a warm water bath; if stirred occasionally, the sauce can be held this way for 15 minutes. To serve the custard cold, stir it over ice until it cools, then refrigerate it.

# 5
# Integral Sauces
## Making the Most of Cooking Liquids

Most methods of cooking a main dish—sautéing, roasting, poaching and braising—offer the chance to make an accompanying sauce from flavoring elements that would otherwise be lost. When meats are sautéed, for example, meat juices coagulate in the bottom of the pan to form savory deposits that can be incorporated into a sauce by being dissolved with liquid. This process—deglazing—is not confined to sautéing. Braised meats, too, are often given a preliminary browning, and the residues that remain in the pan can be deglazed with the braising liquid. And during roasting, meat juices that form a glaze in the bottom of the roasting pan are the starting point for a gravy.

Since the deglazing liquid can be chosen to suit the finished dish, the process permits considerable variation. Plain water may be all that is required to turn the rich residues of a juicy steak or roast into a straightforward and excellent sauce; but red wine, beer, veal stock or suitable combinations of these and other liquids can be used instead. For more delicately flavored meats such as pork, veal or chicken, the harmonious blend of Madeira and cream described on pages 74-75 is one of many options for enriching the finished dish. Sauces for sautés and roasts in particular lend themselves to further elaboration by the addition of herb and vegetable garnishes after the deglazing stage.

In braised dishes, the relatively small amount of liquid used for cooking absorbs enough flavor from the main ingredients to stand as a sauce by itself; no further embellishment is needed for the highly reduced sauce that coats the leg of lamb on pages 80-81. In some braises, however, and in all poached dishes, additional body and flavor is required to turn a dilute cooking medium into a finished sauce. Cream, alone or with egg yolks, will enrich sauces for fish and white meats, while the addition of one of the concentrated savory essences described in Chapter 3 will give substance to sauces for red meats, game and variety meats.

Most of the dishes described in this chapter are composed of two complementary elements: a fluid sauce and a solid main ingredient that share common flavor but retain separate identities. However, when all of the solid ingredients are chopped very fine and cooked together with the liquid, the elements merge. The result is a thick yet pourable blend appropriate for serving over rice, potatoes or pasta (page 86).

A glistening red wine sauce is spooned over slices of tender top-round steak. The sauce was made by using red wine to deglaze the pan in which the steak was sautéed, reducing the liquid until it was concentrated in flavor and then enriching it with butter (pages 76-77).

# Savory Residues from Sautéed and Roasted Meats

## Pork Loin Swathed in Madeira and Cream

As meat and poultry are sautéed or roasted, they release juices that form rich pan deposits; these can be used as savory starting points for sauces. Preparing the sauces entails no more work than deglazing the pan deposits by dissolving them in a liquid. However, despite their culinary simplicity, deglazed sauces can be endlessly varied by adding flavoring ingredients and by changing the choice of liquid—plain or fortified wine, stock, beer or hard cider.

Whatever the liquid, the sauce is made in the same way. After the meat or poultry is cooked, it is removed from the pan. Any excess fat is then poured or spooned off, leaving only the cooking deposits behind. The pan is set over high heat, liquid is added, and the bottom and sides of the pan are scraped vigorously until the caramelized deposits dissolve in the liquid. At this point, the sauce may be enriched with butter, heavy cream or meat glaze; it is now ready to serve.

The choice of deglazing liquid and enrichment depends on the meat you are cooking. Fullness of flavor with a hint of sweetness is the hallmark of sauces made with such fortified wines as Marsala, port or Madeira, and these sauces go especially well with the naturally sweet taste of pork or the richness of game. In this demonstration, for instance, Madeira is the deglazing liquid for sautéed slices of pork loin; for a satiny texture, the sauce is finished with heavy cream.

Red wine contributes a robust taste and a dark color to a deglazing sauce, qualities that make it appropriate for dark, full-flavored meats such as steak (pages 76-77, top). No more enrichment than butter is needed for a steak sauce. For assertive variety meats such as veal kidneys (pages 76-77, bottom) a concentrated reduction of red wine and aromatics makes a distinctive deglazing liquid; an enrichment of meat glaze and butter gives the sauce the appropriate body.

Lighter meats deserve lighter sauces. Deglazing sauces for sautéed or roasted chicken or turkey can be based on water, if you like. However, light veal stock (pages 46-47) or chicken stock (recipe, page 159) will give a greater complexity of flavor. If you choose to deglaze with wine, a mild white one is the best choice.

**1** **Preparing pork.** Trim pork—in this case, a pork loin—of all membranes and fat. Cut the meat into slices 1 inch [2½ cm.] thick. To give the sauce extra body, coat the slices lightly with flour on both sides. In a large, shallow pan set over medium heat, melt butter; when it foams, add the pork slices.

**2** **Turning the pork.** When the pork slices have browned on the underside and partially cooked—after about five minutes—turn them over. Continue to sauté them for five more minutes, and when the slices are evenly colored on both sides, transfer them to a warmed platter. Keep the meat warm in a 200° F. [100° C.] oven.

**5** **Enriching with cream.** To lend volume and richness to the sauce, pour in heavy cream. The amount can be varied according to taste and how much sauce you require. Here, the volume of the cream is equal to about double the volume of the deglazing liquid.

**6** **Blending the sauce.** Stir the cream and deglazing liquid together, scraping the bottom of the pan to bring the syrupy liquid to the surface (above). When the sauce is evenly blended, boil it for a few minutes to concentrate the flavors.

**3** **Adding liquid.** Pour off and discard any excess fat from the pan, leaving behind the pan deposits. Return the pan to high heat and pour in a generous splash of liquid—in this instance, Madeira is used.

**4** **Deglazing.** When the liquid comes to a boil, use a wooden spatula or spoon to scrape up the deposits from the bottom of the pan *(above, left)*. Scrape and stir until the pan bottom is free of deposits and most have dissolved in the liquid. Boil the liquid for a few minutes, drawing the spatula across the bottom of the pan to check the liquid's consistency. When the spatula leaves a clean trail *(right)*, deglazing is complete.

**7** **Straining the sauce.** To ensure that the sauce is entirely smooth and free from any undissolved solids, strain it through a sieve into another pan. Cook the sauce for another minute or two, until it thickens enough to coat the spoon.

**8** **Serving the sauce.** As soon as the sauce has the consistency of heavy cream *(inset)*, it is ready to serve. Spoon it from the pan over each serving of pork. At right, glazed carrots lend a complementary sweetness to the pork, and provide an attractive touch of color.

## Tender Beef Allied with Red Wine

1 **Sautéing steak.** Trim fat from steak—here, a top-round steak 2 inches [5 cm.] thick. Pour a little oil into a skillet set over high heat. When the oil sizzles, drop in the steak and sear one side for two minutes, or until the surface is brown. Reduce the heat and cook the steak for four or five minutes. Turn the steak over and sear the other side.

2 **Pouring off fat.** Reduce the heat and sauté the steak for four or five minutes more, depending on how rare you want the meat to be. Remove the pan from the heat. Transfer the steak to a warmed platter. Pour off and discard the fat in the pan.

3 **Deglazing the pan.** Return the pan to high heat. Pour in a generous amount of full-bodied red wine. With a wooden, flat-edged spatula, scrape up the pan deposits until they have been loosened and partially dissolved in the liquid. Boil the liquid until it is syrupy, then remove the pan from the heat.

## An Aromatic Finish for Veal Kidneys

1 **Sautéing kidneys.** Slit the membrane covering veal kidneys and peel it off. Halve each kidney lengthwise and trim away the core fat. Slice the kidneys into ½-inch [1-cm.] pieces. In a pan set over medium heat, melt butter until it foams. Add the kidneys; sauté them for four minutes, stirring frequently, until they lose their pinkness.

2 **Deglazing.** Tip the kidneys into a strainer to drain off bitter juices released during cooking. Return the pan to the heat; add a little butter to it. Put in chopped shallots; when they are colored, add enough red wine reduction (page 10) to cover the bottom of the pan. Scrape the deposits from the pan until they dissolve in the liquid.

3 **Adding meat glaze.** Boil the liquid until it is a syrupy consistency, then add 2 to 3 tablespoons [30 to 45 ml.] of meat glaze (pages 48-49) for extra flavor and body. Stir until the glaze has melted and the liquids are all blended into a smooth sauce. Add a dash of freshly squeezed lemon juice.

4 **Finishing the sauce.** Add a few cubes of butter, swirling the pan so that the butter is evenly absorbed into the sauce. Carve the steak, cutting it on the bias to make broad slices. Spoon the sauce over the slices and serve them immediately.

4 **Reheating the kidneys.** Put the drained kidneys into the pan of sauce. Over low heat, warm the kidneys for two or three minutes, stirring occasionally; do not let the sauce boil.

5 **Finishing with butter.** When the kidneys are thoroughly reheated, remove the pan from the heat. Add a few cubes of butter. Stir all the ingredients until the butter is completely absorbed.

6 **Serving the kidneys.** Transfer the kidneys and their sauce to a warmed serving platter. If you like, sprinkle some finely chopped fresh chervil over the dish as a garnish before serving.

## Preparing Perfect Pan Gravy

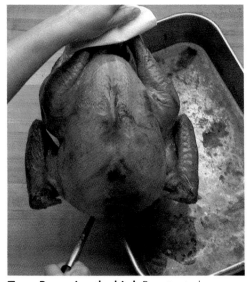

1 **Removing the bird.** Roast a turkey and, when it is done, remove the roasting pan from the oven. Using a broad-bladed spatula, transfer the turkey to a serving platter and keep it warm. Let the juices in the roasting pan cool for a few moments so that the fat rises to the surface of the liquid.

2 **Skimming the fat.** Tilt the roasting pan to collect the juices in one corner. Use a spoon to skim off almost all of the fat, leaving behind the pan deposits and the roasting juices.

3 **Stirring in flour.** Place the pan over low heat and scrape loose the pan deposits with a wooden spatula. When the juices and deposits begin to foam, gradually stir in flour to thicken the gravy. Let the mixture cook for a few minutes, stirring continuously.

4 **Adding liquid.** Stir in hot liquid—in this case, veal stock—in a slow, steady stream and cook until the gravy thickens, about five minutes. Longer cooking is unnecessary: The flavors of the veal stock and the pan deposits will mask any floury taste.

5 **Serving the gravy.** Serve the gravy from a warmed sauceboat. Here, the gravy is ladled over sliced turkey and dressing served with broccoli and glazed sweet potatoes.

Braising means cooking foods in a small amount of liquid for lengthy periods, and ̣oaching means cooking foods ̣in a large amount of liquid for a short time, but ̣oth methods proceed in the same way ̣nd both offer an obvious opportunity for ̣auce making. During cooking, the liq-̣id is imbued with flavors from the main ̣ngredients—meat, poultry, fish or veg-̣tables—and their accompanying aro-̣atics, and this liquid is a natural sauce ̣oundation. The liquid may simply be ̣trained, reduced and cleansed before ̣erving, or it may be enhanced in a va-̣iety of ways.

The most important factor in the taste ̣f the finished sauce is the poaching or ̣raising liquid—water, stock, wine or a ̣ombination. Water leaves the flavor of ̣he poached or braised ingredients unal-̣ered. A rich veal stock enhances the fla-̣ors of meat, poultry or vegetables—as ̣sh stock does fish—and lends body to ̣he final sauce. Wine adds a piquant un-̣ertone. Veal stock is the main cooking ̣quid for the veal sweetbreads at right, ̣r the leg of lamb in the top demonstra-̣on on pages 80-81 and for the artichoke ̣ottoms shown on the bottom of that ̣age. In each case, the stock is rein-̣̣rced—with white wine for the sweet-̣reads and lamb, and with Madeira for ̣e artichokes.

Fish stocks, too, can be varied: Mild-̣asting fish most often are cooked in ̣ock flavored with white wine, stronger-̣asting fish such as salmon in red wine ̣ock. And fish stock can be supplement-̣d with other liquids: Mushroom cooking ̣quid enriches the white wine stock used ̣r sole on pages 82-83.

The enrichments and flavorings used ̣r sauces of this type are legion and may ̣e improvised at will. A sauce based on ̣eal stock, for instance, will gain succu-̣nce from a little meat glaze or *coulis*. A ̣milar effect can be produced by includ-̣g gelatinous calf's or pig's feet in the ̣asic liquid at the start of cooking. These, ̣owever, take at least three hours to ren-̣r their gelatin; use them only in long-̣oked dishes. Cream and flavored but-̣rs are classics among other finishes. ̣nd for a sumptuous sauce, add the cook-̣g liquid to a velouté *(pages 82-83)* fla-̣red to complement the dish at hand.

## Sweetbreads Bathed in Wine and Stock

**1** **Preparing sweetbreads.** Soak veal sweetbreads in several changes of cold water. Simmer them in fresh water for five minutes; drain and rinse them. Peel off membranes, cartilage and fat. Put the sweetbreads between two towels and flatten them under a weighted board for three hours. Place them in a pan on mirepoix *(page 8)*.

**2** **Braising.** Pour in just enough white wine and veal stock to cover the sweetbreads, then press buttered parchment paper on top to hold them in place. Cover the pan. Simmer the sweetbreads for 40 minutes; or bring them to a boil, then transfer them to a 300° to 325° F. [150° to 160° C.] oven to cook for the same period.

**3** **Cleansing.** Remove the sweetbreads from the oven and strain the liquid into a pan. Return the sweetbreads and the mirepoix to the braising pan and set it aside. Simmer the liquid, half off the heat, for approximately 20 minutes, skimming off the thick skin that forms *(page 51, Step 7)*. The sauce is ready when only a thin skin, free of fat, forms. For body, stir in a spoonful of *coulis*.

**4** **Serving.** When the *coulis* has melted and the sauce is smooth, pour it over the sweetbreads. Warm the assembled dish over very low heat before you present it. Serve the sweetbreads straight from the pan, coating each portion with a few spoonfuls of sauce.

## Lamb Glazed with Braising Juices

**1** **Larding.** Remove fat from a leg of lamb. Cut out the pelvic bone; reserve it. Cut chilled pork fatback into ½-inch [1-cm.] strips. Thread a larding needle with a strip and draw it through the surface of the meat, making stitches at 1-inch [2½-cm.] intervals; leave 1 inch of fat protruding. Repeat to lard the leg's upper surface and sides.

**2** **Assembling ingredients.** Tie any loose flesh with string. Split two washed pig's feet lengthwise; parboil them for two to three minutes, then drain and rinse them. Prepare a bouquet garni (page 7). Put coarsely chopped onions and carrots and unpeeled garlic cloves in a deep pot; place the lamb on top.

**3** **Adding veal stock.** Pack the pelvic bone, the pig's feet and the bouquet garni around the meat. Pour in two to three glasses of white wine, then hot veal stock (pages 46-47) until the ingredients are just covered. Cover the contents with buttered parchment paper and a lid; place the pan in a preheated 325° F. [160° C.] oven.

## Artichoke Bottoms Laden with Onions

**1** **Preparing artichokes.** Snap the stem and its fibers off each artichoke. Snap off the tough outer leaves, exposing the tender inner ones. Cut off two thirds of the globe's top and, with a stainless-steel knife, pare away the dark green skin from the base. Scoop out the choke (above). Rub the surfaces with lemon juice to prevent discoloration.

**2** **Adding braising liquid.** To prevent the artichoke bottoms from being spoiled by chemical reactions, place them in a nonreactive vessel—an earthenware dish is shown—packing them tightly in one layer. Add a shallow layer of liquid—in this instance, veal stock and Madeira. Pour some of the liquid inside the artichoke bottoms.

**3** **Braising.** Set the dish on a fireproof pad and bring the liquid to a boil. Then cover and cook the artichokes in a preheated 325° F. [160° C.] oven for about 30 minutes, until they are tender. Transfer them to a plate; pour the liquid into a pan, then return them to the dish. Bring the liquid to a boil; cleanse and reduce it (page 51, Step 7) by half.

4 **Pressing out juices.** Cook the lamb until it is tender, about three hours. Set the lamb and pig's feet aside; discard the bone and the bouquet garni. Strain the liquid and vegetables through a sieve set over a pan, pressing the juices out of the vegetables. Discard the vegetables. Cleanse and reduce the liquid *(page 51, Step 7)* by half.

5 **Glazing the lamb.** Put the lamb in a shallow, ovenproof dish. Remove the bones from the pig's feet, cut each half diagonally into three pieces; arrange them around the meat. Pour the cleansed sauce over the meat and cook it, uncovered, in a 400° F. [200° C.] oven for 30 to 45 minutes, basting every six or seven minutes.

6 **Serving the lamb.** Prepare an accompaniment for the lamb—in this case, a generously buttered mixed purée of rutabaga, onion, celeriac, potato and garlic was chosen. Carve the lamb and transfer the slices, along with pieces of pig's feet and accompaniments, to serving plates. Spoon the sauce over the meat.

4 **Adding cream.** Pour the reduced liquid over the artichokes, then add heavy cream—here, an amount about equal to the braising liquid. Cover the dish and return it to the oven for 20 to 30 minutes, basting regularly. Transfer the artichokes to a warm plate, draining them of all liquid, and keep them warm.

5 **Finishing the sauce.** Strain the cream-enriched braising liquid through a sieve set over a small pan. Over high heat, boil the liquid briskly until it has the consistency of thick syrup.

6 **Serving.** Prepare a garnish to go inside each artichoke. In this case, tiny onions were parboiled, then cooked gently in butter. Arrange the artichokes and the garnish on a warmed serving dish. Ladle the sauce over them and serve them at once.

## Spirals of Fish with a Seafood Garnish

**1 Preparing sole.** Make and chill a spinach-flavored fish mousseline *(recipe, page 164)*. Rinse, dry and flatten sole fillets. To prevent curling, score each fillet in three or four places on the skinned side. Spread the mousseline thick on the scored sides. Roll the fillets; pack them in a buttered heavy pan.

**2 Adding the liquid.** Blanch mushrooms *(page 11)*, set them aside, and ladle their liquid and white-wine fish stock *(page 46)* around the fillets. Add just enough to cover the fillets.

**3 Poaching.** Cover the fillets with buttered parchment paper. Then set the pan, covered, on medium heat and bring the liquid to a boil. Remove the pan from the heat and allow the fillets to steep for about 10 minutes, or until the mousseline is firm to the touch. Using a spatula or spoon, transfer the fillets to a warmed serving platter.

## Salmon Steaks in a Wine-dark Sauce

**1 Enriching velouté.** Prepare a basic fish velouté *(page 53, Steps 1 and 2)*, using a fish stock flavored with red wine *(page 46)*. Pour an equal quantity of red wine reduction *(page 10)* into the fish velouté, stirring as you pour. Then boil the mixture briskly until it has reduced by about half.

**2 Poaching salmon.** Slice fresh salmon into steaks 2 inches [5 cm.] thick and arrange them in a buttered heavy pan. Cover them with red-wine fish stock and place buttered parchment paper on top; cover the pan. Bring the stock to a boil, then turn off the heat and let the steaks steep in the hot liquid for about 15 minutes to complete their cooking.

**3 Straining the liquid.** Transfer the salmon steaks to a warmed plate with a little of their poaching liquid; cover them and keep them warm. Strain the remaining poaching liquid through a sieve set over a small pan. Over high heat, boil the strained liquid until it has reduced by about half.

4 **Reducing the liquid.** Set the pan over high heat, and boil the liquid briskly until it has reduced by about half. Add heavy cream to taste, then swirl the pan gently to mix the cream into the liquid.

5 **Adding a garnish.** Prepare a garnish for the sauce—here, steamed, shelled mussels *(page 10)* and the blanched mushrooms. Add the garnish ingredients to the sauce. Stir the sauce gently over low heat for a couple of minutes to warm the garnish, then pour the sauce into a warmed sauceboat.

6 **Serving.** Slice the rolled sole fillets in half horizontally; arrange three halves on each serving plate. Ladle a little of the garnished sauce around each portion and serve the rest separately.

4 **Combining the two liquids.** Pour the reduced poaching liquid into the pan containing the velouté. Stir the liquids to amalgamate them. Over high heat, bring the liquid to a boil. Set the pan half off the heat, then cleanse and reduce the sauce *(page 51, Step 7)*.

5 **Adding anchovy butter.** Remove the pan from the heat. Add chilled anchovy butter *(page 12)* a few pieces at a time, whisking to blend it smoothly into the sauce. In this case, about 2 tablespoons [30 ml.] of butter are used for each cup [¼ liter] of sauce.

6 **Serving.** Immediately pour the sauce into a warmed sauceboat. Remove the skin from the salmon steaks and place them on individual serving plates. Ladle a generous helping of sauce over them.

# Meat Stew: An Intricate Assembly of Flavors

For some braised dishes, the meat is browned in fat before liquid is added, and this browning yields savory deposits that may be deglazed by the method used for sautéed and roasted meats. When the meat is then braised in its deglazed pan, the meat's flavor is drawn into the braising liquid, where it mingles with the dissolved pan deposits to form a rich, concentrated sauce. The procedure is shown here with veal, but the same technique could be applied—with the proper adjustments of cooking time—to pieces of lean beef, lamb, rabbit or chicken.

The sauce for a stew of this type owes much to the character of the liquids employed for deglazing and braising. These can include red or white wine, beer, stock or plain water, depending on taste. Here, a dash of brandy and a generous amount of red wine are used to deglaze the pan in which pieces of veal knuckle have been browned with flour. Melted veal stock is employed for braising. The stock tenderizes the meat while it is stewing, and the gelatin in the liquid gives body to the final sauce.

The dish is by no means finished when the meat is done. Lengthy cooking draws fat and solids from the meat; these rise to the surface, where they are trapped in a thick skin. This skin must be repeatedly skimmed off, just as for a stock *(page 47, Step 2, top)*. During the cleansing period, the sauce reduces and becomes thicker.

Garnishes for these stews can include a variety of vegetables—carrots, peas, green beans, onions, turnips and mushrooms, for example. Garnish vegetables should be cooked in advance. Once they are added to the braised meat, the assembled dish should be gently reheated in its sauce before serving. Pasta, rice or potatoes, which will soak up the rich sauce, all make suitable accompaniments.

1 **Sautéing onions.** Heat butter in a wide, shallow pan until the butter foams, then gently sauté finely chopped onions in it. When they are soft, remove the onions with a slotted spoon, put them on a plate and set them aside.

2 **Browning veal.** Put veal—in this case, thick pieces from the knuckle—in the pan. Over medium heat, cook the pieces on one side for about 10 minutes until they are brown. Turn them over, and cook them for a further 15 minutes to brown the undersides.

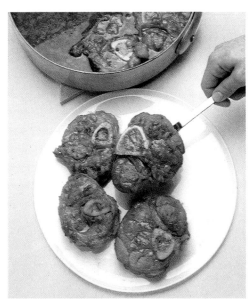

6 **Transferring the meat.** Remove the pan from the heat. With a slotted spoon, transfer the veal to a plate *(above)*. Press juices from the bouquet garni into the pan, then discard it.

7 **Puréeing the onions.** Pour the braising liquid and onions from the pan into a fine-meshed sieve set over a bowl. To add body to the sauce, press the onions through the sieve with a pestle. Transfer the liquid to a small pan. Return the meat to the braising pan and keep it covered.

3 **Adding flour.** Return the softened onions to the pan with the veal. To thicken the sauce and deepen the color, sprinkle a little flour over the ingredients. With a wooden spatula, lift the pieces of meat slightly and stir the flour into the pan juices, then turn the meat over.

4 **Deglazing.** Pour in 1 to 2 tablespoons [15 to 30 ml.] of brandy; then, over high heat, add red wine (above)—here, about 1 cup [¼ liter]. With the wooden spatula, deglaze the pan by scraping up the residues from underneath the meat.

5 **Braising.** Pour in enough hot veal stock (pages 46-47) just to cover the meat. Prepare a bouquet garni (page 7) and tuck it under the meat. Put a lid on the pan and simmer the meat gently, over low heat, for approximately one and one half hours.

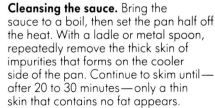

8 **Cleansing the sauce.** Bring the sauce to a boil, then set the pan half off the heat. With a ladle or metal spoon, repeatedly remove the thick skin of impurities that forms on the cooler side of the pan. Continue to skim until—after 20 to 30 minutes—only a thin skin that contains no fat appears.

9 **Reassembling the stew.** Add a garnish to the meat in the braising pan—in this case, blanched mushrooms (page 11); chopped and parboiled carrots; and tiny onions that were plunged briefly into boiling water to loosen their skins, then cooled, peeled and parboiled for 10 minutes. Pour the sauce into the pan.

10 **Serving the stew.** Cover the pan and simmer the stew gently for 15 to 20 minutes so that its elements heat through and the flavors intermingle. Here, the stew is served from the pan, with pasta.

# Ragù: Pasta's Perfect Partner

When finely chopped or ground meat is braised for long periods, the resulting stew is so fine in texture that it constitutes a sauce in itself, a perfect partner for such starchy, sauce-absorbing foods as boiled potatoes, rice or pasta.

The meat for such a sauce should be lean and well flavored, but there is no need to choose an expensive cut, since the combination of fine chopping and slow cooking will tenderize it. You can choose any raw lean meat, poultry or game; here, for instance, beef is braised until it is meltingly tender (recipe, page 141). To minimize any loss of juices, you can chop the meat by hand, using two heavy knives of equal size and weight. Alternatively, pass the meat through a meat grinder or simply cut it into small pieces.

The ground beef in this demonstration is cooked with aromatic vegetables, stock and tomato purée, with finely chopped prosciutto incorporated for extra flavor. Other possible supplements include celery, dried mushrooms or chopped chicken livers. The cooked sauce may be enriched with a few spoonfuls of cream.

**1** **Browning meat.** Chop onions and carrots fine. Warm butter or oil in a heavy pan over low heat. Then sauté the vegetables, stirring them until they are soft—about five minutes. Increase the heat and add raw ground beef. Brown the beef, stirring it so that the heat sears it on all sides.

**2** **Adding flavorings.** When the meat is well browned, reduce the heat and stir in any flavoring ingredients you wish to add, such as diced cooked ham, leftover meat or, as here, prosciutto. Season the mixture; in this case, salt, pepper, lemon peel and a grating of nutmeg are used.

**3** **Adding liquid.** Add a little tomato purée (pages 34-35) or puréed canned tomatoes. Pour in enough melted veal stock (pages 46-47) to half-cover the meat, scraping the pan to dissolve any meaty deposits. Cook the mixture over low heat, with the lid set slightly ajar so that you can control the simmer.

**4** **Finishing the sauce.** Cook the sauce for about one and one half hours, until the meat is tender and the sauce has reduced to the desired consistency; if the sauce dries too much, add a little more liquid during cooking. The sauce should have sufficient body for the meat and liquid not to separate. To enrich the sauce, stir in heavy cream.

**5** **Serving the sauce.** Cook rice, polenta or pasta—here, spaghetti. Transfer the drained spaghetti to a warmed serving dish, spreading it evenly with a fork. Ladle the sauce over the pasta and serve the dish immediately.

# Anthology of Recipes

In choosing the 220 recipes that make up the Anthology, the editors and consultants have drawn upon the cooking literature of 19 countries. A large number of the recipes are French; among them are sauces from the classic tradition as well as recipes from masters of the *nouvelle cuisine*. Recipes from other countries include both simple mixtures, such as the uncooked English mint sauce or the Mexican fresh vegetable *salsa cruda,* and elaborate concoctions such as a Polish fish dish with gingerbread sauce or a spiced Indian lamb dish called *shahi raan.*

Many of the recipes were written by world-renowned exponents of the culinary art, but there are also selections from rare and out-of-print books and from works that have never been published in English. Whatever the sources, the emphasis is always on fresh, natural ingredients that blend harmoniously and on techniques that are practical for the home cook.

Since many early recipe writers did not specify amounts of ingredients or cooking times and temperatures, the missing information has been judiciously added. In some cases, clarifying introductory notes have also been supplied; they are printed in italics. Modern terms have been substituted for archaic language and some instructions have been expanded; but to preserve the character of the original recipes, the authors' texts have been changed as little as possible. Some instructions have necessarily been expanded, but anywhere the cooking directions still seem somewhat abrupt, the reader need only refer to the appropriate demonstrations in the front of the book.

In keeping with the organization of the first half of the book, the recipes in the Anthology are categorized according to their major ingredients. Standard preparations—basic meat and fish stocks, for example—appear at the end of the Anthology. Unfamiliar cooking terms and uncommon ingredients are explained in the combined General Index and Glossary.

Apart from the primary components, all ingredients are listed in order of use, with both the customary U.S. measurements and the metric measurements provided. All quantities reflect the American practice of measuring such solid ingredients as flour by volume rather than by weight, as Europeans do.

To make the quantities simpler to measure, many of the figures have been rounded off to correspond to the gradations on U.S. metric spoons and cups. (One cup, for example, equals 237 milliliters; however, wherever practicable in these recipes, the metric equivalent of 1 cup appears as a more readily measured 250 milliliters—¼ liter.) Similarly, the weight, temperature and linear metric equivalents have been rounded off slightly. Thus the American and metric figures do not exactly match, but using one set or the other will produce the same good results.

# Simple Sauces

## Warm Chive Sauce

### Warme Schnittlauchsauce

*This rich sauce is suitable for boiled or steamed vegetables and poached chicken or fish.*

To make about 1 ¼ cups [300 ml.]

| | | |
|---|---|---|
| 3 tbsp. | finely cut fresh chives | 45 ml. |
| 1 tbsp. | butter | 15 ml. |
| 1 | small onion, very finely chopped | 1 |
| 1 tbsp. | flour | 15 ml. |
| 1 cup | milk | ¼ liter |
| | salt and pepper | |
| | freshly grated nutmeg | |
| 2 tbsp. | sour cream | 30 ml. |

In a saucepan, melt the butter and fry the onion in it for about one minute, without letting the onion brown. Stir in the flour, then pour in the milk and season the mixture with salt and pepper and a pinch of nutmeg. Bring the sauce to a boil, then let it simmer for five minutes. Finally, add the chives and the sour cream.

HANS GUSTL KERNMAYR
SO KOCHTE MEINE MUTTER

## Ibizan Parsley Sauce

### Salsa de Juvert

This sauce is especially good with poached or grilled fish. If you serve it with poached fish, thin the sauce with a few spoonfuls of the liquid in which the fish was cooked.

To make about 2 cups [½ liter]

| | | |
|---|---|---|
| 2 cups | fresh parsley leaves | ½ liter |
| 2 | garlic cloves | 2 |
| | salt | |
| | cayenne pepper | |
| 3 tbsp. | fresh lemon juice | 45 ml. |
| ½ cup | oil | 125 ml. |

In a mortar, pound the parsley, garlic, a pinch of salt and a little cayenne pepper to a paste. Gradually add the lemon juice and oil, beating the mixture well.

JUAN CASTELLÓ GUASCH
BON PROFIT!

## The Perfect Mint Sauce

*This sauce is a classic accompaniment for lamb.*

To make about ⅓ cup [75 ml.]

| | | |
|---|---|---|
| 40 | fresh mint leaves | 40 |
| about 1 tsp. | superfine sugar | about 5 ml. |
| about 1 tbsp. | boiling water | about 15 ml. |
| about 1 tbsp. | fresh lemon juice or wine vinegar | about 15 ml. |

Pound the mint leaves with a mortar and pestle. Cover the mint with the sugar to absorb all the juice. Add just enough boiling water to dissolve the sugar. Sharpen the sauce with lemon juice or wine vinegar to taste.

BEE NILSON (EDITOR)
THE WI DIAMOND JUBILEE COOKBOOK

## Cold Tomatoes with Hot Curry Sauce

The success of the recipe depends entirely on the contrast between the cold, cold tomato and the superhot spicy sauce. Although this recipe works best when good tomatoes are in season, it can give even pale winter tomatoes some semblance of glamour.

To serve 6

| | | |
|---|---|---|
| 6 | medium-sized ripe tomatoes | 6 |
| 4 tsp. | curry powder | 20 ml. |
| 3 tbsp. | butter | 45 ml. |
| 3 tbsp. | flour | 45 ml. |
| 2 cups | light cream | ½ liter |
| 3 tbsp. | finely chopped chutney | 45 ml. |
| | salt and pepper | |
| 6 | slices firm-textured white bread with the crusts removed | 6 |

Plunge the tomatoes into boiling water for a few seconds and remove them with a skimmer, peel them and cut out the stem ends. Chill the prepared tomatoes in the refrigerator for at least three hours.

To prepare the sauce, melt the butter in a saucepan, add the flour and curry powder, and stir until this roux is smooth, making certain that none clings to the edges of the pan. Cook the mixture for a minute or two, stirring constantly. Remove the pan from the heat and slowly stir in the cream, beating constantly with a whisk. When the sauce is smooth, return it to the heat. Add the chutney and its liquid to the sauce and sprinkle on salt and pepper. Simmer the sauce for two minutes.

Toast the bread and place the slices on individual plates. Place a tomato on each slice and spoon a tablespoon [15 ml.]

of the hot sauce over it. Pass the rest of the sauce separately to keep it as hot as possible. Serve at once.

CAROL CUTLER
THE SIX-MINUTE SOUFFLÉ AND OTHER CULINARY DELIGHTS

## Cold Horseradish Sauce with Sour Cream

### Umak od Hrena

Serve this sauce with ham, fish or boiled beef.

To make 1 cup [¼ liter]

| | | |
|---|---|---|
| ½ cup | freshly grated horseradish | 125 ml. |
| ¼ cup | sour cream | 50 ml. |
| | salt | |
| 1 tsp. | sugar | 5 ml. |
| 2 tbsp. | vinegar or fresh lemon juice | 30 ml. |
| 1 | hard-boiled egg yolk | 1 |

Pour the sour cream over the horseradish. Add salt to taste, the sugar, and the vinegar or lemon juice. Press the egg yolk through a sieve into the sauce and mix well.

INGE KRAMARZ
THE BALKAN COOKBOOK

## Mustard Cream Sauce

### Sauce Moutarde à la Crème

This sauce can accompany many hors d'oeuvre dishes.

To make ¾ cup [175 ml.]

| | | |
|---|---|---|
| 3 tbsp. | Dijon mustard | 45 ml. |
| ⅔ cup | heavy cream or crème fraîche (recipe, page 158) | 150 ml. |
| | salt and pepper | |
| 3 tbsp. | fresh lemon juice | 45 ml. |

In a bowl, mix the mustard with salt and pepper and the lemon juice. Gradually whisk in the cream, in the same way that you would whisk oil into a mayonnaise.

EUGENIE BRAZIER
LES SECRETS DE LA MÈRE BRAZIER

## Yogurt Raita

*The volatile oils in the chili may irritate your skin. Wear rubber gloves when handling it or wash your hands immediately afterward.*

To balance spicy Indian grills there is nothing better than a refreshing yogurt sauce. For a spicy *raita* add one or more of the following to taste: about 1 teaspoon [5 ml.] of paprika; a pinch of cayenne pepper; the juice of a ½-inch [1-cm.] piece of fresh ginger, squeezed in a garlic press; a pinch of *garam masala;* a pinch of ground cumin; a pinch of ground coriander; a few chopped coriander leaves.

To make about 2½ cups [625 ml.]

| | | |
|---|---|---|
| 2 cups | yogurt | ½ liter |
| 1½ tbsp. | fresh lemon juice | 22½ ml. |
| 2 | garlic cloves, crushed to a paste | 2 |
| 2 tbsp. | chopped fresh mint leaves | 30 ml. |
| 1 | hot green chili, stemmed, seeded and finely chopped | 1 |

Beat all the ingredients together in a bowl. Chill the mixture thoroughly before serving.

CLAUDIA RODEN
PICNIC: THE COMPLETE GUIDE TO OUTDOOR FOOD

## Whipped Cream Dressing for Salads

### Punajuurikermakastike

*To make beet juice, grate a beet onto a double thickness of cheesecloth. Gather the cloth and squeeze it vigorously.*

This sauce is fluffy and light pink. Serve it in a small bowl or arranged in a mound on a beet salad or red cabbage slaw. It also goes well with a herring-and-beet salad.

To make 2 cups [½ liter]

| | | |
|---|---|---|
| 1 cup | heavy cream, whipped | ¼ liter |
| 2 tbsp. | fresh lemon juice | 30 ml. |
| 2 tsp. | beet juice | 10 ml. |
| | salt | |
| | sugar | |

Combine the cream with the lemon juice, beet juice and a pinch each of salt and sugar. Blend the sauce thoroughly.

BEATRICE A. OJAKANGAS
THE FINNISH COOKBOOK

## Blue Cheese Sauce for Steaks

This sauce works well for hamburgers, too.

To make about ¾ cup [175 ml.]

| | | |
|---|---|---|
| ¼ lb. | blue cheese, softened | 125 g. |
| 1 | garlic clove, crushed and macerated in 1 to 2 tbsp. [15 to 30 ml.] brandy for 15 minutes | 1 |
| ¼ cup | olive oil | 50 ml. |

Pound the garlic clove and brandy to a paste, and blend in the blue cheese and the olive oil. Grill a thick steak, slice it, spread it with this mixture and slip it under the broiler just long enough to melt the cheese.

HELEN BROWN
HELEN BROWN'S WEST COAST COOK BOOK

## Lemon-Wine Steak Sauce

*To make about 1 ½ cups [375 ml.]*

| | | |
|---|---|---|
| ¼ cup | fresh lemon juice | 50 ml. |
| 2 cups | red wine | ½ liter |
| ¼ cup | finely chopped onion | 50 ml. |
| 1 | garlic clove, lightly crushed | 1 |
| 2 tbsp. | butter | 30 ml. |
| 2 tbsp. | olive oil | 30 ml. |
| | salt and pepper | |
| 1 tbsp. | finely chopped fresh parsley | 15 ml. |

Cook the chopped onion and the crushed garlic clove in the red wine until the liquid is reduced by one half. Remove the garlic, stir in the butter, olive oil, lemon juice, salt and pepper, and the chopped parsley.

HELEN BROWN
HELEN BROWN'S WEST COAST COOK BOOK

## Spaghetti with Lemon Sauce

### Spaghetti al Limone

*Grappa is a potent, unaged brandy distilled from the pulpy residue left when grapes are crushed and pressed for wine.*

The name may suggest a pungent taste, but the dish has only the fragrance of lemon. The original recipe uses grappa; we have substituted vodka not only because it is more readily available, but also because it has a more delicate flavor. If you can find a good grappa, however, be daring and use it.

*To serve 4*

| | | |
|---|---|---|
| 14 oz. | spaghetti | 425 g. |
| 1 ½ tbsp. | fresh lemon juice | 22 ½ ml. |
| 2 tsp. | grated lemon peel | 10 ml. |
| 1 cup | heavy cream | ¼ liter |
| ¼ cup | vodka or grappa | 50 ml. |
| ⅛ tsp. | freshly grated nutmeg | ½ ml. |

In a large skillet over very low heat, steep the lemon peel in the cream for five minutes. Add the lemon juice and vodka or grappa, and stir in the nutmeg.

Cook the pasta in at least 4 quarts [4 liters] of boiling salted water. Drain the pasta when it is barely *al dente* and add it to the sauce in the skillet. Raise the heat to medium, then stir and toss the spaghetti until it has absorbed most of the liquid and the sauce is thick and creamy. Serve hot.

MARGARET AND G. FRANCO ROMAGNOLI
THE NEW ITALIAN COOKING

## Sea Urchin Butter

### Beurre d'Oursins

*To open a sea urchin, cut a circular piece from the dimpled underside with scissors. Shake the urchin to empty out the viscera; discard them. Scoop out the pink roe with a spoon.*

Use this butter to coat poached fish fillets or lobster. It will melt as it comes into contact with the heat of the seafood.

*To make about ½ cup [125 ml.]*

| | | |
|---|---|---|
| 3 or 4 | sea urchins | 3 or 4 |
| 4 tbsp. | butter, softened | 60 ml. |

Open the sea urchins and remove the roe from each one. Purée the roe by pushing it through a fine-meshed sieve. Then work the purée into the softened butter.

JEAN AND PAUL MINCHELLI
CRUSTACÉS, POISSONS ET COQUILLAGES

## My Special Butter Sauce

### Mon Beurre Blanc

*This rich sauce is suitable for poached fish and shellfish or for steamed or boiled vegetables.*

*To make about 1 ½ cups [375 ml.]*

| | | |
|---|---|---|
| ½ lb. | butter, chilled and cut into 10 slices | ¼ kg. |
| 4 | shallots, very finely chopped | 4 |
| ¾ cup | dry white wine | 175 ml. |
| 3 tbsp. | white wine vinegar | 45 ml. |
| ½ tsp. | salt | 2 ml. |
| 6 | black peppercorns, crushed | 6 |
| 1 tbsp. | *crème fraîche (recipe, page 158)* or heavy cream | 15 ml. |

Place the shallots in a heavy saucepan. Add the wine, vinegar, salt and peppercorns, and place the pan over medium heat. Bring the liquid to a boil, then reduce the heat and let the liquid boil very gently, until only a tablespoon [15 ml.] remains. This will take about 10 minutes.

Add the *crème fraîche* or heavy cream and stir it in. Let the mixture boil for one minute, then take the pan away from the heat and let it cool until you can place your hand on the pan without burning yourself.

Place the pan back on very low heat and add two pieces of the butter. Mix them in with a whisk until they have been completely incorporated into the mixture. Whisking continuously, incorporate another piece of butter into the sauce, and—when it has been completely amalgamated—whisk in another. Continue until all the butter has been whisked in and you have a fine, smooth sauce. Adjust the seasoning if necessary and strain the sauce through a very fine-meshed sieve into a sauceboat. Serve it immediately.

MICHEL OLIVER
MES RECETTES À LA TÉLÉ

# Meat-based Béchamel Sauce

## Sauce Béchamel

*This rich sauce is suitable for meat or poultry croquettes and for boiled vegetables or vegetable puddings.*

*To make about 2 cups [ ½ liter]*

| 8 tbsp. | butter | 120 ml. |
|---|---|---|
| ½ lb. | veal scraps and trimmings, chopped (about 1 cup [ ¼ liter]) | ¼ kg. |
| ¼ lb. | ham, chopped (about ½ cup [125 ml.]) | 125 g. |
| 2 | carrots, sliced | 2 |
| 2 | onions, thinly sliced | 2 |
| 2 | whole cloves, crushed | 2 |
| 1 | bay leaf, crumbled | 1 |
| 2 | shallots, thinly sliced | 2 |
| 1 tbsp. | finely chopped fresh parsley | 15 ml. |
| 1 tbsp. | finely chopped scallion | 15 ml. |
| ½ tsp. | coarsely ground white pepper | 2 ml. |
| ¼ tsp. | freshly grated nutmeg | 1 ml. |
| ¼ tsp. | salt | 1 ml. |
| 1 tbsp. | flour | 15 ml. |
| 2½ cups | milk | 625 ml. |

Melt the butter in a heavy pan, and add the meats, vegetables and seasonings. Cook over medium heat, stirring frequently, until the meats have stiffened but not browned. Stir in the flour, then gradually add the milk. Simmer the sauce gently, stirring constantly, until it is very thick—about 40 minutes. Strain the sauce through a fine-meshed sieve.

B. ALBERT
LE CUISINIER PARISIEN

# Gascony Butter

## Beurre de Gascogne

*This butter is suitable for broiled or grilled meats or poultry.*

*To make 1 ¼ cups [300 ml.]*

| 12 | large garlic cloves | 12 |
|---|---|---|
| about ½ lb. | butter | about ¼ kg. |
| | salt | |
| | freshly grated nutmeg | |
| | cayenne pepper | |

Cook the garlic cloves in a large quantity of boiling water until they are very soft—12 to 15 minutes. Drain them, then pound them in a mortar with four times their volume of butter. Season with salt, a grating of nutmeg and a pinch of cayenne pepper. Pass the butter through a drum sieve.

URBAIN DUBOIS AND ÉMILE BERNARD
LA CUISINE CLASSIQUE

# Norman White Sauce

## Sauce Blanche Normande

*This mild sauce is suitable for boiled or steamed vegetables.*

*To make 1 cup [ ¼ liter]*

| 1 tsp. | cornstarch or flour | 5 ml. |
|---|---|---|
| 1 to 2 tbsp. | water | 15 to 30 ml. |
| 2 tbsp. | butter | 30 ml. |
| 1 cup | heavy cream | ¼ liter |
| 1 tsp. | white wine vinegar (optional) | 5 ml. |

Mix together the cornstarch or flour and the water; add the butter and cream and place the mixture over low heat. Stir until the sauce boils. Serve.

You may acidulate this sauce with a little vinegar, but do not add it until you have removed the sauce from the heat.

ÉMILE DUMONT
LA BONNE CUISINE FRANÇAISE

# Bound Butter Sauce

## Sauce au Beurre Lié

*This delicate sauce is suitable for boiled or steamed vegetables or for poached fish, shellfish or poultry.*

*To make 1 ½ cups [375 ml.]*

| 12 tbsp. | butter, 10 tbsp. [150 ml.] cut into small pieces | 180 ml. |
|---|---|---|
| ¼ cup | flour, sifted | 50 ml. |
| 1 cup | water | ¼ liter |
| 3 to 4 tbsp. | fresh lemon juice | 45 to 60 ml. |
| | salt and pepper | |

Place 2 tablespoons [30 ml.] of the butter in a saucepan. Add the flour and mix the ingredients with a wooden spoon to form a smooth paste. Gradually stir in the water and 2 tablespoons of the lemon juice. Then season the butter mixture to taste with salt and pepper.

Place the saucepan over medium heat and stir the butter mixture constantly. When the mixture comes to a boil, remove it from the heat and stir it vigorously while adding the remaining butter, a few pieces at a time. The sauce will become creamy. Finish by beating in 1 to 2 more tablespoons [15 to 30 ml.] of lemon juice to taste.

F. BARTHÉLÉMY
LES MENUS EXPLIQUÉS DE CUISINE PRATIQUE

## White Sauce for Boiled Fowl

To serve, put some of the sauce in a tureen and the remainder in the dish with the bird.

| | To make 3 cups [¾ liter] | |
|---|---|---|
| 1 | large blade mace | 1 |
| 2 | whole cloves | 2 |
| 15 | peppercorns | 15 |
| 1¼ cups | water | 300 ml. |
| 4 | salt anchovies, soaked, filleted, rinsed, dried and finely chopped | 4 |
| 8 tbsp. | butter, kneaded with 1 tbsp. [15 ml.] flour | 120 ml. |
| 1¼ cups | heavy cream | 300 ml. |

Boil the mace, cloves and peppercorns in the water until the water is flavored with the spices—about 10 minutes. Strain the liquid into a saucepan and add the chopped anchovies, the kneaded butter and flour, and the cream. Boil the sauce, stirring it well, for two minutes.

MRS. RUNDELL
MODERN DOMESTIC COOKERY

## Real Sauce à la King

*This rich sauce can be used as a base for making chicken, turkey or ham à la king.*

| | To make about 3 cups [¾ liter] | |
|---|---|---|
| 4 tbsp. | butter | 60 ml. |
| ¼ cup | flour | 50 ml. |
| ½ tsp. | salt | 2 ml. |
| ¼ tsp. | pepper | 1 ml. |
| 1½ cups | milk | 375 ml. |
| ¾ cup | light cream | 175 ml. |
| ¼ cup | finely chopped green pepper | 50 ml. |
| 2 | pimientos, chopped | 2 |
| ½ cup | sliced fresh mushrooms | 125 ml. |
| 2 | egg yolks | 2 |
| 2 tbsp. | dry sherry | 30 ml. |

In a double boiler, melt the butter. Stir in the flour and the seasonings. Gradually stir in the milk and light cream. Add the green pepper, pimientos and mushrooms. Stirring occasionally, cook the mixture for 10 minutes, or until it has thickened. Without stirring, cook gently for 10 minutes longer. Beat the egg yolks and sherry together. Add this mixture gradually to the sauce.

IDA BAILEY ALLEN
BEST LOVED RECIPES OF THE AMERICAN PEOPLE

## Buttermilk Sauce

*Karnemelksaus*

Serve this sauce warm with a salad of lettuce, potato and hard-boiled eggs, or Belgian endive and potato. Each diner should mix the salad and sauce together on his own plate.

| | To make 2 cups [½ liter] | |
|---|---|---|
| 2 cups | buttermilk | ½ liter |
| 3 | slices fatty bacon, cut into squares | 3 |
| ⅓ cup | flour | 75 ml. |
| | salt | |

Fry the bacon slowly to extract the fat, stirring it occasionally. In a small pan, mix the flour with ⅓ cup [75 ml.] of the buttermilk to form a smooth paste, then stir in the remaining buttermilk. Bring the buttermilk mixture to a boil, stirring it all the time, and cook it until the sauce thickens—about four minutes. Stir in the bacon and its fat. Season the sauce to taste with salt.

RIA HOLLEMAN
UIT GROOTMOEDERS KEUKEN

## English Bread Sauce

*This spicy sauce is traditionally served with game birds.*

| | To make about 1½ cups [375 ml.] | |
|---|---|---|
| 2 cups | soft white bread crumbs | ½ liter |
| 1 | onion, stuck with 4 whole cloves | 1 |
| 1 cup | milk | ¼ liter |
| | ground mace | |
| 6 | peppercorns | 6 |
| 1 tbsp. | butter | 15 ml. |
| 2 tbsp. | heavy cream | 30 ml. |
| | salt and pepper | |

Put the onion into a saucepan with the milk, a pinch of ground mace and the peppercorns. Bring the mixture to a boil, then remove it from the heat and let it stand for 30 minutes. Strain the milk into another pan and add the bread crumbs. Heat the sauce until it boils, stirring it gently. Stir in the butter and the cream, and season the sauce to taste with salt and pepper.

MARY NORWAK
THE FARMHOUSE KITCHEN

## Bread Sauce for Poultry

*The author suggests that, instead of the milk, this sauce can be made with a stock prepared from the giblets, neck and legs of the poultry that the sauce is to accompany.*

To make about 1 cup [¼ liter]

| ½ cup | fresh white bread crumbs | 125 ml. |
|---|---|---|
| about ¾ cup | milk | about 175 ml. |
| 1 | onion | 1 |
| 12 | peppercorns or whole allspice tied in cheesecloth, or ½ tsp. [2 ml.] ground mace | 12 |
| 2 tbsp. | cream, melted butter or chicken stock (recipe, page 159) | 30 ml. |

Put the bread crumbs into a saucepan and pour on as much milk as they will soak up and a little more. Put the pan over gentle heat and add the onion and the pepper, allspice or mace. Bring the mixture to a boil, then stir it well and let it simmer until it is quite stiff. Remove the pan from the heat and stir in the cream, melted butter or stock. Take out the onion and the peppercorns or allspice, and the sauce is ready.

DR. KITCHINER
THE COOK'S ORACLE

---

## Marseilles Sauce

### Sauce Marseillaise

*This pungent sauce is suitable for poached meats, roasted game, poached fish or shellfish.*

To make ⅔ cup [150 ml.]

| 1 tbsp. | olive oil | 15 ml. |
|---|---|---|
| 2 | garlic cloves, crushed to a paste | 2 |
| 1 tbsp. | flour | 15 ml. |
| 1 cup | dry white wine | ¼ liter |
| 1 | sprig fresh parsley | 1 |
| ⅛ tsp. | powdered saffron | ½ ml. |
| | salt and pepper | |

Place the olive oil in a saucepan with half of the garlic paste. Stirring constantly, heat the oil without letting the garlic brown. When it is very hot, sprinkle in the flour. Cook and stir the mixture until it begins to brown.

Gradually stir in the wine; add the parsley, the saffron, the remaining garlic, and salt and pepper. Bring the mixture to a boil, then reduce the heat and move the pan to the side of

the burner. Simmer for 20 minutes, removing the skin that will repeatedly form on the surface of the liquid.

Skim all traces of grease from the surface of the liquid, pour the sauce through a fine-meshed sieve into a sauceboat and serve it hot.

F. BARTHÉLÉMY
LES MENUS EXPLIQUÉS DE CUISINE PRATIQUE

## Crab Sauce or Dip

### Poo Lon

*To make the coconut milk, steep the grated flesh of one coconut in 2½ cups [625 ml.] of boiling water for one hour. Strain the milk through a sieve lined with a double layer of cheesecloth and squeeze the coconut flesh remaining in the cheesecloth until all the liquid is extracted.*

**Lon** are boiled sauces that are commonly served with fresh vegetables and small dried and fried fish of the herring family. This combination of vegetables, fish and sauce eaten with rice provides the basic meal of the Thai.

To make about 2½ cups [625 ml.]

| 6 oz. | cooked crab meat, picked over and flaked (about ¾ cup [175 ml.]) | 175 g. |
|---|---|---|
| 1¾ cups | coconut milk | 425 ml. |
| ½ tsp. | salt | 2 ml. |
| 3 | shallots, finely chopped | 3 |
| 1 tsp. | sugar | 5 ml. |
| 1 tbsp. | tamarind water, made by soaking ½ oz. [15 g.] of dried tamarind pulp in 1 tbsp. [15 ml.] hot water for 1 hour and pressing the liquid through a sieve | 15 ml. |
| 2 | green serrano chilies, stemmed, seeded and thinly sliced | 2 |
| 1 tbsp. | chopped fresh coriander leaves | 15 ml. |

In a medium-sized saucepan, mix the crab meat, coconut milk and salt. Bring the mixture to a boil, stirring constantly. Reduce the heat and simmer it for five minutes, stirring it occasionally. Add the shallots, sugar, tamarind water and chilies and continue to cook the mixture, stirring, for another five minutes until it forms a thick, homogeneous sauce. Transfer the sauce to a serving bowl and sprinkle it with the chopped coriander.

JENNIFER BRENNAN
THAI COOKING

## To Make a Good Fish Sauce

This is the best sauce for skate and ray.

*To make about 1 ¼ cups [300 ml.]*

| 2 | salt anchovies, soaked, filleted, rinsed and dried | 2 |
|---|---|---|
| 1 cup | water | ¼ liter |
| 1 | whole clove | 1 |
| 1 | blade mace | 1 |
| 2 | strips lemon peel | 2 |
| 1 tsp. | black peppercorns | 5 ml. |
| 1 tbsp. | dry red wine | 15 ml. |
| 1 tbsp. | butter | 15 ml. |
| 2 tbsp. | flour | 30 ml. |

Boil all the ingredients except the butter and flour together until your anchovy is dissolved—about 10 minutes. Then strain the liquid. Roll the butter in the flour, add the mixture to the sauce, and heat gently for a few minutes until the fish sauce has thickened.

SUSANNAH CARTER
THE FRUGAL COLONIAL HOUSEWIFE

## Crayfish Sauce

*La Sauce Nantua*

Crayfish sauce accompanies all kinds of fish simply poached in white wine or a court bouillon.

*To make 3 ½ cups [875 ml.]*

| 3 lb. | small live crayfish, rinsed | 1 ½ kg. |
|---|---|---|
| 7 cups | court bouillon (recipe, page 164) | 1 ¾ liters |
| 20 tbsp. | butter, softened or beaten until light | 300 ml. |
| 3 tbsp. | flour | 45 ml. |
| 2 cups | heavy cream | ½ liter |
| | salt | |
| | cayenne pepper | |

Bring the court bouillon to a boil, throw in the crayfish and let them cook for eight minutes over high heat. Drain, shell and devein them. Reserve the tails and keep them hot.

Put the shells into a mortar with the butter and pound them together. When they are well amalgamated, put this mixture into a saucepan and cover it with cold water. Bring it to a boil and simmer it for 15 minutes. Take the pan from the heat to let the crayfish butter rise and spread out over the surface. Skim off the butter with a ladle and pour it through a fine-meshed sieve into a bowl of cold water with a few ice cubes floating in it. The iced water will quickly make the crayfish butter solidify. Lift out the solidified butter, turn it over on the kitchen table, and use a knife to scrape off any scum sticking to it.

Put half of the crayfish butter into a sauté pan, let it melt, add the crayfish tails and heat them without letting the butter bubble. Sprinkle in the flour, mix it in carefully, pour in the cream and bring the sauce to a boil, stirring it all the time. Cook the sauce until it thickens—about 10 minutes. Season the sauce with salt and a pinch of cayenne pepper, and incorporate the remaining crayfish butter, stirring constantly. Do not let the sauce boil again. The crayfish sauce is now ready to serve.

PAUL BOUILLARD
LA GOURMANDISE À BON MARCHÉ

## Spanish Mussel Sauce

*Salsa Marinera*

*Toast the almonds in a shallow pan in a preheated 350° F. [180° C.] oven for 10 minutes, turning them frequently to brown them evenly.*

Use this sauce to accompany fish and egg dishes.

*To make 1 cup [ ¼ liter]*

| 1 dozen | small live mussels, scrubbed and debearded | 1 dozen |
|---|---|---|
| ¾ cup | water | 175 ml. |
| 2 tbsp. | dry white wine | 30 ml. |
| 1 | onion, finely chopped | 1 |
| 2 | garlic cloves, finely chopped | 2 |
| 1 tbsp. | olive oil | 15 ml. |
| 2 | small tomatoes, peeled, seeded and chopped | 2 |
| 2 tbsp. | flour | 30 ml. |
| | salt and pepper | |
| 2 | sprigs fresh parsley, finely chopped | 2 |
| 12 | almonds, blanched, peeled and toasted | 12 |
| ⅛ tsp. | powdered saffron | ½ ml. |

Combine the mussels, water and wine in a heavy, nonreactive pot, cover, and cook over high heat until the mussels open—about three minutes. Shuck the mussels; strain and reserve the cooking liquor.

Fry the onion and garlic in the oil until they start to brown. Add the tomatoes and, when they have softened, stir in the flour and the reserved mussel cooking liquor. Season the mixture with salt and pepper, add the parsley and simmer gently until the sauce thickens—about five minutes.

Pound the almonds and the saffron together in a mortar. Add the almond mixture to the sauce and cook it for a few minutes. Finally, add the mussels.

MAGDALENA ALPERI
TRATADO COMPLETO DE COMIDAS Y BEBIDAS

## A Traveling Sauce

*This recipe dates from the early 18th Century. "Verjuice" usually meant the juice of unripe grapes, although in Britain the juice of unripe apples or crab apples was sometimes used instead. Fresh lemon juice may be substituted for verjuice.*

This general sauce is always ready to be used with all kinds of meat, fowl or fish that require rich sauces. It is a good companion for travelers, who more frequently find good meat than good cooks. Those who are admirers of the taste of garlic may add it to this sauce, or diminish or leave out any particular ingredient that they do not approve of. The sauce may also be made of water only, or of verjuice, or of wine, or of orange or lemon juice; but if it is made of water, it will keep only a month; if it is made of verjuice, it will last three months; if it is made of vinegar it will last a year; or of wine it will last as long. You must keep it in a dry place. Use a little of this sauce at a time, stirring it well when you use it.

*To make about 3 quarts [3 liters]*

| 2 quarts | red Bordeaux | 2 liters |
|---|---|---|
| ⅔ cup | wine vinegar | 150 ml. |
| ⅔ cup | verjuice | 150 ml. |
| ½ cup | salt | 125 ml. |
| 2 tbsp. | black peppercorns | 30 ml. |
| ½ tsp. | freshly grated nutmeg | 2 ml. |
| ½ tsp. | ground cloves | 2 ml. |
| ¼ tsp. | ground ginger | 1 ml. |
| 2 or 3 | strips dried orange peel | 2 or 3 |
| 1 tbsp. | mustard seeds, bruised with a pestle | 15 ml. |
| 6 | shallots, pounded lightly | 6 |
| 5 or 6 | bay leaves | 5 or 6 |
| 1 | small sprig basil or marjoram | 1 |
| 1 | sprig thyme | 1 |
| 4-inch | cinnamon stick | 10-cm. |

Place the wine, vinegar and verjuice together in a clean stone jar that can be tightly closed. Add to this the salt, peppercorns, nutmeg, cloves, ginger, orange peel, mustard seeds, shallots, bay leaves, herbs and cinnamon. Close the jar tightly and let the mixture infuse for 24 hours in the oven at its lowest possible setting.

When this is done, strain your composition through a linen cloth until you have pressed out as much liquor as possible, and put it in a dry stone bottle or jar. Close the jar tightly as soon as the liquid is cold.

RICHARD BRADLEY
THE COUNTRY HOUSEWIFE AND LADY'S DIRECTOR

## A Sauce for Boiled Fish

### Salsa per Condire il Pesce Lessato

*To make 2 cups [½ liter]*

| ½ lb. | salt anchovies, soaked, filleted, rinsed and dried | ¼ kg. |
|---|---|---|
| ¾ cup | oil | 175 ml. |
| 2 tbsp. | capers, rinsed and drained, or tomato purée (recipe, page 159) (optional) | 30 ml. |

In a saucepan combine the anchovies with the oil, and cook over low heat, stirring with a spoon until the anchovies dissolve. Take care that the oil does not come to a boil. Add the capers or the tomato purée if you wish.

G. B. RATTO
LA CUCINIERA GENOVESE

# Savory Vegetable, Fruit and Nut Sauces

## Avocado Sauce for Fish and Shellfish

Avocado makes a good sauce for salmon and salmon trout in particular, though it also goes well with crab and lobster. If the sauce is to be served with cold fish, mix in two chopped scallions after the sauce has been seasoned. If the sauce is for hot fish, omit the scallions and warm the sauce in a bowl over a pan of simmering water until the sauce is hot, but not boiling.

*To make 2 cups [½ liter]*

| 2 | ripe avocados, halved, pitted and peeled | 2 |
|---|---|---|
| 3 tbsp. | fresh lemon juice· | 45 ml. |
| 1 | large garlic clove, crushed to a paste | 1 |
| 1¼ cups | sour cream | 300 ml. |
| | salt and pepper | |

Mash the avocados with the lemon juice and garlic. Mix in the sour cream gradually. Taste the sauce and season it with salt and pepper.

JANE GRIGSON
JANE GRIGSON'S VEGETABLE BOOK

## Mexican Avocado Sauce

### *Guacamole*

*If serrano chilies are not obtainable, any other small hot green chilies may be substituted. The volatile oils in chilies may irritate your skin. Wear rubber gloves when handling them or wash your hands immediately afterward.*

Use this as a sauce or a salad. It also makes an excellent dip with fried tortilla chips. Including the avocado pit in the dish is supposed to keep the *guacamole* from turning a dark color. If you are not using the *guacamole* immediately, cover it tightly with aluminum foil or plastic wrap and refrigerate it (possibly a more reliable formula than the retention of the avocado pit).

*To make about 4 cups [1 liter]*

| | | |
|---|---|---|
| 2 | large, very ripe avocados, halved, pitted and peeled | 2 |
| 1 | medium-sized tomato, peeled, seeded and finely chopped | 1 |
| ½ | small onion, finely chopped | ½ |
| 2 or 3 | serrano chilies, stemmed, seeded and chopped | 2 or 3 |
| 3 or 4 | sprigs fresh coriander, finely chopped | 3 or 4 |
| | salt and freshly ground pepper | |
| | sugar | |

Mash the avocados in a large bowl. Mix in the tomatoes, onion, chilies and coriander and season with salt, pepper and a pinch of sugar. Pile the *guacamole* into a serving dish and place an avocado pit in the center of the mixture.

ELISABETH LAMBERT ORTIZ
THE COMPLETE BOOK OF MEXICAN COOKING

## Onion Sauce

*This assertive sauce is suitable for roast lamb or pork.*
Some cooks mix the pulp of apples or turnips with the onions; others add mustard to them.

*To make about ⅔ cup [150 ml.]*

| | | |
|---|---|---|
| 2 | large onions, unpeeled | 2 |
| 4 tbsp. | butter, melted | 60 ml. |

Put the onions into a bowl of salted cold water and let them soak for one hour. Then wash them, put them into a saucepan with plenty of salted water, and boil them until they are tender—30 to 40 minutes. Now peel them, pass them through a sieve and mix the melted butter with them.

DR. KITCHINER
THE COOK'S ORACLE

## Lyonnaise Sauce

### *Sauce Lyonnaise*

*This pungent sauce is suitable for grilled meats and fish.*

*To make about 3 cups [¾ liter]*

| | | |
|---|---|---|
| 3 | onions, chopped | 3 |
| 2 tbsp. | butter | 30 ml. |
| ¾ cup | white wine vinegar | 175 ml. |
| ¾ cup | dry white wine | 175 ml. |
| 2 cups | tomato purée *(recipe, page 159)* | ½ liter |

In a heavy saucepan, cook the onions in the butter over low heat for about 30 minutes, or until the onions are golden and very soft. Add the vinegar and wine and let the mixture reduce to one third its original volume.

Stir in the tomato purée. Cook the sauce very gently for five to six more minutes, removing the skin as it forms. Sieve the finished sauce or leave it unsieved, as you wish.

EUGENIE BRAZIER
LES SECRETS DE LA MÈRE BRAZIER

## Picardy Onion Sauce

### *La Sauce ou Soubise Picarde*

This sauce is an excellent accompaniment to roast pork, grilled pork chops or fried pork sausages.

*To make about 2 cups [½ liter]*

| | | |
|---|---|---|
| 2 | large onions, preferably Spanish onions, thinly sliced | 2 |
| 4 tbsp. | butter | 60 ml. |
| ⅓ cup | flour | 75 ml. |
| | water | |
| about 1 tbsp. | vinegar | about 15 ml. |
| | salt and pepper | |
| | pork roasting juices or pork stock *(recipe, page 159)* | |

In a heavy saucepan, make a pale roux with the butter and the flour. Take care that the roux does not color at all. Add a very little water, the onions, the vinegar, and salt and pepper. Cover the pan and let the onions cook over very low heat, stirring occasionally to prevent the mixture from coloring, until the onions have disintegrated almost to a purée—about one hour. Then add enough pork roasting juices or stock to give the sauce the consistency of thick cream. Stir the sauce well, but do not sieve it.

AUSTIN DE CROZE
LES PLATS RÉGIONAUX DE FRANCE

## Shallot and Parsley Butter
### Sauce Valentinoise

This sauce is served as an accompaniment to all meats, white or red, grilled over glowing charcoal.

*To make about ⅔ cup [150 ml.]*

| | | |
|---|---|---|
| 6 | shallots, finely chopped, wrapped in a cloth, washed in running water and squeezed dry | 6 |
| ¼ cup | finely chopped fresh parsley | 50 ml. |
| 1 | ripe tomato, peeled, seeded and finely chopped | 1 |
| 4 tbsp. | butter, chilled | 60 ml. |
| | salt and pepper | |
| 3 tbsp. | fresh lemon juice | 45 ml. |
| 1 tbsp. | jellied meat roasting juices | 15 ml. |

Put the shallots and the parsley in a long, fairly deep platter. Add the tomato and the butter. Season with salt and pepper, and add the lemon juice and the jellied meat juices. With a fork, mix all the ingredients together well. Take the grilled meat from the hot grill and place it on top of the sauce.

PAUL BOUILLARD
LA GOURMANDISE À BON MARCHÉ

## Potato Sauce
### Salsa de Patatas

This sauce is typical of the Sierra Morena region of Andalusia, and goes very well with fish dishes.

*To make about 2 cups [½ liter]*

| | | |
|---|---|---|
| 2 | medium-sized potatoes, peeled and sliced | 2 |
| ¼ cup | olive oil | 50 ml. |
| 2 | red peppers, halved, seeded, deribbed and chopped | 2 |
| 2 | medium-sized tomatoes, peeled, seeded and finely chopped | 2 |
| | salt | |
| 4 | cumin seeds | 4 |
| 1 | bay leaf | 1 |
| ⅔ cup | water | 150 ml. |

Heat the oil in a pan, add the potato slices and fry them for five minutes. Add the red peppers and the tomatoes and cook the vegetables for about 15 minutes, or until the potatoes are soft. Add salt to taste and the cumin seeds, bay leaf and water. Let the mixture boil for five minutes, then discard the bay leaf and rub the mixture through a fine-meshed sieve. Return the sauce to the heat for two minutes, skimming off any froth that appears.

ANA MARIA CALERA
COCINA ANDALUZA

## Sorrel Sauce
### Zuringsaus

Serve this sauce with fish. There is an even simpler and more old-fashioned way to make this sauce: Boil some finely chopped sorrel with a little water and salt and then stir in some butter and crumbled brown bread until you have a smooth sauce.

*To make 3 cups [¾ liter]*

| | | |
|---|---|---|
| ½ lb. | chopped or thinly sliced sorrel leaves | ¼ kg. |
| 2 tbsp. | thinly sliced leek | 30 ml. |
| 4 tbsp. | butter | 60 ml. |
| 2 cups | veal stock *(recipe, page 159)* | ½ liter |
| ¼ cup | flour | 50 ml. |
| | pepper | |
| 2 tbsp. | heavy cream or butter (optional) | 30 ml. |

Sauté the leek in 1 tablespoon [15 ml.] of the butter, add the sorrel and let them cook together for five minutes. Add the stock and cook the mixture for another 15 minutes. Purée the sorrel mixture by pressing it through a sieve.

Melt the remaining butter over low heat, stir in the flour and let it cook without browning for a few minutes. Then whisk in the sorrel purée and let the sauce cook gently for five minutes. Season it with pepper. Add a dash of cream or a little extra butter, if desired, just before serving the sauce.

RIA HOLLEMAN
UIT GROOTMOEDERS KEUKEN

## Green or Sorrel Sauce

Serve this sauce with lamb, veal and sweetbreads. Cayenne pepper, nutmeg and fresh lemon juice are sometimes added.

*To make about ⅔ cup [150 ml.]*

| | | |
|---|---|---|
| ½ lb. | fresh sorrel leaves, washed | ¼ kg. |
| 4 tbsp. | butter | 60 ml. |
| | salt and pepper | |
| | confectioners' sugar | |

Put the sorrel into a pan that will just hold it. Add the butter. Cover the pan tightly and set it over low heat for 15 minutes. Then pass the sorrel through a fine sieve with the back of a wooden spoon. Season the purée with salt, pepper and a small pinch of confectioners' sugar. Return the sorrel purée to the pan, heat and serve it.

DR. KITCHINER
THE COOK'S ORACLE

## Spaghetti with Tomato Sauce

### Spaghetti all'Amatriciana

*Pecorino Romano is an Italian cheese made from sheep's milk. If it is not available, use Parmesan cheese instead.*

*To serve 4*

| | | |
|---|---|---|
| 1 lb. | spaghetti, boiled in plenty of salted water for 4 to 8 minutes and drained | ½ kg. |
| 3 | medium-sized tomatoes, peeled, seeded and coarsely chopped | 3 |
| 1 | garlic clove | 1 |
| 1 tbsp. | lard | 15 ml. |
| 1 | onion, finely chopped | 1 |
| ¼ lb. | lean salt pork with the rind removed, cut into cubes | 125 g. |
| ½ cup | dry white wine | 125 ml. |
| | salt | |
| | cayenne pepper | |
| ⅓ cup | grated pecorino Romano cheese | 75 ml. |

Fry the garlic in the lard. When the garlic is golden, remove and discard it and add the onion and salt pork cubes to the pan. Then add the wine. Cook until the liquid is reduced to half its original volume—about three minutes—then add the tomatoes. Season with salt and cayenne pepper and heat through. Mix the sauce with the spaghetti and sprinkle with the cheese before serving.

FRANCA FESLIKENIAN
CUCINA E VINI DEL LAZIO

## Thick Provençal Tomato Sauce

### Coulis de Tomates à la Provençale

This *coulis* goes well with any pasta or rice, and with boiled chicken, veal or beef; it is also excellent on hamburgers or with meat loaf. Obviously the sauce should be made when tomatoes are at their peak in flavor; it would be a shame to put out all the work and time if the product is inferior to begin with. The recipe can be easily halved, but since it is so tasty and versatile, and also freezes perfectly, this larger quantity is suggested.

*To make 5 to 6 cups [1¼ to 1½ liters]*

| | | |
|---|---|---|
| 6 lb. | tomatoes | 3 kg. |
| ⅓ cup | oil | 75 ml. |
| 1 cup | finely chopped onions | ¼ liter |
| ⅓ cup | flour | 75 ml. |
| ½ tsp. | sugar | 2 ml. |
| 5 | garlic cloves, crushed to a paste | 5 |
| 3 | 1-inch [2½-cm.] pieces orange peel, without the bitter white pith | 3 |
| 1 | bouquet garni of 6 parsley sprigs tied around 2 bay leaves | 1 |
| ½ tsp. | fennel seeds | 2 ml. |
| ½ tsp. | dried basil | 2 ml. |
| ¼ tsp. | dried coriander | 1 ml. |
| 1 tsp. | salt | 5 ml. |
| ½ tsp. | pepper | 2 ml. |
| ½ tsp. | celery salt | 2 ml. |
| | powdered saffron | |
| 2 to 4 tbsp. | tomato paste | 30 to 60 ml. |

Plunge the tomatoes into boiling water for a few seconds; peel them, then cut them in half and gently squeeze out the seeds and juice. Chop the remaining pulp coarse. There should be 7 to 8 cups [1¾ to 2 liters] of tomato pulp.

Heat the oil in a heavy pot and add the onions; cover and cook them slowly for about 15 minutes, until they are transparent but not brown. Remove the lid and stir in the flour. Cook the mixture for two to three minutes, still not letting it brown. Add the tomato pulp, sugar, garlic, orange peel, bouquet garni and all of the herbs. Season the mixture with the salt, pepper, celery salt and a pinch of saffron. Cover the pot and simmer the mixture slowly for 15 minutes.

Add 2 tablespoons [30 ml.] of the tomato paste and simmer the mixture very slowly, partially covered, for one to one and one half hours. Stir it occasionally, making certain to scrape the bottom of the pot so the mixture does not stick or scorch as it thickens. As you stir, press the tomato pulp against the sides of the pot to make the sauce smoother. If there is any risk of scorching, add a little tomato juice or water. Cook the sauce until it is very thick and will stand up in a mass on a spoon. Remove the bouquet garni and orange peel. If the color of the sauce seems a little pale, or you would like to intensify the tomato flavor, add the other 2 tablespoons of tomato paste. Taste the sauce for seasoning and add more salt and pepper if necessary.

CAROL CUTLER
HAUTE CUISINE FOR YOUR HEART'S DELIGHT

# Mexican Tomato Sauce

## Salsa de Jitomate

*This zesty sauce is suitable for grilled or broiled meats as well as for burritos, tacos or enchiladas. If serrano chilies are not obtainable, any other small hot green chilies may be substituted. The volatile oils in chilies may irritate your skin. Wear rubber gloves when handling them or wash your hands immediately afterward.*

*To make about 2 cups [ ½ liter]*

| | | |
|---|---|---|
| 2 | large tomatoes, peeled, seeded and finely chopped | 2 |
| 2 tbsp. | olive oil | 30 ml. |
| 1 | onion, finely chopped | 1 |
| 1 | garlic clove, finely chopped | 1 |
| ½ tsp. | sugar | 2 ml. |
| 2 or 3 | serrano chilies, stemmed, seeded and chopped | 2 or 3 |
| | salt and freshly ground pepper | |
| 1 tbsp. | chopped fresh coriander leaves | 15 ml. |

Heat the oil in a skillet and fry the onion and garlic until limp. Add all of the other ingredients, except the coriander, and cook them gently for 15 minutes. Season the sauce to taste with salt and pepper. Add the coriander and cook the sauce for a minute or two longer. This sauce can be served either hot or cold.

ELISABETH LAMBERT ORTIZ
THE COMPLETE BOOK OF MEXICAN COOKING

# Tomato Sauce

## Salsa di Pomodoro

*This hearty sauce is suitable for gnocchi or pasta.*

Out of season, you can use canned tomatoes for this sauce. It should be served hot.

*To make 2 cups [ ½ liter]*

| | | |
|---|---|---|
| 2 lb. | ripe tomatoes, chopped | 1 kg. |
| 2 tbsp. | butter | 30 ml. |
| 1 | celery rib, diced | 1 |
| ½ | carrot, diced | ½ |
| ½ | onion, sliced | ½ |
| 1 tbsp. | olive oil | 15 ml. |
| ½ tsp. | salt | 2 ml. |

In a saucepan, melt the butter and cook the celery, carrot and onion in it for five minutes, or until they are softened. Add the tomatoes, oil and salt. Simmer the sauce, uncovered, for 30 minutes, or until it is thick and all of the excess liquid has evaporated. Sieve the sauce.

GINO BRUNETTI
CUCINA MANTOVANA DI PRINCIPI E DI POPOLO

# Spanish Cold Tomato Sauce

Serve this sauce as a relish with cold pork or veal.

*To make about 1 ½ cups [375 ml.]*

| | | |
|---|---|---|
| 4 to 6 | tomatoes, peeled, seeded and chopped | 4 to 6 |
| | salt | |
| 2 tbsp. | vinegar | 30 ml. |
| 1 tsp. | sugar | 5 ml. |
| 1 tbsp. | water | 15 ml. |
| 1 tbsp. | finely chopped fresh parsley leaves | 15 ml. |
| 1 tsp. | finely chopped fresh marjoram leaves | 5 ml. |
| 2 tbsp. | finely chopped onion | 30 ml. |
| ¼ cup | olive oil | 50 ml. |

Sprinkle the tomatoes with salt. Mix together the vinegar, sugar and water, and add them to the tomatoes. Sprinkle the mixture with the chopped herbs and the onion. Put the olive oil in here and there, and stir gently.

CORA, ROSE AND BOB BROWN
SOUPS, SAUCES AND GRAVIES

## Fresh Mexican Sauce

*Salsa Mexicana Cruda*

*The volatile oils in chilies may irritate your skin. Wear rubber gloves when you are handling them or wash your hands immediately afterward.*

Although this can be made up to three hours ahead, it is best made at almost the last minute. You will find this sauce on Mexican tables at any time of the day, for it goes well with breakfast eggs, with roast or grilled meat at lunchtime, or tacos in the evening, and there are people who put a spoonful of it into their *frijoles de olla* (stewed beans). It is marvelously crunchy and refreshing served just with tortillas. The Sinaloa version calls for some scallions and lime juice in place of the onions and water, and the Yucatan version substitutes Seville orange juice for the water.

*To make about 1 ½ cups [375 ml.]*

| | | |
|---|---|---|
| 1 | medium-sized tomato, finely chopped but not peeled | 1 |
| ¼ cup | finely chopped onion | 50 ml. |
| 6 | sprigs fresh coriander, finely chopped | 6 |
| 3 | fresh hot green chilies, preferably serranos, stemmed and finely chopped | 3 |
| about ½ tsp. | salt | about 2 ml. |
| ⅓ cup | cold water | 75 ml. |

Mix the tomato, onion, coriander and chilies together in a bowl and add the salt and the water.

DIANA KENNEDY
THE CUISINES OF MEXICO

---

## Tomato and Yogurt Sauce

*Tomaten-Joghurt-Sauce*

*This tangy sauce is suitable for green salads, cold boiled or steamed vegetables and cold fish.*

*To make about 1 ½ cups [375 ml.]*

| | | |
|---|---|---|
| 2 | tomatoes, peeled, seeded and finely chopped | 2 |
| 1 ¼ cups | yogurt | 300 ml. |
| ¼ cup | finely chopped fresh parsley | 50 ml. |
| 1 tbsp. | white wine vinegar | 15 ml. |
| | salt and freshly ground black pepper | |

Stir the yogurt until it is smooth. Mix in the tomatoes and parsley. Season the sauce with the vinegar and some salt and freshly ground black pepper.

BERND NEUNER-DUTTENHOFER
DIE NEUE DEUTSCHE KÜCHE

---

## Samfaina Sauce

*Salsa Samfaina*

Serve this sauce hot with either meat or fish.

*To make about ¾ cup [175 ml.]*

| | | |
|---|---|---|
| 1 | onion, cut into large pieces | 1 |
| 4 tbsp. | oil or lard | 60 ml. |
| 1 | red or green pepper, halved, seeded, deribbed and cut into strips | 1 |
| 1 | eggplant or zucchini, cut into strips | 1 |
| 2 or 3 | ripe tomatoes, peeled and chopped | 2 or 3 |
| | salt | |

Heat the oil or lard in a large skillet and fry the onion until it is transparent. Add the red or green pepper and, after cooking it for seven to eight minutes, add the eggplant or zucchini. Cook this mixture for three minutes, then add the tomatoes. Season the sauce with salt and let it cook for five more minutes over low heat.

MARÍA DOLORES CAMPS CARDONA
COCINA CATALANA

---

## Genoese Piquant Sauce

*Salsa Piccante*

Use this to season a small capon, beans cooked in herbs, cauliflower or fish.

*To make about 3 cups [¾ liter]*

| | | |
|---|---|---|
| 2 | medium-sized tomatoes, peeled, seeded and chopped | 2 |
| 2 tbsp. | finely chopped fresh parsley | 30 ml. |
| ¼ cup | pine nuts | 50 ml. |
| 1 tbsp. | capers, rinsed and drained | 15 ml. |
| 1 | garlic clove | 1 |
| 2 | salt anchovies, soaked, filleted, rinsed and dried | 2 |
| 2 cups | fresh white bread crumbs | ½ liter |
| ¾ cup | vinegar | 175 ml. |
| ¾ cup | oil | 175 ml. |
| | salt | |

Put the tomatoes, parsley, pine nuts, capers, garlic and anchovies in a mortar. Soak the bread crumbs in ⅔ cup [150 ml.] of the vinegar and add them to the tomato mixture. Pound everything together, then press it through a sieve. Dilute the sieved mixture with the oil and the rest of the vinegar, and season the sauce with a little salt.

G. B. RATTO
LA CUCINIERA GENOVESE

# Catalan Sauce

## Sauce à la Catalane

*The author suggests serving this sauce with pork or with dishes of game such as wild boar, hare or venison.*

*To make 3 cups [¾ liter]*

| | | |
|---|---|---|
| 1 | onion, sliced | 1 |
| 10 | garlic cloves | 10 |
| ⅓ cup | oil | 75 ml. |
| 2 cups | tomato purée (recipe, page 159) | ½ liter |
| 1 cup | fresh orange juice | ¼ liter |
| ¼ cup | grated orange peel | 50 ml. |
| 3 tbsp. | fresh lemon juice | 45 ml. |
| 2 tsp. | grated lemon peel | 10 ml. |
| | cayenne pepper | |
| 2 tbsp. | finely chopped fresh parsley | 30 ml. |
| 2 tbsp. | chopped fresh mint leaves | 30 ml. |
| | dry mustard | |
| ⅓ cup | Madeira | 75 ml. |

In a saucepan over medium heat, fry the onion and garlic in the oil. Stir in the tomato purée, orange juice and peel, lemon juice and peel, a pinch of cayenne pepper, the parsley and mint, a little mustard and the Madeira. Heat the sauce through before serving.

JOSEPH FAVRE
DICTIONNAIRE UNIVERSEL DE CUISINE PRATIQUE

# Provençal Anchovy Sauce

## Anchoïade

This sauce can accompany raw vegetables, cold meats and poached fish. You can also spread it on slices of toasted bread and reheat the bread very gently before serving.

*To make about 1 cup [¼ liter]*

| | | |
|---|---|---|
| 10 | salt anchovies, soaked, filleted, rinsed and dried | 10 |
| 3 | garlic cloves | 3 |
| ⅔ cup | olive oil | 150 ml. |
| | pepper | |

In a mortar, pound the anchovy fillets with the garlic cloves. When they have been reduced to a paste, pour in the olive oil in a thin trickle, beating the mixture all the time, as though you were making mayonnaise. Season the sauce with pepper and serve it chilled.

LUCETTE REY-BILLETON
LES BONNES RECETTES DU SOLEIL

# Andalusia Sauce

## Salsa Andaluza

*This thick sauce is suitable for asparagus or broccoli and for roast pork. Any winter squash—acorn or Hubbard, for example—can replace the pumpkin.*

*To make about 1 ½ cups [375 ml.]*

| | | |
|---|---|---|
| ½ lb. | pumpkin, peeled, seeded and cut into ½-inch [1-cm.] squares (about 2 cups [½ liter]) | ¼ kg. |
| 1 | garlic clove | 1 |
| 2 | black peppercorns | 2 |
| 1 | large tomato, peeled and seeded | 1 |
| 3 tbsp. | white wine vinegar | 45 ml. |
| | salt | |

Boil the pumpkin in a little water until tender—10 to 15 minutes—then drain it and set it aside. Pound the garlic and the peppercorns together in a mortar. Then add the tomato and the pumpkin. Pound the ingredients well, then add the vinegar and a little salt.

ANA MARIA CALERA
COCINA ANDALUZA

# Catalan Vegetable Sauce

## Samfaina

*This tangy sauce is suitable for grilled fish or meat.*

*To make about 2 ½ cups [625 ml.]*

| | | |
|---|---|---|
| 1 | Spanish onion, sliced | 1 |
| 2 tbsp. | olive oil or lard | 30 ml. |
| 2 or 3 | green or half-red peppers, halved, seeded, deribbed and cut into 1-inch [2½-cm.] squares | 2 or 3 |
| 1 | eggplant, cubed, salted and drained for 30 minutes | 1 |
| 3 | medium-sized tomatoes, peeled, seeded and diced | 3 |

Fry the onion in the oil or lard until it is soft but not browned. Add the peppers; cook for eight minutes, then add the eggplant. After cooking the mixture for five minutes, add the tomatoes. Cook the sauce for 15 minutes, until all the vegetables are soft and any excess liquid has evaporated.

FERRAN AGULLÓ
LLIBRE DE LA CUINA CATALANA

## Italian Green Sauce

### Salsa Verde

*This pungent sauce is suitable for boiled or steamed cauliflower or broccoli and for poached or grilled strong-flavored fish such as swordfish or mackerel.*

To make about 3 cups [¾ liter]

| | | |
|---|---|---|
| ½ cup | Italian mixed pickled vegetables, rinsed and drained | 125 ml. |
| 2 | salt anchovies, soaked, filleted, rinsed and dried | 2 |
| 1 | hard-boiled egg | 1 |
| ¼ cup | flaked cooked tuna | 50 ml. |
| 1 | green pepper, halved, seeded and deribbed | 1 |
| 3 cups | fresh parsley leaves | ¾ liter |
| 1 cup | fresh basil leaves | ¼ liter |
| 3 tbsp. | fresh lemon juice | 45 ml. |
| ⅔ cup | olive oil | 150 ml. |
| 1 tsp. | prepared mustard (optional) | 5 ml. |

Put all the solid ingredients through a food grinder or chop them fine in a food processor. Add the lemon juice, oil and, if you wish, the mustard, and let the sauce stand for several hours before serving it.

GINO BRUNETTI
CUCINA MANTOVANA DI PRINCIPI E DI POPOLO

## Italian Mixed Green Sauce

### Salsa Verde Composta

*This pungent sauce is suitable for hot or cold smoked tongue and cold lamb or beef.*

To make about 3 cups [¾ liter]

| | | |
|---|---|---|
| 2½ cups | finely chopped fresh parsley | 625 ml. |
| ½ | garlic clove, finely chopped | ½ |
| ¼ cup | finely chopped sour gherkins | 50 ml. |
| 1 tbsp. | finely chopped capers | 15 ml. |
| ¼ cup | finely chopped green pepper | 50 ml. |
| ⅓ cup | finely chopped onion | 75 ml. |
| 1 tbsp. | fresh white bread crumbs | 15 ml. |
| | salt and pepper | |
| ¼ cup | vinegar | 50 ml. |
| 1 cup | olive oil | ¼ liter |

Mix together the parsley, garlic, gherkins, capers, green pepper end onion. Add the bread crumbs. Season the mix-

ture with salt and pepper, then stir in the vinegar and the olive oil. Mix all of the ingredients together very thoroughly.

ARMIDO FERRANDINI
ONESTÀ IN CUCINA

## Genoese Green Sauce or Basil Sauce

### Pesto alla Genovese

*Toast the pine nuts in a shallow pan in a preheated 350° F.[180° C.] oven for 10 minutes, turning them frequently to brown them evenly.*

There is a saying that he who eats pesto never leaves Genoa. This famous sauce is considered an invention of the Ligurians. It is used in all kinds of pasta dishes and is an essential and traditional part of *trenette* (a dish of egg noodles) and Genoese vegetable soup. The housewives of Liguria collect the fresh young leaves of the basil plant (they insist it is the best in Italy), put the leaves into a mortar with garlic, and pound with great patience and diligence until they have a piquant, delicious paste. Some cooks insist that only a marble mortar can be used; others, more modern, use a blender, which is quick and very effective.

To make about 3 cups [¾ liter]

| | | |
|---|---|---|
| 4 cups | fresh basil leaves | 1 liter |
| 2 | garlic cloves | 2 |
| | coarse salt | |
| 1 tbsp. | pine nuts, toasted | 15 ml. |
| 3 to 4 tbsp. | freshly grated Parmesan cheese | 45 to 60 ml. |
| 3 to 4 tbsp. | freshly grated pecorino Romano cheese | 45 to 60 ml. |
| 1 cup | olive oil | ¼ liter |

Put the basil, garlic, a pinch of coarse salt and the pine nuts in a mortar. Pound them to a paste. Continue pounding, gradually adding the cheeses. When the paste is smooth, slowly stir in the olive oil.

ADA BONI
ITALIAN REGIONAL COOKING

# Chili and Garlic Sauce

## Rouille

*The volatile oils in chilies may irritate your skin. Wear rubber gloves when you are handling them or wash your hands immediately afterward.*

This sauce should be served from the mortar, to accompany fish soup.

| | To make 1½ cups [375 ml.] | |
|---|---|---|
| 2 | fresh hot chilies, stemmed and seeded, or substitute ½ tsp. [2 ml.] cayenne pepper | 2 |
| 2 | garlic cloves | 2 |
| 2 cups | fresh white bread crumbs | ½ liter |
| ⅔ cup | fish stock (recipe, page 164) or liquid from the soup being served with the sauce | 150 ml. |
| | powdered saffron | |
| ⅔ cup | olive oil | 150 ml. |

Put the chilies or cayenne and garlic into a wood or marble mortar, and crush them together. Soak the bread crumbs in the fish stock or soup, then add them to the garlic-and-chili mixture and continue to pound until the mixture has a thick, creamy consistency. Add a pinch of saffron, then pour in the olive oil, a little at a time, in a thin stream, stirring all the time. If the sauce is too thick, dilute it with a little more stock or soup.

JEAN AND PAUL MINCHELLI
CRUSTACÉS, POISSONS ET COQUILLAGES

———————◆———————

# Garlic and Potato Sauce

## Skordalia

*Skordalia is traditionally served with fried or broiled seafood or with cold sliced beets.*

| | To make about 2 cups [½ liter] | |
|---|---|---|
| 2 tbsp. | chopped garlic | 30 ml. |
| 6 | small potatoes (about 1 lb. [½ kg.]), boiled and peeled | 6 |
| 2 tsp. | salt | 10 ml. |
| 1 to 1½ cups | olive oil | 250 to 375 ml. |
| ¼ cup | fresh lemon juice | 50 ml. |
| | white or freshly ground black pepper | |

With a large mortar and pestle or the back of a spoon, mash the garlic and salt together to a fine paste. Add the warm potatoes a little at a time, stirring and mashing vigorously until the ingredients are well combined. Beat in the oil, a tablespoon [15 ml.] at a time, making sure each addition of oil is absorbed before adding more. The mixture will absorb from 1 to 1½ cups [250 to 375 ml.] of oil, depending on the texture of the potatoes.

Beat in the lemon juice, taste the sauce and add as much pepper and salt as you think it needs. The sauce should be highly seasoned and dense enough to hold its shape almost solidly in a spoon. If you prefer a thinner sauce, beat in a little lukewarm water a few drops at a time.

FOODS OF THE WORLD/MIDDLE EASTERN COOKING

# Piquant Garlic and Hazelnut Sauce

## Salvitjada

*To toast and peel the hazelnuts called for in this recipe, place them in a shallow pan in a preheated 350° F. [180° C.] oven for 10 minutes, turning them frequently to brown them evenly. Roll them in a towel to remove their skins. The volatile oils in chilies may irritate your skin. Wear rubber gloves when handling them or wash your hands immediately afterward.*

This sauce, usually garnished with grilled and peeled scallions, accompanies grilled chops or sausages.

| | To make 1½ cups [375 ml.] | |
|---|---|---|
| 4 | garlic cloves | 4 |
| 12 | hazelnuts, toasted and peeled | 12 |
| 6 | fresh mint leaves | 6 |
| | salt | |
| 2 | dried hot chilies, stemmed, seeded and soaked in hot water, or 1 tbsp. [15 ml.] cayenne pepper | 2 |
| 3 | slices firm-textured white bread with the crusts removed, moistened in ⅓ cup [75 ml.] vinegar | 3 |
| 1 cup | olive oil | ¼ liter |
| | pepper (optional) | |

In a mortar, pound the garlic, mint and a little salt. Add the hazelnuts and pound again. When the mixture has formed a smooth paste, add the chilies or cayenne pepper and the bread. Continue pounding to form a very fine paste. Finally, add the oil, drop by drop, until the sauce is thick but runny. Add salt and pepper if necessary.

NESTOR LUJAN AND JUAN PERUCHO
EL LIBRO DE LA COCINA ESPAÑOLA

# Garlic Sauce

## La Sauce d'Ail

*This pungent sauce is suitable for pasta, boiled vegetables and poached fish.*

Chopped chervil, hyssop or marjoram may be added to the sauce; avoid chives and tarragon.

|  | *To make ½ cup [125 ml.]* |  |
|---|---|---|
| 6 | garlic cloves, any green center shoots removed | 6 |
| 12 | walnuts | 12 |
| 1 tsp. | Armagnac | 5 ml. |
|  | salt and pepper |  |
| about ⅓ cup | olive oil | about 75 ml. |
|  | chopped herbs (optional) |  |

In a mortar, pound the garlic, walnuts and Armagnac to a smooth paste. Season with salt and pepper, and gradually add oil, turning the mixture with the pestle. The amount of oil should equal the combined volume of the garlic and nuts. Finally, if you wish, add herbs of your choice.

ANDRÉ DAGUIN
LE NOUVEAU CUISINIER GASCON

# Catalan Garlic Sauce

## Picada

*This sauce is used to flavor soups and fish or meat stews. It is usually added to the main dish about halfway through the cooking time. Toast the nuts in a shallow pan in a preheated 350° F. [180° C.] oven for five to 10 minutes, turning them frequently to brown them evenly.*

|  | *To make 1 cup [¼ liter]* |  |
|---|---|---|
| 6 | garlic cloves | 6 |
| 4 | sprigs fresh parsley | 4 |
| ¼ cup | blanched and peeled almonds, hazelnuts or walnuts, toasted, or ¼ cup [50 ml.] toasted pine nuts | 50 ml. |
| 1 | slice firm-textured white bread with the crust removed, sautéed in olive oil until lightly browned | 1 |
| ⅓ cup | tepid water or veal stock (recipe, page 159) | 75 ml. |

Pound the garlic cloves in a mortar until they form a paste. Add the parsley and continue to pound. When the parsley is combined with the garlic, pound in the nuts, then the fried bread. Gradually work in the water or stock. When the sauce is smooth, add it to the dish it is to flavor.

FERRAN AGULLÓ
LLIBRE DE LA CUINA CATALANA

# Garlic and Anchovy Sauce from Provence

## Bagna Caudà

This sauce provides a pleasant accompaniment to cooked vegetables such as parsnips and turnips, or raw vegetables such as celery and fennel.

|  | *To make about 1 cup [¼ liter]* |  |
|---|---|---|
| 3 | garlic cloves | 3 |
| 6 | salt anchovies, soaked, filleted, rinsed and dried | 6 |
|  | olive oil |  |
| 5 tbsp. | butter, cut into small cubes | 75 ml. |

Heat the oil in a saucepan and fry the garlic in it, without letting it brown. Add the anchovy fillets and cook them until they dissolve. Stir the ingredients together to form a paste. Take the saucepan off the heat and stir in the cubes of butter with a wooden spoon. Serve the sauce hot.

LUCETTE REY-BILLETON
LES BONNES RECETTES DU SOLEIL

# Greek Garlic Sauce

## Skorthaliá

This is the famous *skorthaliá* made in Greek villages, and usually served over fried cod or fried eggplant slices. It is powerful—a delight for garlic fanciers. It is always served chilled, even over hot foods. In addition to being used over fried foods, it is good as a dip with an assortment of crisp raw vegetables. With boiled whole artichokes, serve 3 tablespoons [45 ml.] alongside each artichoke as a dip. The mixture may be a bit thick if you use a blender; if it is, turn the machine off every couple of seconds and mix with a rubber spatula, then turn the blender on again.

|  | *To make 2 cups [½ liter]* |  |
|---|---|---|
| 4 | garlic cloves, crushed to a paste | 4 |
| ¼ cup | water | 50 ml. |
| ½ tsp. | salt | 2 ml. |
| 2 | medium-sized potatoes, boiled, peeled and mashed | 2 |
| ½ cup | almonds, blanched, peeled and ground | 125 ml. |
| ¼ cup | wine vinegar | 50 ml. |
| 1 cup | olive oil | ¼ liter |

Place all of the ingredients in the bowl of an electric mixer or the container of a blender. Mix or blend at high speed. When the sauce is white and creamy, pour it into a bowl, cover and refrigerate it for at least two hours.

ANNE THEOHAROUS
COOKING AND BAKING THE GREEK WAY

# Rocambole, Garlic and Anchovy Sauce

## Sauce Perlée

*Rocambole is also known as giant garlic because of the size of its stems, not its bulbs. The bulbs are slightly larger than those of garlic, and have brown skins and flesh. Rocambole is somewhat milder in taste than garlic. If it is not available, use an extra garlic clove. The author states that this sauce is particularly good for bland meats.*

To make 2 ¼ cups [550 ml.]

| | | |
|---|---|---|
| 1 | bulb rocambole, cloves separated and peeled | 1 |
| 2 | garlic cloves | 2 |
| 3 | salt anchovies, soaked, filleted, rinsed, dried and pounded | 3 |
| ⅔ cup | white wine vinegar | 150 ml. |
| ⅔ cup | Champagne | 150 ml. |
| ⅓ cup | oil | 75 ml. |
| 3 tbsp. | fresh lemon juice or ⅓ cup [75 ml.] fresh orange juice | 45 ml. |
| | salt and coarsely ground black pepper | |

Place the rocambole, garlic, anchovies, vinegar, Champagne, oil and lemon or orange juice in a pan and bring the mixture to a boil. Set the mixture aside to cool and let the flavors infuse. When it is cold, pass it through a sieve. Serve the sauce cold or hot with whatever you wish, adding salt and pepper to taste.

LOUIS AUGUSTE DE BOURBON
LE CUISINIER GASCON

---

# Applesauce with Madeira

## Sauce Dino

This is a sauce for cold game, and was created in honor of the Duke of Dino by his chef, Bichot, in 1877.

To make about 2 cups [½ liter]

| | | |
|---|---|---|
| ¾ cup | thick apple purée | 175 ml. |
| 1 ¼ cups | Madeira | 300 ml. |
| 2 | oranges, the peel thinly pared and the juice strained | 2 |
| 2 tbsp. | fresh lemon juice | 30 ml. |

Heat the Madeira with the orange peel until the liquid has reduced by half. Add the apple purée and stir it over low heat to reduce the sauce to the thickness you desire. Let it cool. Finally, stir in the orange and lemon juices.

JOSEPH FAVRE
DICTIONNAIRE UNIVERSEL DE CUISINE PRATIQUE

---

# Applesauce

This goes well with goose, roast pork and other pork dishes.

To make about 1 ¼ cups [300 ml.]

| | | |
|---|---|---|
| 3 | cooking apples, peeled, cored and sliced | 3 |
| 6 | almonds, blanched, peeled and sautéed in butter until lightly browned | 6 |
| 1 | onion, chopped | 1 |
| 2 tbsp. | grated orange peel | 30 ml. |
| 1 | slice firm-textured white bread with the crust removed, toasted and dipped in white wine vinegar | 1 |
| | pepper | |
| ½ tsp. | ground mixed spices | 2 ml. |
| 3 tbsp. | white wine | 45 ml. |
| 3 tbsp. | white wine vinegar | 45 ml. |

Place the apple slices in a saucepan with the almonds, onion, grated orange peel and bread. Season the mixture with pepper and mixed spices, moisten it with the wine and vinegar and boil it until the apple slices are soft—about 15 minutes. Pass the sauce through a sieve and serve it hot.

PAUL DINNAGE
THE BOOK OF FRUIT AND FRUIT COOKERY

---

# German Applesauce

## Apfelsauce

Should the sauce be too thick, dilute it with white wine. This is an excellent sauce for game and poultry.

To make about 3 cups [¾ liter]

| | | |
|---|---|---|
| 4 | large apples, peeled, cored and cut into pieces | 4 |
| 2 tbsp. | butter | 30 ml. |
| 2 tbsp. | dark rye bread crumbs | 30 ml. |
| ½ cup | white wine | 125 ml. |
| ¼ cup | seedless white raisins, chopped | 50 ml. |
| | ground cinnamon | |
| 1 tsp. | grated lemon peel | 5 ml. |
| about 1 tbsp. | sugar | about 15 ml. |

In a saucepan, sauté the apple pieces in the butter until they are soft. Remove them and fry the bread crumbs in the butter that remains. Return the apples to the pan, add the wine, raisins and a pinch of cinnamon, and bring the sauce to a boil with the lemon peel and sugar to taste.

HANS GUSTL KERNMAYR
SO KOCHTE MEINE MUTTER

# Cumberland Sauce

*This sauce is reputedly named after Ernest, Duke of Cumberland, who was the brother of King George IV. It is traditionally served with roast venison or such cold meats as ham, corned beef or tongue.*

To make about ¾ cup [175 ml.]

| | | |
|---|---|---|
| 2 | shallots, finely chopped | 2 |
| 1 | lemon, the peel thinly pared and cut into short julienne, and the juice strained | 1 |
| 1 | orange, the peel thinly pared and cut into short julienne, and the juice strained | 1 |
| about 2 tbsp. | red currant jelly | about 30 ml. |
| 2 to 3 tbsp. | port | 30 to 45 ml. |
| 1 tbsp. | wine vinegar | 15 ml. |
| | ground ginger | |
| | salt | |
| | cayenne pepper | |

Blanch the chopped shallots in boiling water for two minutes, then drain them. Blanch the lemon and orange julienne for one minute and drain them. Melt the currant jelly in a heatproof bowl set over a pan of boiling water. Add the shallots, lemon and orange julienne, port, vinegar, a pinch of ground ginger and the orange and lemon juices. Season the sauce to taste with a little salt and a pinch of cayenne pepper.

ALFRED SUZANNE
A BOOK OF SALADS

# Gooseberry Mint Sauce

Serve this gooseberry and mint sauce with lamb.

To make about 1 cup [¼ liter]

| | | |
|---|---|---|
| 1 cup | gooseberries, topped and tailed | ¼ liter |
| 1 tbsp. | finely chopped fresh mint leaves | 15 ml. |
| 2 tbsp. | water | 30 ml. |
| 1 tbsp. | butter | 15 ml. |
| | salt and pepper | |
| | sugar | |

Put the gooseberries in a pan with the water and butter, salt and pepper to taste and a pinch of sugar. Bring the mixture to a boil, cover and simmer it gently until the fruit is cooked and tender—about 20 minutes. Either rub the mixture through a sieve or purée it in a blender. Just before serving, reheat the purée and stir in the finely chopped mint leaves.

JOAN CATLIN AND JOY LAW (EDITORS)
ROYAL COLLEGE OF ART COOK BOOK

# Green Gooseberry Sauce

*To make the spinach juice, pound cleaned spinach leaves in a mortar until they form a paste. Place the paste on a square of cheesecloth and fold the cloth around the spinach. Twist the cloth to squeeze the juice out of the spinach.*

This is the standard sauce for grilled mackerel. It is best when served very hot.

To make about ¾ cup [175 ml.]

| | | |
|---|---|---|
| 1 cup | gooseberries (about ½ lb. [¼ kg.]) | ¼ liter |
| ¼ cup | spinach juice, or 4 fresh sorrel leaves, finely chopped | 50 ml. |
| 1 tbsp. | butter | 15 ml. |
| | freshly grated nutmeg | |
| | sugar | |
| | salt and pepper | |

Boil the gooseberries in water until they are soft—about 20 minutes. Drain the gooseberries and pass them through a sieve. Put the purée into a nonreactive saucepan and add the spinach juice or sorrel. Add the butter and a pinch of nutmeg. Season the mixture with sugar, salt and pepper to taste, then heat it through.

PAUL DINNAGE
THE BOOK OF FRUIT AND FRUIT COOKERY

# Prune Sauce
## *Zwetschgensauce*

This sauce traditionally accompanies pork or dumplings.

To make 2 cups [½ liter]

| | | |
|---|---|---|
| ½ lb. | dried prunes, soaked overnight and drained | ¼ kg. |
| | water | |
| 1 tbsp. | butter | 15 ml. |
| 1 tbsp. | flour | 15 ml. |
| 1 tsp. | grated lemon peel | 5 ml. |
| 1 tbsp. | rum | 15 ml. |
| | ground cinnamon | |
| 2 tbsp. | sugar (optional) | 30 ml. |
| 1 tbsp. | fresh lemon juice | 15 ml. |
| | salt | |

Cover the prunes with water and boil them for about 20 minutes, or until they are soft. Then drain them and reserve 1¼ cups [300 ml.] of the cooking liquid. Pit the prunes and chop them fine.

Melt the butter in a pan and stir in the flour. Let it cook for a minute, without browning. Pour in the reserved cooking liquid and add the lemon peel, rum and a pinch of cinnamon. Add the sugar, if desired, then the prunes. Bring the sauce to a boil and season it with the lemon juice and salt.

HANS GUSTL KERNMAYR
SO KOCHTE MEINE MUTTER

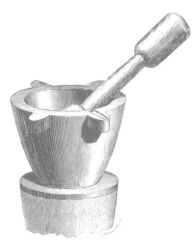

## Pounded Almond Sauce
### Romesco
This is very good with whelks and with all kinds of fish and shellfish, grilled or poached.

To make about 1 ¼ cups [300 ml.]

| ½ cup | almonds, blanched and peeled | 125 ml. |
|---|---|---|
| 1 | slice firm-textured white bread with the crusts removed, cut into cubes | 1 |
| about ¾ cup | olive oil | about 175 ml. |
| 4 to 6 | garlic cloves | 4 to 6 |
| 4 | small tomatoes, peeled, seeded and coarsely chopped | 4 |
|  | salt and black pepper |  |
| ¼ tsp. | cayenne pepper | 1 ml. |
| ¼ cup | sherry | 50 ml. |

Fry the bread cubes in a little of the oil until they are golden. Take them out of the pan and fry the almonds and garlic cloves, adding a little more oil if necessary. When the almonds and garlic cloves are golden, remove them from the pan and fry the tomatoes for a few minutes.

Place all of the fried ingredients in a mortar and pound them with salt and black pepper, the cayenne pepper and the sherry. Stir in enough of the remaining oil, a little at a time, to make a thick sauce.

JAUME CIURANA AND LLORENÇ TORRADO
ELS OLIS DE CATALUNYA

## Yogurt Almond Sauce
### Skorthaliá me Yaoúrti
This mild variation of *skorthaliá* has a unique flavor and the consistency of sour cream. It should be served cold or at room temperature. Greeks almost always serve it with fried vegetables. It also makes an unusual dip when served chilled with lots of crisp raw vegetables.

To make 2 cups [½ liter]

| 2 cups | yogurt | ½ liter |
|---|---|---|
| 8 | almonds, blanched, peeled and finely ground | 8 |
| ¼ tsp. | almond extract | 1 ml. |
| 1 | small garlic clove, crushed to a paste | 1 |
| 2 tbsp. | olive oil | 30 ml. |
| 1 ½ tbsp. | white wine vinegar | 22 ½ ml. |
| ¼ tsp. | salt | 1 ml. |
| ¼ cup | finely chopped fresh parsley | 50 ml. |

Combine the almonds, almond extract, garlic, olive oil and vinegar in a bowl. Drain off any excess water from the yogurt. Add the yogurt, salt and parsley to the bowl, and whisk the sauce until it is smooth.

ANNE THEOHAROUS
COOKING AND BAKING THE GREEK WAY

## A Delicate Green Sauce
### Salsa Verde Delicata
This sauce is served with cauliflower or capon.

To make 1 ¾ cups [425 ml.]

| ½ cup | pine nuts | 125 ml. |
|---|---|---|
| ⅓ cup | pistachios, blanched and peeled | 75 ml. |
|  | salt |  |
| ⅓ cup | white wine vinegar | 75 ml. |
| ⅔ cup | oil | 150 ml. |

Cover the pine nuts and pistachios with tepid water and soak them for two hours to soften them. Drain them, then pound the nuts in a mortar until they are reduced to a paste. Add a pinch of salt and the vinegar. Gradually stir in the oil.

G. B. RATTO
LA CUCINIERA GENOVESE

## Horseradish and Almond Sauce

### *Mandelkren*

*This tangy sauce is a suitable accompaniment for boiled beef, pot roast or baked ham.*

| | To make 1 ½ cups [375 ml.] | |
|---|---|---|
| 3 tbsp. | freshly grated horseradish | 45 ml. |
| ½ cup | almonds, finely ground | 125 ml. |
| 3 tbsp. | butter | 45 ml. |
| ⅓ cup | flour | 75 ml. |
| 1 ¼ cups | milk or ¾ cup [175 ml.] milk and ½ cup [125 ml.] veal stock (recipe, page 159) | 300 ml. |
| | salt | |
| 1 tbsp. | sugar | 15 ml. |
| ¼ cup | heavy cream | 50 ml. |
| 1 tbsp. | fresh lemon juice | 15 ml. |

Prepare a white sauce with the butter, flour and milk (or milk and stock). Season the sauce with salt and the sugar, and cook it over low heat for about 20 minutes, or until all taste of raw flour has disappeared. Stir in the ground almonds and cream, and add the lemon juice gradually to avoid curdling the sauce.

Stir in the grated horseradish, then check the seasoning. Serve the sauce hot.

ROSL PHILPOT
VIENNESE COOKERY

## Walnut Sauce

### *Salsa di Noci*

*Toast the pine nuts in a shallow pan in a 350° F. [180° C.] oven for 10 minutes, turning them frequently to brown evenly.* Use this sauce to season *gnocchi* and pasta.

| | To make 1 ¾ cups [425 ml.] | |
|---|---|---|
| ¾ cup | walnuts, blanched and peeled | 175 ml. |
| ¼ cup | pine nuts, toasted | 50 ml. |
| ⅔ cup | oil | 150 ml. |
| ¼ cup | finely chopped fresh parsley | 50 ml. |
| 1 | garlic clove, finely chopped | 1 |
| ⅔ cup | hot water | 150 ml. |

Crush the walnuts and the pine nuts together in a mortar. Heat half of the oil and sauté the parsley and garlic until soft but not brown. Add the pounded nuts. When the mixture is light brown in color, dilute it by stirring in the remaining oil and the hot water.

G. B. RATTO
LA CUCINIERA GENOVESE

## Turkish Nut Sauce

### *Khiyàr Tèrèturu*

Present this sauce with cucumber, cauliflower or another such salad, with a dribbling of olive oil poured over it.

| | To make about 2 ½ cups [625 ml.] | |
|---|---|---|
| ½ lb. | walnuts or blanched and peeled almonds | ¼ kg. |
| 1 or 2 | slices firm-textured white bread with the crusts removed, soaked in water and squeezed dry | 1 or 2 |
| 1 or 2 | garlic cloves, crushed to a paste | 1 or 2 |
| about ¼ cup | wine vinegar or fresh lemon juice | about 50 ml. |
| | salt and pepper | |
| about ⅓ cup | water | about 75 ml. |

Grind the nuts in a blender; add the bread, garlic, wine vinegar or lemon juice, and salt and pepper to taste. Blend all of the ingredients, adding enough water to bring the mixture to the consistency of light cream.

CLAUDIA RODEN
PICNIC: THE COMPLETE GUIDE TO OUTDOOR FOOD

# Stock-based Sauces

## Curry Sauce

This sauce is used for curried vegetables and fish. Three apples, peeled, cored, sliced and added to the onions in the pan, are an improvement.

| | To make about 2 cups [ ½ liter] | |
|---|---|---|
| 1 tbsp. | curry powder | 15 ml. |
| 4 tbsp. | butter | 60 ml. |
| 6 | onions, sliced | 6 |
| 2 cups | beef stock (recipe, page 159) or concentrated brown sauce (recipe, page 160) | ½ liter |
| 1 tbsp. | flour or arrowroot (optional) | 15 ml. |

Melt the butter in a pan, add the onions, and let them stew without browning for five minutes. Add the curry powder and mix them all together. Then moisten them with the stock or brown sauce and, stirring often, cook the mixture for 20 minutes. Rub the sauce through a sieve. If it needs further thickening, stir a little of the sauce into the flour or arrow-root to make a thin paste. Return this to the rest of the sauce in a pan and cook it, stirring, for two minutes, or until the sauce has the desired consistency.

C. F. LEYEL AND OLGA HARTLEY
THE GENTLE ART OF COOKERY

# Cardoons with Beef Marrow Sauce

## Cardons à la Moelle

*Cardoons are a stalky relative of the artichoke. If they are unavailable, fennel or celery can be substituted. The techniques for extracting bone marrow from beef shank bones and poaching the marrow is shown on page 11.*

| | To serve 4 | |
|---|---|---|
| 2 lb. | cardoons, trimmed and cooked in boiling salted water for 40 to 50 minutes | 1 kg. |
| ¼ lb. | beef marrow, sliced, poached in salted water for 1 to 2 minutes and drained | 125 g. |
| 2 tbsp. | butter | 30 ml. |
| 1 tbsp. | flour | 15 ml. |
| ¼ cup | meat glaze (recipe, page 160) or jellied roasting juices | 50 ml. |
| about 2 cups | beef stock (recipe, page 159) | about ½ liter |
| 1 tbsp. | fresh lemon juice | 15 ml. |
| | salt and pepper | |
| | chopped fresh parsley | |

Melt the butter in a saucepan, stir in the flour, then the meat glaze or roasting juices and enough stock to make a light sauce. Start on the liquid side and then boil it down steadily. When the sauce has thickened, pour in the lemon juice, then add the marrow to reheat it. Check the seasoning and stir in a little chopped parsley.

Put the cardoons into a hot serving dish, pour the sauce over them and serve immediately.

JANE GRIGSON
JANE GRIGSON'S VEGETABLE BOOK

# Frothy Shallot Sauce

## Sauce aux Échalotes

Serve this sauce with grilled beef tenderloin or poached fish.

| | To make ¾ cup [175 ml.] | |
|---|---|---|
| 2 | shallots, very finely chopped | 2 |
| 2 tbsp. | white wine vinegar | 30 ml. |
| 8 tbsp. | butter, 7 tbsp. [105 ml.] cut into small pieces | 120 ml. |
| 1 | sprig fresh parsley, chopped | 1 |
| | salt and pepper | |
| 2 tbsp. | dry white wine | 30 ml. |
| 2 to 3 tbsp. | beef stock (recipe, page 159) or fish stock (recipe, page 164) | 30 to 45 ml. |

Put the shallots and vinegar into a small enameled saucepan and cook them over low heat for 10 minutes, or until only about 1 teaspoon [5 ml.] of liquid remains. Watch carefully to ensure that the liquid does not dry up completely. Add 1 tablespoon [15 ml.] of butter and the chopped parsley, season the mixture with salt and pepper and stir in the wine and stock. Simmer the mixture for seven to eight minutes. Before serving the sauce, whisk in the remaining butter, a few pieces at a time. The sauce should be thick and frothy.

PIERRE NOLOT
À LA RECHERCHE DES CUISINES OUBLIÉES

# French Sorrel Sauce

## La Sauce à l'Oseille

Serve this sauce as a garnish for grilled fish or as an accompaniment to a pot-au-feu.

| | To make about 1 cup [¼ liter] | |
|---|---|---|
| 1 lb. | sorrel, stems removed, leaves washed | ½ kg. |
| 3 tbsp. | butter | 45 ml. |
| ½ cup | beef stock (recipe, page 159) | 125 ml. |
| 1 tbsp. | sugar | 15 ml. |
| | salt and pepper | |
| 2 | egg yolks, lightly beaten | 2 |

In a saucepan over low heat, cook the sorrel in the butter until it has reduced almost to a purée. Stir in the beef stock. Strain the mixture through a sieve into another saucepan and put it back on the heat. Add the sugar and season the mixture with salt and pepper. Let the sauce reduce for about 20 minutes, until it has the consistency of a light purée. Remove the pan from the heat. Gradually stir in the egg yolks and mix them in well.

ÉDOUARD DE POMIANE
LE CODE DE LA BONNE CHÈRE

## To Make Sauce for Roasted Meat

*This hearty sauce is suitable for beef, lamb or pork—and for game and game birds.*

*To make about 1½ cups [375 ml.]*

| 1 | salt anchovy, soaked, filleted, rinsed and dried | 1 |
|---|---|---|
| ¾ cup | red wine | 175 ml. |
| ⅓ cup | beef stock (recipe, page 159) or concentrated brown sauce (recipe, page 160) | 75 ml. |
| ¼ tsp. | freshly grated nutmeg | 1 ml. |
| 1 | shallot, thinly sliced | 1 |
| ½ cup | Seville orange juice | 125 ml. |
|  | meat roasting juices |  |

Take the anchovy and put to it the red wine, stock or brown sauce, nutmeg, shallot and orange juice. Stew these together for about 10 minutes, then pour the sauce into the juices that run from your roasted meat.

SUSANNAH CARTER
THE FRUGAL COLONIAL HOUSEWIFE

## Sauce for Boiled Fowl or Turkey

*To make about 6 cups [1½ liters]*

| 3 | cucumbers, peeled, halved, seeded and thinly sliced | 3 |
|---|---|---|
| 3 | small heads lettuce, boiled for 2 or 3 minutes in salted water, drained and the leaves cut into thin shreds | 3 |
| 1 | small onion, thinly sliced | 1 |
| 4 cups | concentrated brown sauce (recipe, page 160) | 1 liter |
| 3 tbsp. | heavy cream | 45 ml. |
| 2 tbsp. | butter | 30 ml. |
| 1½ tbsp. | fresh lemon juice | 22½ ml. |
|  | salt |  |

Put the cucumber, lettuce and onion in a saucepan with the concentrated brown sauce and cook them until they become quite tender—about 10 minutes. Just before serving, stir in the cream, butter and lemon juice; add salt to taste.

IGNOTUS
CULINA FAMULATRIX MEDICINAE

## Aromatic Sauce

*This sauce goes well with pan-fried chicken breasts, roast veal or pork and poached sweetbreads or brains. Morels are a delicate wild mushroom. Although fresh morels are rarely available, imported dried morels are generally obtainable where fine foods are sold. Fresh morels should be split and washed under running water to rid them of trapped sand. If you are substituting the dried ones, submerge them in hot water, let them soak for 30 minutes and drain them well.*

*To make about 1 cup [¼ liter]*

| 2 | sprigs each of fresh winter savory, basil and lemon thyme | 2 |
|---|---|---|
| 6 | fresh sage leaves | 6 |
| 2 | bay leaves | 2 |
| 2 | shallots, chopped | 2 |
|  | freshly grated nutmeg |  |
|  | pepper |  |
| ⅔ cup | beef stock (recipe, page 159) | 150 ml. |
| ⅓ cup | white sauce (recipe, page 156) | 75 ml. |
| 24 | morels, sliced | 24 |
| 4 tbsp. | butter, 2 tbsp. [30 ml.] cut into small pieces | 60 ml. |
| 4 | egg yolks, beaten | 4 |
| 1½ tbsp. | fresh lemon juice | 22½ ml. |
| 1 tbsp. | mixed chopped fresh tarragon and chervil leaves, blanched for 5 seconds and drained | 15 ml. |

Put into a saucepan the whole herbs, chopped shallots, a little nutmeg and pepper and the beef stock; boil rapidly for 10 minutes. Sieve this mixture into another saucepan, add the white sauce and reduce this by a quarter. Meanwhile, in a heavy pan, stew the morels in 2 tablespoons [30 ml.] of butter for about five minutes, or until they have given up their juice.

Remove the pan from the heat, gradually whisk in the egg yolks, and transfer this sauce to the pan containing the morels. Stirring constantly, simmer the sauce over low heat until it is thick. Just before serving the sauce, add the butter pieces, the lemon juice and the chopped tarragon and chervil leaves.

CHARLES ELMÉ FRANCATELLI
THE MODERN COOK

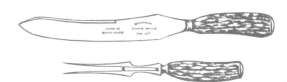

# Brown Sauce with Gherkins and Mustard

## Sauce Charcutière

*This piquant sauce is traditionally served with pork, sausages and variety meats.*

To make 1 cup [¼ liter]

| | | |
|---|---|---|
| 1 cup | concentrated brown sauce (recipe, page 160) | ¼ liter |
| ¼ cup | finely sliced small sour gherkins | 50 ml. |
| 1 tbsp. | Dijon mustard | 15 ml. |
| ½ cup | wine vinegar | 125 ml. |
| 1 tbsp. | finely chopped shallot | 15 ml. |

Place the vinegar and chopped shallot in a small, nonreactive pan and simmer them over low heat until the liquid is reduced to half its original volume. Add the concentrated brown sauce and continue to cook the mixture gently for 10 minutes. Stir in the gherkins, then the mustard. Do not let the sauce boil after the mustard is added.

ÉDOUARD NIGNON
ÉLOGES DE LA CUISINE FRANÇAISE

# Chicken-Liver Sauce

## Salsa di Fegatini

*This rich sauce is suitable for pasta or gnocchi.*

To make about 2½ cups [625 ml.]

| | | |
|---|---|---|
| 4 | chicken livers, finely chopped | 4 |
| 4 tbsp. | butter | 60 ml. |
| ¼ lb. | prosciutto, finely chopped (about ½ cup [125 ml.]) | 125 g. |
| 1 | onion, chopped | 1 |
| 1 cup | chopped fresh parsley | ¼ liter |
| 1 tbsp. | flour | 15 ml. |
| ¾ cup | chicken stock (recipe, page 159) | 175 ml. |
| ⅓ cup | Marsala | 75 ml. |
| | ground mixed spices or grated nutmeg (optional) | |
| | salt (optional) | |

Melt the butter in a pan, add the chicken livers, prosciutto, onion and parsley, and sauté them lightly. Stir in the flour and cook the mixture—stirring constantly—until it colors a little. Stir in the chicken stock and the Marsala. Add a pinch of mixed spices or nutmeg, if desired. Taste the sauce and add salt if necessary.

GIUSEPPE OBEROSLER
IL TESORETTO DELLA CUCINA ITALIANA

# Caper Sauce

*This spicy sauce is suitable for either lamb or fish.*

To make 1½ cups [375 ml.]

| | | |
|---|---|---|
| 3 tbsp. | capers, rinsed and drained | 45 ml. |
| 2 tbsp. | butter | 30 ml. |
| 2 tbsp. | flour | 30 ml. |
| 1 cup | chicken stock (recipe, page 159) | ¼ liter |
| 1 tsp. | dry mustard | 5 ml. |
| 1 tsp. | Worcestershire sauce | 5 ml. |
| 1½ tbsp. | fresh lemon juice | 22½ ml. |
| 1 | egg yolk | 1 |
| ½ cup | cream | 125 ml. |

In a saucepan over low heat, melt the butter and stir in the flour. Gradually add the chicken stock, then the mustard, Worcestershire sauce and lemon juice, and stir until the mixture is thick and smooth. Remove the pan from the heat and add the egg yolk, cream and capers, and again stir until the sauce is smooth. Serve the sauce at once.

SARA B. B. STAMM AND THE LADY EDITORS OF YANKEE MAGAZINE
YANKEE MAGAZINE'S FAVORITE NEW ENGLAND RECIPES

# Almond Sauce for Turkey

To make about 1 cup [¼ liter]

| | | |
|---|---|---|
| ½ cup | almonds, blanched, peeled and finely chopped | 125 ml. |
| 1 tbsp. | butter | 15 ml. |
| 1 tbsp. | flour | 15 ml. |
| ⅔ cup | chicken stock (recipe, page 159) or broth made by cooking the turkey giblets in water for 20 minutes, then straining the mixture | 150 ml. |
| | salt | |
| | ground mace | |
| | sugar | |
| 1 tbsp. | heavy cream | 15 ml. |

Melt the butter in a small saucepan and put the almonds into this, stirring them until they brown. Then sift in the flour and stir in the stock or broth. Flavor the mixture with a pinch each of salt, mace and sugar. Bring the sauce to a boil, then keep it hot by setting the pan in a large pan of simmering water. Do not strain this sauce. Before serving, stir the cream into the sauce.

C. F. LEYEL AND OLGA HARTLEY
THE GENTLE ART OF COOKERY

## Game with Tomato and Chocolate Sauce

I have based this recipe on the Spanish *perdices a la bilbaina*, partridges Bilbao-style, adapting it to a casserole method for hare, pigeon and older game birds. The unusual interest of the sauce depends on two items that the Spaniards brought back from the New World: tomatoes and chocolate. The flavor of unsweetened chocolate and the essences of game give splendor to the tomato.

*To serve 6*

| | | |
|---|---|---|
| 3 | partridges, or 6 squab or 1 hare, cut into serving pieces | 3 |
| 2 | huge tomatoes, peeled, seeded and chopped | 2 |
| 2 to 3 tsp. | grated unsweetened chocolate | 10 to 15 ml. |
| 3 | thick slices bacon, chopped | 3 |
| | lard, rendered bacon fat or oil | |
| 2 | large onions, sliced | 2 |
| 2 | carrots, chopped | 2 |
| 2 | garlic cloves, crushed to a paste | 2 |
| | beef or game stock (recipe, page 159) | |
| 1 tbsp. | finely chopped fresh parsley | 15 ml. |
| | salt and freshly ground pepper | |
| 2 | whole cloves | 2 |
| | freshly grated nutmeg | |
| 1 tbsp. | sherry vinegar or wine vinegar | 15 ml. |
| 1 cup | dry sherry | ¼ liter |

In a large skillet, brown the game and bacon quickly in a little lard, bacon fat or oil. Put the game pieces into a heavy casserole, breast down if you are cooking birds. Add the tomatoes, onions, carrots, garlic and enough stock to barely cover them. Stir in the parsley and season with salt and pepper; add the cloves, a pinch of nutmeg and the vinegar. Bring the mixture to a boil, cover and simmer it until the game is tender—about 30 to 50 minutes.

Transfer the game to a dish, carving the birds into two pieces each. Keep the game warm. Strain the sauce remaining in the casserole into a saucepan and reheat it. Add the grated chocolate slowly to taste; stir in the sherry. Simmer the sauce for five to 10 minutes, then taste it again and adjust the seasoning if necessary. Pour the sauce over the game. Scatter a little extra parsley over the game and serve with buttered noodles.

JANE GRIGSON
JANE GRIGSON'S VEGETABLE BOOK

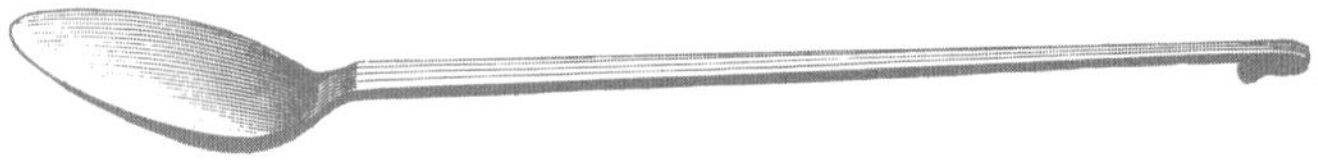

## Moscow Sauce for Venison

*Sauce Moscovite pour Venaison*

*Malaga wine is a sweet, fortified wine from Spain. If it is unavailable, substitute port or Madeira. Toast the almonds in a shallow pan in a preheated 350° F. [180° C.] oven for 10 minutes, turning them frequently to brown them evenly.*

*To make about 3 cups [¾ liter]*

| | | |
|---|---|---|
| ⅔ cup | game stock (recipe, page 159), boiled to reduce it to ⅓ cup [75 ml.] | 150 ml. |
| ⅓ cup | Malaga wine | 75 ml. |
| 2 cups | pepper sauce (recipe, page 161) | ½ liter |
| 1 tbsp. | juniper berries, crushed and steeped in ⅓ cup [75 ml.] boiling water for 5 minutes | 15 ml. |
| ⅓ cup | almonds, blanched, peeled, slivered and toasted | 75 ml. |
| ¼ cup | raisins, soaked in warm water for 15 minutes and drained | 50 ml. |

Add the stock and the wine to the pepper sauce. Strain the juniper-berry infusion through a cloth and add the liquid to the sauce with the almonds and raisins. Heat the sauce without allowing it to boil.

EUGENIE BRAZIER
LES SECRETS DE LA MÈRE BRAZIER

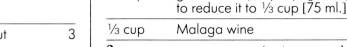

## Tarragon Sauce

*Sauce Purée d'Estragon*

This sauce goes particularly well with white meats such as veal and chicken and with eggs.

*To make about 1½ cups [375 ml.]*

| | | |
|---|---|---|
| 3 cups | freshly picked tarragon leaves, stems removed | ¾ liter |
| ½ lb. | spinach, the stems removed and the leaves washed | ¼ kg. |
| 1 cup | chicken stock (recipe, page 159) | ¼ liter |
| ½ tsp. | white peppercorns, crushed | 2 ml. |
| 2 tbsp. | butter | 30 ml. |
| | salt | |

Drop the spinach into boiling salted water and cook it for three minutes, uncovered. Then drain and plunge it into cold water. Drain it again.

Place the tarragon leaves in a sieve and blanch them for one minute in boiling salted water. Then refresh the tarragon immediately under cold running water.

In a small casserole, bring the chicken stock to a boil. Add the peppercorns, then the tarragon. Boil rapidly, uncovered, until the liquid barely covers the bottom of the casserole—about 15 minutes. Add the spinach and reheat it.

Pour the spinach-and-tarragon mixture into a fine sieve set over a bowl; press down hard on the leaves with a wooden spoon to force them through the sieve. Scrape the bottom of the sieve well with the back of a knife. There should be about 1½ cups [375 ml.] of purée.

Heat the butter in a heavy saucepan. When it begins to brown, quickly whisk in the tarragon-spinach purée. Hold the pan over the heat just until the sauce has warmed. Do not let it boil. Taste for seasoning; it may need salt.

JEAN AND PIERRE TROISGROS
THE NOUVELLE CUISINE OF JEAN AND PIERRE TROISGROS

## Wild Duck Sauce

*This sauce is intended to accompany roast wild duck, though the author suggests that it also provides a good accompaniment to any kind of grilled meat.*

*To make about ½ cup [125 ml.]*

| | | |
|---|---|---|
| 1½ tbsp. | fresh lemon juice | 22½ ml. |
| 2 tsp. | prepared mustard | 10 ml. |
| 1 tsp. | salt | 5 ml. |
| | cayenne pepper | |
| | black pepper | |
| 2 tbsp. | port | 30 ml. |
| ⅓ cup | duck gravy or game stock (recipe, page 159) | 75 ml. |

Mix together the lemon juice, mustard and salt. Add a good deal of cayenne pepper and black pepper with the port and duck gravy or game stock. Mix the whole till quite smooth; let the sauce be heated through and send it to the table hot.

LADY MURIEL BECKWITH
SAUCES, SWEET AND SAVOURY

## Italian Sweet-and-Sour Sauce

*Salsa Agrodolce*

*This sauce goes well with poultry, pork and game.*

Seedless white raisins, pine nuts and a squeeze of lemon juice can be substituted for the capers.

*To make about ¾ cup [175 ml.]*

| | | |
|---|---|---|
| 4 tbsp. | butter | 60 ml. |
| 1 tbsp. | flour | 15 ml. |
| ¾ cup | chicken stock (recipe, page 159) | 175 ml. |
| 2 tbsp. | superfine sugar | 30 ml. |
| 2 tbsp. | boiling white wine vinegar | 30 ml. |
| 1 tbsp. | capers, rinsed and drained | 15 ml. |

Melt the butter in a saucepan and add the flour, stirring until it dissolves. Stir in the stock.

Heat the sugar in a small saucepan. When it turns brown, add the boiling vinegar and stir to dissolve the sugar in the liquid. Pour the sugar-and-vinegar mixture into the pan containing the sauce. Simmer the sauce for 30 minutes. Just before serving, add the capers.

GIUSEPPE OBEROSLER
IL TESORETTO DELLA CUCINA ITALIANA

## Lemon White Sauce for Boiled Fowl

*To make about 3½ cups [875 ml.]*

| | | |
|---|---|---|
| 1 | small lemon, the peel thinly pared, and the juice strained | 1 |
| 2 cups | heavy cream | ½ liter |
| 1 | sprig lemon thyme | 1 |
| 10 | white peppercorns | 10 |
| 8 tbsp. | butter, kneaded with 2 tbsp. [30 ml.] flour | 120 ml. |
| ½ cup | velouté sauce (recipe, page 162), heated until almost boiling | 125 ml. |
| | salt | |

Place the lemon peel, cream, lemon thyme and peppercorns in a saucepan. Simmer the mixture very gently until it has a good taste of lemon—about 10 minutes. Strain the sauce and thicken it by whisking in the kneaded butter and flour. Bring the sauce to a boil and pour in the lemon juice, stirring well. Pour the hot stock into the sauce; do not let the mixture boil. Add salt to taste.

MRS. RUNDELL
MODERN DOMESTIC COOKERY

# Macaroni with Mushrooms

## *Maccheroni coi Funghi*

*Cepes are edible wild mushrooms. They are available dried at specialty markets.*

|  | To serve 4 |  |
|---|---|---|
| 1 lb. | macaroni | ½ kg. |
|  | salt and pepper |  |
| ⅓ cup | freshly grated Parmesan cheese | 75 ml. |
| 8 | butter curls | 8 |
| | **Mushroom sauce** | |
| ¼ lb. | dried cepes, covered with tepid water, soaked for 1 hour, then drained | 125 g. |
| ¼ cup | olive oil | 50 ml. |
| 3 tbsp. | butter | 45 ml. |
| 3 | garlic cloves | 3 |
| 1 | small onion, chopped | 1 |
|  | salt |  |
| ⅓ cup | chopped fresh parsley | 75 ml. |
| ⅓ cup | dry white wine | 75 ml. |
| about ¾ cup | chicken stock *(recipe, page 159)* | about 175 ml. |
| 2 tsp. | flour | 10 ml. |

To make the mushroom sauce, set a casserole over medium heat and put in the oil, butter, garlic and onion. When the onions begin to brown, add the mushrooms and stir the mixture so that it does not stick. Add salt and the parsley.

After two minutes of cooking, moisten the mushrooms with the white wine. Continue cooking the mushrooms, adding the stock a little at a time. When only 2 tablespoons [30 ml.] of stock remain, stir this into the flour to make a paste. Add the paste to the mushrooms and let them cook for about one hour.

Cook the macaroni in boiling salted water for 10 to 15 minutes. Drain and season it with salt and pepper. Add the Parmesan cheese and toss well. Transfer the macaroni to a serving dish and scatter the curls of butter here and there.

Remove the garlic cloves from the mushroom sauce and serve the sauce with the macaroni.

GIUSEPPE OBEROSLER
IL TESORETTO DELLA CUCINA ITALIANA

# Reduced Chicken Stock

## *Le Jus de Volaille Réduit*

*This stock is used in the same way as meat glaze (recipe, page 160). To skin chicken feet, hold one foot at a time over an open flame and turn the foot frequently until the skin has blistered all over—approximately five minutes. Using a paper towel to protect your hands, pull off the pieces of skin and discard them. Trim off the nail from the base of each toe with kitchen shears or with a sharp, heavy knife.*

Collect chicken carcasses, necks, gizzards and skinned feet, and store them in your freezer until you have enough to make this stock, which can be kept for up to two weeks if refrigerated and brought to a boil every two days.

|  | To make about 2½ cups [625 ml.] |  |
|---|---|---|
| 9 lb. | cleaned chicken carcasses, necks, gizzards and skinned feet | 4½ kg. |
| 1 lb. | rendered goose fat | ½ kg. |
| 9 lb. | carrots, onions, celery and turnips, in equal quantities, coarsely chopped | 4½ kg. |
|  | cold water |  |
| 3 | garlic bulbs | 3 |
| 6 | tomatoes, halved crosswise and seeded | 6 |
| 2 | sprigs thyme | 2 |
| 12 | black peppercorns | 12 |
| 3 cups | red wine | ¾ liter |

Melt the goose fat in a very large, deep stockpot. Add the chopped vegetables and sauté them gently in the fat just until they start to brown. Meanwhile, roast the chicken pieces for about 30 minutes in a preheated 475° F. [250° C.] oven so that they also brown.

Place the meat in the stockpot and pour in cold water to twice the height of the meat and vegetables. Add the garlic, tomatoes, thyme and peppercorns. Heat the mixture gently until the surface of the water just trembles; do not let it boil. For the first 30 minutes of cooking, skim off the scum that rises to the surface from time to time. Then let the stock cook gently, uncovered and undisturbed, for at least six hours.

Check the level of the liquid in the pot, skim it again and remove any fat. Make sure the liquid is not boiling. Pour in the red wine, then let the stock cook for another two hours.

At the end of this time, strain the contents of the stockpot through a fine sieve into a clean pan. Bring the stock to a boil, cool it, then refrigerate it overnight. The next day you can easily remove the remaining fat, which will have solidified lightly on the surface of the stock.

Bring the stock to a boil and let it bubble vigorously for two hours. You will then have a strongly flavored, richly colored stock that has been thickened by reduction.

Do not salt the stock; salt would upset the seasoning of the preparations of which the stock will form a part.

ANDRÉ DAGUIN
LE NOUVEAU CUISINIER GASCON

## Rich Oyster Sauce

### Austernsauce

*This rich sauce goes well with poached fish.*

To make about 3 cups [¾ liter]

| | | |
|---|---|---|
| 8 | live oysters, shucked, their liquor reserved | 8 |
| 1 cup | dry white wine | ¼ liter |
| 2 cups | fish velouté sauce (recipe, page 162) | ½ liter |
| 1 | egg yolk | 1 |
| 1 tbsp. | heavy cream | 15 ml. |
| 4 tbsp. | butter, cut into small pieces | 60 ml. |
| | fresh lemon juice | |
| | cayenne pepper | |

In a nonreactive pan, simmer the oysters in the wine until they are firm—about five minutes. Pour the oyster liquor into the pan, then slowly stir in the fish velouté sauce. Bring the mixture to a boil, then remove the pan from the heat.

Whisk together the egg yolk and cream. Gradually whisk in about ⅓ cup [75 ml.] of the sauce, then stir this mixture slowly into the pan of sauce. Stirring all the time, heat the sauce very gently until it thickens—about two minutes. Remove the sauce from the heat and stir in the butter, a little at a time. Season with lemon juice and cayenne pepper to taste.

THEODOR BÖTTIGER
SCHALEN UND KRUSTENTIERE

## Sauce from Bilbao

### Salsa a la Bilbaína

*This fragrant sauce is suitable for poached fish and steamed shellfish. Toast the almonds in a shallow pan in a preheated 350° F. [180° C.] oven for 10 minutes, turning them frequently to brown them evenly.*

To make about 1½ cups [375 ml.]

| | | |
|---|---|---|
| 1 | large onion, finely chopped | 1 |
| 1 | garlic clove, finely chopped | 1 |
| ¼ cup | olive oil | 50 ml. |
| 2 | medium-sized ripe tomatoes, peeled and crushed | 2 |
| 12 | almonds, blanched, peeled and toasted | 12 |
| 4 | sprigs fresh parsley | 4 |
| 1 cup | fish stock (recipe, page 164) | ¼ liter |
| | salt | |

In a heavy skillet, sauté the onion and garlic in the oil. When the onion begins to brown, add the tomatoes and simmer the mixture over low heat. Meanwhile, pound the almonds and parsley in a mortar, until they form a coarse paste. Add this to the skillet. Pour in the stock, season with salt and let the sauce reduce for 10 minutes. Pass the sauce through a sieve and serve it very hot.

ANA MARIA CALERA
365 RECETAS DE COCINA VASCA

## Fillets of John Dory in White Wine Sauce with Tomatoes

### Filets de St. Pierre sans Nom

*John Dory, a fish commonly found in the Mediterranean, has firm, white flesh that is finely flaked. The American counterpart can be found between Nova Scotia and North Carolina although it is not widely marketed. Flounder or sole make suitable substitutes.*

To serve 4

| | | |
|---|---|---|
| two 3 lb. | John Dory, skinned and filleted | two 1½ kg. |
| | salt and freshly ground pepper | |
| ½ cup | dry white wine | 125 ml. |
| ¼ cup | fish stock (recipe, page 164) | 50 ml. |
| 3 tbsp. | fresh lemon juice | 45 ml. |
| ⅓ cup | dry vermouth | 75 ml. |
| 2 | egg yolks, lightly beaten | 2 |
| 1 tbsp. | finely cut fresh chives | 15 ml. |
| | cayenne pepper | |
| 1 cup | heated tomato purée (recipe, page 159), well seasoned | ¼ liter |

Butter a nonreactive baking pan large enough to hold the fish fillets in one layer. Season the fillets with salt and pepper and place them in the pan. Add ¼ cup [50 ml.] of the white wine and the fish stock, and sprinkle on 2 tablespoons [30 ml.] of the lemon juice. Cover the pan with buttered parchment paper, bring the liquid to a boil, then poach the fish in a preheated 400° F. [200° C.] oven until it is just tender—three to four minutes. Remove the fish fillets from the pan and keep them warm.

Reduce the fish poaching liquid a little and strain it into a nonreactive saucepan. Add the vermouth and the remaining white wine and reduce the liquid to half its original volume. Allow it to cool a little, then gradually stir in the egg yolks. Put the saucepan on a rack set in a pot of gently simmering water, and whisk the sauce mixture until it is very stiff, like a sabayon. Flavor the sauce with lemon juice to taste, stir in the chives, and season the sauce well with salt, pepper and cayenne pepper.

Coat a platter with the tomato purée. Place the fillets on top and cover them with the sauce. Serve immediately.

ANTON MOSIMANN
CUISINE À LA CARTE

## Salmon in Basil Sauce

*Escalope de Saumon au Basilic*

*Salmon roe, preserved in salt, can be purchased where fine foods are sold.*

This sauce must be served on ovenproof plates at room temperature so that it does not separate. Because the salmon is so easy to overcook, watch it carefully during the cooking.

*To serve 6*

| | | |
|---|---|---|
| 18 | thin salmon steaks, each weighing about 2 oz. [60 g.] | 18 |
| 2 cups | fresh basil leaves, 1 cup [¼ liter] thinly sliced | ½ liter |
| 10 tbsp. | butter, cut into 10 equal pieces | 150 ml. |
| 3 | medium-sized shallots, sliced | 3 |
| 2 | fresh mushrooms, sliced | 2 |
| 2 cups | dry white wine | ½ liter |
| 2 cups | fish stock (recipe, page 164) | ½ liter |
| 2 cups | heavy cream | ½ liter |
| | salt (optional) | |
| | salmon roe (optional) | |

Melt two of the pieces of butter in a nonreactive saucepan. Add the shallots and mushrooms, and sweat them over low heat for 10 minutes. Add the wine and sliced basil. Over medium heat, reduce the liquid to half its original volume. Add the fish stock and again reduce the liquid by half. Stir in the cream and continue to reduce the sauce over medium heat until it has thickened enough to coat the spoon. Strain the sauce into a clean saucepan.

Saving a few nice basil leaves for a garnish, purée the remaining basil and ½ cup [125 ml.] of the sauce in a blender or food processor. Whisk the purée into the remaining sauce and, over low heat, whisk in the remaining pieces of butter, one at a time. Season the sauce with salt if necessary.

Coat the bottom of six ovenproof plates with the sauce. Place the salmon steaks on top of the sauce and bake them in a preheated 450° F. [230° C.] oven or broil them under a preheated broiler for one minute, or until just cooked. Garnish each plate with fresh basil leaves and—if you like—salmon roe, and serve immediately.

WOLFGANG PUCK
WOLFGANG PUCK'S MODERN FRENCH COOKING FOR THE
AMERICAN KITCHEN

## Rich Red Wine Sauce

*Sauce Genevoise*

Serve this sauce with fresh-water fish or salmon.

*To make about 2 cups [½ liter]*

| | | |
|---|---|---|
| 1 bottle | red Bordeaux or other full-bodied red wine | 1 bottle |
| 1 | onion, chopped | 1 |
| | chopped fresh parsley | |
| 4 | shallots, chopped | 4 |
| 2 | garlic cloves, crushed to a paste | 2 |
| 1 | bay leaf | 1 |
| 2 | sprigs thyme | 2 |
| 1 cup | chopped fresh mushrooms | ¼ liter |
| 1 cup | enriched veal stock (recipe, page 160) | ¼ liter |
| 2 cups | fish stock (recipe, page 164) | ½ liter |
| 2 tbsp. | compound butter (recipe, page 157) | 30 ml. |
| 8 tbsp. | butter, cut into small pieces | 120 ml. |

Pour the wine into a nonreactive pan, add the onion, parsley, shallots, garlic, bay leaf, thyme and mushrooms. Place the pan over medium heat and reduce the mixture to a quarter of its original volume. Pour in the enriched veal stock and fish stock. Increase the heat and boil the sauce rapidly, stirring and scraping it with a wooden spatula, until it is reduced by half. Strain the sauce, then whisk in the compound butter and the butter pieces to make the sauce thick and smooth.

VIARD AND FOURET
LE CUISINIER ROYAL

## A Sauce for Cod

*Sauce à la Morue*

*To make 2½ cups [625 ml.]*

| | | |
|---|---|---|
| ½ lb. | fresh mushrooms, sliced | ¼ kg. |
| 1 | bouquet garni | 1 |
| 2 | garlic cloves | 2 |
| 4 tbsp. | butter | 60 ml. |
| 1 tbsp. | flour | 15 ml. |
| 2 cups | cream | ½ liter |
| 1 | sprig fresh parsley, blanched for 5 seconds, drained and finely chopped | 1 |
| 1 cup | fish stock (recipe, page 164), boiled to reduce it to ½ cup [125 ml.] | ¼ liter |

Sauté the mushrooms, bouquet garni and garlic in the butter until the mushrooms give off their liquid and color lightly. Sprinkle in the flour and mix in the cream. Stirring the mixture continuously, cook it until it is thick—about 10 minutes. Discard the bouquet garni, then strain the mixture through a cloth-lined sieve into another pan. Add the parsley, stir in the reduced fish stock and cook the sauce gently until it is hot.

LOUIS AUGUSTE DE BOURBON
LE CUISINIER GASCON

## White Lamb Stew with Saffron Sauce

### Blanquette d'Agneau au Safran

*To "turn" carrots and turnips, cut them into chunks about 1 inch [2½ cm.] long, then use a sharp vegetable knife to pare them into the shape of olives. To glaze pearl onions, place the peeled onions in a pan with a little butter and sugar—in the proportion of 2 tablespoons [30 ml.] of butter and 1 tablespoon [15 ml.] of sugar for every 1 pound [½ kg.] of onions. Season the onions with salt and pour in enough cold water to partially cover them. Bring the water to a boil, cover the pan and simmer until the onions are tender and the liquid is reduced to a glaze—about 15 minutes.*

*To serve 4*

| | | |
|---|---|---|
| 2 lb. | boneless lamb breast and shoulder, trimmed of excess fat and connective tissue and cut into 1-inch [2½-cm.] pieces | 1 kg. |
| ⅛ tsp. | powdered saffron | ½ ml. |
| 2 cups | lamb stock *(recipe, page 159)*, well seasoned | ½ liter |
| ½ cup | dry white wine | 125 ml. |
| 1 | large bouquet garni, consisting of onions, carrots, celery, ¼ bay leaf, 1 whole clove and some parsley sprigs | 1 |
| 2 | egg yolks | 2 |
| 1 cup | heavy cream | ¼ liter |
| 4 tbsp. | butter, cut into small pieces | 60 ml. |
| 1 tbsp. | fresh lemon juice | 15 ml. |
| | salt and freshly ground pepper | |
| ½ cup | turned carrots, boiled in salted water for 5 minutes | 125 ml. |
| ½ cup | turned turnips, boiled in salted water for 5 minutes | 125 ml. |
| ½ cup | green beans, boiled in salted water for 2 minutes | 125 ml. |
| ¼ cup | pearl onions, glazed | 50 ml. |

Blanch the lamb pieces in boiling salted water for two minutes; drain and immediately rinse them under running water to arrest the cooking. Place the lamb in a large pan, add the lamb stock and the white wine, bring the liquid to a boil and skim off the surface scum. Add the bouquet garni and the saffron. Cover and simmer the lamb until it is tender—about one hour—occasionally skimming off the fat. Remove the lamb and keep it warm. Strain the stock through a fine-meshed sieve into a clean pan. Boil the stock to reduce it to half its original volume. Remove the pan from the heat.

Mix the egg yolks with the cream. Stir in a few spoonfuls of the stock, then gradually stir this mixture into the stock. Heat this sauce gently, without boiling, until it is thick. Strain the sauce through a cloth-lined sieve, then carefully whisk in the butter. Add the lemon juice and season to taste with salt and pepper.

Arrange the lamb pieces on a serving dish and cover them with the sauce. Garnish the lamb with the carrots, turnips, green beans and the freshly glazed pearl onions.

ANTON MOSIMANN
CUISINE À LA CARTE

## Shallot Sauce for Scrag of Mutton Boiled

*"Scrag" is the English name for the neck of mutton or lamb.*

*To make about ½ cup [125 ml.]*

| | | |
|---|---|---|
| 2 or 3 | shallots, thinly sliced | 2 or 3 |
| 2 tbsp. | lamb stock *(recipe, page 159)* | 30 ml. |
| 2 tbsp. | white wine vinegar | 30 ml. |
| | salt | |
| 2 tbsp. | butter | 30 ml. |
| ¼ cup | flour | 50 ml. |

Pour the stock and vinegar into a saucepan and add the shallots and a little salt. Roll the butter in the flour and add it to the shallot mixture. Stir everything together over low heat and bring the sauce to a boil.

SUSANNAH CARTER
THE FRUGAL COLONIAL HOUSEWIFE

## Almond Sauce with Horseradish

### Sos de Migdale cu Hrean

Serve this sauce with boiled or roast meats.

| To make about 2 cups [½ liter] | | |
|---|---|---|
| ⅔ cup | almonds, blanched, peeled and finely chopped | 150 ml. |
| 1 tbsp. | freshly grated horseradish | 15 ml. |
| 1 tsp. | flour | 5 ml. |
| 1 cup | sour cream | ¼ liter |
| ⅓ cup | veal stock (recipe, page 159) | 75 ml. |
| 1 tsp. | sugar | 5 ml. |

In a heavy saucepan, mix the flour and sour cream together well. Thin the mixture with the stock, adding it slowly to avoid lumps. Add the almonds and sugar and simmer the sauce for five minutes. Just before serving the sauce, add the horseradish.

ANISOARA STAN
THE ROMANIAN COOK BOOK

## German Anchovy Sauce

### Sardellen-Sauce

*This pungent sauce is suitable for braised veal, poached fish or hot cheese preparations.*

| To make about 1½ cups [375 ml.] | | |
|---|---|---|
| 3 | salt anchovies, soaked and rinsed, each cut into 3 pieces | 3 |
| 4 tbsp. | butter | 60 ml. |
| 1 tsp. | flour | 5 ml. |
| 1 cup | veal stock (recipe, page 159) | ¼ liter |
| 2 | egg yolks, beaten | 2 |

Put the anchovies in a small saucepan and fry them gently in the butter for two minutes. Stir in the flour and then pour on the stock. Stirring constantly, let the sauce boil until it is slightly thickened—about four minutes. Pour some of the boiling sauce into the egg yolks, stirring constantly. Stir the egg-yolk mixture into the saucepan. Quickly remove the sauce from the heat and pour it through a fine sieve into the sauceboat in which it is to be served.

RATH SCHLOSSER
URGROSSMUTTERS KOCHBUCH

## Sour-Cream Sauce for Veal Brain

### Sos Mózgowy

Serve this sauce with veal cutlets. It is excellent when it is reheated.

| To make about 4 cups [1 liter] | | |
|---|---|---|
| 1 | veal brain | 1 |
| | salt | |
| 1 | onion | 1 |
| 1 | bay leaf | 1 |
| 6 | peppercorns | 6 |
| | dried thyme leaves | |
| 1 | celery rib | 1 |
| 1 | lemon, the peel grated, and the juice strained | 1 |
| 1 tbsp. | butter | 15 ml. |
| 1 tbsp. | flour | 15 ml. |
| ½ cup | veal stock (recipe, page 159) | 125 ml. |
| 2 cups | sour cream | ½ liter |
| 2 | egg yolks, beaten | 2 |

Place the veal brain in a saucepan of boiling salted water. Add the onion, bay leaf, peppercorns, a pinch of thyme, the celery and half of the grated lemon peel and lemon juice. Bring the water back to a boil, then simmer the brain for approximately 10 minutes.

Drain the brain and, when it is cool enough to handle, remove the membranes and cut the brain into small pieces.

Melt the butter in a saucepan, blend in the flour and then pour in the stock, stirring until the mixture is smooth. Add the sour cream and the remaining lemon peel and juice, and let the sauce boil. Remove the pan from the heat, slowly stir ⅓ cup [75 ml.] of the sauce into the egg yolks, then add this mixture gradually to the rest of the sauce. Reheat the mixture gently until it thickens—a minute or two. Finally, add the brain and heat the sauce through.

MARJA OCHOROWICZ-MONATOWA
POLISH COOKERY

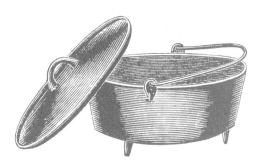

## Rumanian Bread Sauce

### Semmelsosse

*This mild-flavored sauce goes well with roast chicken or veal.*

| | To make about 2 cups [ ½ liter] | |
|---|---|---|
| 2 | bread rolls, crumbled | 2 |
| 2 | garlic cloves, crushed to a paste | 2 |
| ⅓ cup | oil | 75 ml. |
| 1 cup | veal stock (recipe, page 159) | ¼ liter |
| | salt and pepper | |

Soak the rolls in water, then squeeze them well. Fry the garlic lightly in the oil. Add the rolls. Pour in the stock, season with salt and pepper, and boil the sauce until it is thick—about five minutes. Sieve the sauce and reheat it before serving.

MARIA HORVATH
BALKAN-KÜCHE

## Lamb Chops Bourdaloue

### Noix d'Agneau des Landes Bourdaloue

Accompany this dish with a rice pilaf served separately.

| | To serve 6 | |
|---|---|---|
| 18 | small lamb chops, trimmed of excess fat | 18 |
| 12 | 1-inch [2½-cm.] cubes of lean lamb shoulder, trimmed of excess fat | 12 |
| 12 | eggs | 12 |
| | salt and pepper | |
| 1 cup | heavy cream | ¼ liter |
| ¼ cup | peas, boiled for 5 minutes and puréed | 50 ml. |
| 8 tbsp. | butter, 2 tbsp. [30 ml.] cut into small pieces | 120 ml. |
| 12 | fresh button mushrooms, stems discarded | 12 |
| ¼ cup | port | 50 ml. |
| ½ cup | meat glaze (recipe, page 160) | 125 ml. |
| 3 tbsp. | Madeira | 45 ml. |

Thickly butter a 10-inch [25-cm.] ring mold. Beat the eggs thoroughly with a pinch each of salt and pepper. Beat in 2 tablespoons [30 ml.] of the cream and all of the pea purée.

Pour this custard mixture into the mold. Cover the mold with buttered parchment paper and put it into a shallow pan partly filled with hot water. Cook the custard in a preheated 325° F. [160° C.] oven for 45 minutes, or until it is set and a knife inserted into the ring comes out clean.

Meanwhile, blanch the lamb cubes in boiling water for one minute. Drain them and pat them dry. Heat 2 tablespoons [30 ml.] of the butter in a skillet. When it has melted, add the lamb cubes and the mushrooms. When the meat is light beige in color, add the port and cover the skillet tightly so that the vapor from the port condenses and falls back into the mixture. Cook the mixture for five minutes, then stir in the rest of the cream and ⅓ cup [75 ml.] of the meat glaze. Simmer very gently, uncovered, for about 20 minutes, or until a thick glaze forms over the meat and mushrooms.

While the lamb cubes simmer, melt 4 tablespoons [60 ml.] of butter in a large skillet and sauté the lamb chops—in batches if necessary—over high heat for five minutes on each side, or until they are lightly browned. Remove the lamb chops from the skillet and keep them warm. Then set the skillet aside.

When the custard is done, unmold it onto a heated round platter. Arrange the lamb chops around the ring. Pile the meat-and-mushroom mixture into the center of the ring. Working quickly, use the Madeira and the rest of the meat glaze to deglaze the pan in which the chops were cooked. Let this sauce simmer for a few seconds. Remove the skillet from the heat and whisk in the butter pieces. Pour the sauce over the custard and chops.

ÉDOUARD NIGNON
ÉLOGES DE LA CUISINE FRANÇAISE

## White Bread Sauce

### Sos de Piine Albă

Serve this sauce with either cold or warm fish.

| | To make about 2 cups [ ½ liter] | |
|---|---|---|
| 4 | thick slices firm-textured white bread with the crusts removed, cubed | 4 |
| ½ cup | hot water | 125 ml. |
| 2 | garlic cloves, crushed to a paste | 2 |
| 1 tbsp. | oil | 15 ml. |
| 1 cup | veal stock (recipe, page 159) | ¼ liter |
| | salt and pepper | |

Soak the bread in the hot water, then squeeze the bread until dry. Over low heat, sauté the garlic in the oil until golden—about three minutes. Stir in the bread. Pour in the stock and bring the mixture to a boil, stirring it all the time until it is smooth. Season to taste and serve.

INGE KRAMARZ
THE BALKAN COOKBOOK

# Golden Sauce

## *Sauce Dorée*

*This luxurious sauce is suitable for any roast meat or game. The technique of deglazing a roasting pan is shown on page 8.*

*To make 1 ¼ cups [300 ml.]*

| | | |
|---|---|---|
| 2 cups | meat gravy made by deglazing a roasting pan with wine, or substitute veal stock (recipe, page 159) | ½ liter |
| ⅓ cup | dry white wine | 75 ml. |
| 3 tbsp. | fresh lemon juice | 45 ml. |
| 5 or 6 | hard-boiled egg yolks | 5 or 6 |

Boil the gravy or stock together with the white wine until the mixture is reduced to half its original volume. Add the lemon juice. Remove the pan from the heat. Press the egg yolks through a fine-meshed sieve so that they fall in fine threads into the sauce. Serve the sauce without reheating.

B. ALBERT
LE CUISINIER PARISIEN

# Chopped Sauce

## *Sauce Hachée*

*To make ½ cup [125 ml.]*

| | | |
|---|---|---|
| 1 tsp. | chopped shallots, blanched | 5 ml. |
| 1 tsp. | finely chopped fresh mushrooms | 5 ml. |
| 1 tsp. | finely chopped fresh parsley | 5 ml. |
| ¼ cup | Spanish brown sauce (recipe, page 160) | 50 ml. |
| ¼ cup | veal stock (recipe, page 159) | 50 ml. |
| 3 tbsp. | red wine vinegar | 45 ml. |
| | pepper | |
| 1 tbsp. | chopped capers | 15 ml. |
| 1 tbsp. | chopped sour gherkins | 15 ml. |
| 2 tbsp. | compound butter (recipe, page 157) | 30 ml. |

Place the shallots, mushrooms and parsley in a saucepan and pour in the Spanish brown sauce, stock and vinegar. Add a pinch of pepper. Bring the mixture to a boil, skim, and simmer it for several minutes. Sieve the sauce and, just before serving, add the capers, gherkins and compound butter. The sauce should not boil after these additions.

ALEXANDRE DUMAS
LE GRAND DICTIONNAIRE DE CUISINE

# Essence of Sage and Onions

Serve with goose, duck and pork chops.

*To make about ⅓ cup [75 ml.]*

| | | |
|---|---|---|
| 12 | fresh sage leaves, chopped | 12 |
| 2 | large onions, chopped | 2 |
| 2 tbsp. | butter | 30 ml. |
| | salt and pepper | |
| ⅔ cup | veal stock (recipe, page 159) | 150 ml. |

Fry the sage and onions in a small saucepan over low heat with the butter and a little salt and pepper. As soon as the onion becomes lightly colored, add the veal stock. Boil the sauce for 15 minutes, or until it is reduced to half its original volume. Sieve the sauce into a small saucepan for use.

CHARLES ELMÉ FRANCATELLI
THE MODERN COOK

# Green Sauce, Languedoc-Style

## *La Sauce Verte Languedocienne*

This is an excellent sauce for serving with crustaceans, mollusks, fish and grilled meats.

*To make about 2 cups [½ liter]*

| | | |
|---|---|---|
| 2 cups | dry white wine | ½ liter |
| 1 cup | veal stock (recipe, page 159) | ¼ liter |
| 1 tbsp. | olive oil | 15 ml. |
| 2 | garlic cloves, finely chopped | 2 |
| 1 | shallot, finely chopped | 1 |
| 2 or 3 | scallions, finely chopped | 2 or 3 |
| 10 | sprigs watercress, finely chopped | 10 |
| 3 | sprigs tarragon, finely chopped | 3 |
| 2 | sprigs fresh parsley, finely chopped | 2 |
| 1 | sprig chervil, finely chopped | 1 |
| 1 | sprig rosemary or wild thyme, finely chopped | 1 |
| | salt and pepper | |

In a small, nonreactive saucepan, boil together the white wine, stock and olive oil. When the liquid has been reduced to a little less than half its original volume, turn the heat to low and add the remaining ingredients. Cook the sauce just until it boils, then pour it into a very hot sauceboat.

AUSTIN DE CROZE
LES PLATS RÉGIONAUX DE FRANCE

## Devil's Sauce

### Sauce à la Diable

*To make red-pepper butter, prepare a red-pepper purée as shown on page 9 and beat the purée into 8 tablespoons [120 ml.] of creamed butter. Press the flavored butter through a drum sieve before use.*

*To make 1 ½ cups [375 ml.]*

| | | |
|---|---|---|
| 6 | large shallots, very finely chopped | 6 |
| ⅔ cup | white wine vinegar | 150 ml. |
| 1 | garlic clove, crushed to a paste | 1 |
| 1 | bay leaf | 1 |
| ⅔ cup | meat glaze (recipe, page 160) | 150 ml. |
| ⅔ cup | veal stock (recipe, page 159) | 150 ml. |
| 4 tbsp. | red-pepper butter, chilled and cut into pieces | 60 ml. |
| 1 tbsp. | olive oil | 15 ml. |

Wash the chopped shallots, then press them gently in a towel to dry them. Put the shallots in a heavy, nonreactive pan, pour in the vinegar, and add the garlic, bay leaf and meat glaze. Over low heat, reduce the mixture until it has a thick, syrupy consistency—about 10 to 15 minutes. Dilute the mixture with the stock, then whisk in the red-pepper butter and the olive oil.

VIARD AND FOURET
LE CUISINIER ROYAL

---

## Celery Sauce

### Sauce Céleri

*This rich sauce is suitable as an accompaniment for vegetables, eggs, fish or chicken.*

*To make about 2 cups [½ liter]*

| | | |
|---|---|---|
| 4 | celery ribs, cut into 1-inch [2½-cm.] pieces | 4 |
| 1 | onion, stuck with a whole clove | 1 |
| 1 | small bouquet garni | 1 |
| 2 cups | veal stock (recipe, page 159) | ½ liter |
| 1½ tbsp. | butter | 22½ ml. |
| 2 tbsp. | flour | 30 ml. |
| ¼ cup | heavy cream | 50 ml. |
| | salt and pepper | |

Place the celery, onion and bouquet garni in a saucepan and pour in the stock. Cover the pan and cook the mixture over medium heat until the celery is soft enough to be crushed easily—approximately 15 minutes. Strain the cooking liquid through a sieve; discard the onion and bouquet garni and set the celery aside in the sieve.

In another pan, melt the butter over medium heat and stir in the flour. Stir in the strained cooking liquid and continue stirring until the sauce comes to a boil. Reduce the heat to very low.

While the sauce simmers, press the celery through the sieve. Stir the puréed celery into the sauce. Add the cream and season the sauce to taste with salt and pepper. Stirring occasionally, cook the celery sauce for a few minutes more, until it is creamy.

F. BARTHÉLÉMY
LES MENUS EXPLIQUÉS DE CUISINE PRATIQUE

## Poor Man's Hot Sauce

### Sauce au Pauvre Homme Chaude

*This aromatic sauce goes well with grilled or broiled meats.*

*To make about ¾ cup [175 ml.]*

| | | |
|---|---|---|
| 2 tbsp. | olive oil | 30 ml. |
| 6 | shallots, chopped | 6 |
| | bouquet garni | |
| | salt and pepper | |
| 1 | garlic clove | 1 |
| 1 tbsp. | fresh white bread crumbs | 15 ml. |
| 1½ cups | veal stock (recipe, page 159) | 375 ml. |
| 1 tbsp. | chopped fresh parsley | 15 ml. |

Heat the oil in a saucepan and brown the shallots in the oil. Add the bouquet garni, salt and pepper, the garlic clove and the bread crumbs. Stir in the stock and bring the mixture to a boil; then simmer over very low heat for 20 minutes to let the sauce reduce to about half its original volume. Discard the bouquet garni. Just before serving the sauce, stir in the chopped parsley.

ALOÏDE BONTOU
TRAITÉ DE CUISINE BOURGEOISE BORDELAISE

## Piquant Sauce

### *Sauce Piquante*

*This sauce goes well with pork and variety meats of all kinds.*

*To make about ¾ cup [175 ml.]*

| | | |
|---|---|---|
| 6 | shallots, chopped | 6 |
| 1 tbsp. | butter | 15 ml. |
| 1 tbsp. | flour | 15 ml. |
| 1½ cups | veal stock (recipe, page 159) | 375 ml. |
| | salt and pepper | |
| 2 tbsp. | vinegar, reduced over low heat to 1 tbsp. [15 ml.] | 30 ml. |
| 1 tbsp. | chopped sour gherkins | 15 ml. |
| 1 tbsp. | chopped capers | 15 ml. |
| 1 tsp. | chopped fresh parsley | 5 ml. |

Sauté the chopped shallots in the butter for five minutes, then stir in the flour and let it brown lightly. Whisk in the stock, season with salt, pepper and the vinegar, and cover. Cook the sauce over low heat for 20 minutes, or until it is reduced to about half its original volume. Just before serving, stir in the gherkins, capers and parsley.

ALOÏDE BONTOU
TRAITÉ DE CUISINE BOURGEOISE BORDELAISE

## Sharp Sauce

### *La Sauce Pointue*

This sauce goes well with hot meat pâtés and cold terrines.

*To make about 1¼ cups [300 ml.]*

| | | |
|---|---|---|
| 1 tbsp. | butter | 15 ml. |
| 3 | shallots, chopped | 3 |
| 1 tbsp. | Dijon mustard | 15 ml. |
| 1 tsp. | white wine vinegar | 5 ml. |
| 12 | capers, rinsed and drained | 12 |
| 2 cups | veal stock (recipe, page 159) | ½ liter |
| 2 tbsp. | heavy cream | 30 ml. |

In a heavy, tin-lined copper pan, melt the butter over medium heat and add the shallots and mustard. Stirring frequently, cook the mixture for three to four minutes, then deglaze the pan with the vinegar and add the capers. Stir in the stock, and simmer for 40 to 45 minutes.

Just before serving, pour the cream into the middle of the pan and allow it to disappear without stirring. The sauce will be smooth, shiny and thick.

ANDRÉ DAGUIN
LE NOUVEAU CUISINIER GASCON

## Sweet-and-Sour Sauce, Genoa-Style

### *Sauce Génoise*

*If you want to make a Génoise sauce to serve with poached fish or vegetables, the authors suggest the following variation on this recipe: Omit the sugar, substitute 2 tablespoons [30 ml.] of mock hollandaise sauce (recipe, page 166) for the enriched veal stock or tomato purée, then thicken the sauce by whisking in 2 tablespoons of compound butter (recipe, page 157).*

Serve this sauce with grilled or roast chicken.

*To make about 1 cup [¼ liter]*

| | | |
|---|---|---|
| 4 | sour gherkins, finely chopped | 4 |
| 2 tbsp. | capers, rinsed and drained | 30 ml. |
| ¼ cup | seedless white raisins | 50 ml. |
| ¼ cup | dried currants | 50 ml. |
| | cayenne pepper | |
| | freshly grated nutmeg | |
| | pepper | |
| 2 tbsp. | chopped fresh parsley | 30 ml. |
| 2 | shallots, chopped | 2 |
| 1 tbsp. | meat glaze (recipe, page 160) | 15 ml. |
| ⅓ cup | vinegar | 75 ml. |
| 1 tbsp. | sugar | 15 ml. |
| 2 tbsp. | enriched veal stock (recipe, page 160) or tomato purée (recipe, page 159) | 30 ml. |
| ⅓ cup | veal stock (recipe, page 159) | 75 ml. |

Put the gherkins, capers, raisins, dried currants, a pinch each of the cayenne pepper, grated nutmeg and pepper, and the parsley and shallots into a nonreactive pan; add the meat glaze. Pour in the vinegar and add the sugar. Stirring frequently, cook the mixture until it is reduced to a thick syrup, then moisten it with the enriched veal stock or tomato purée, and finally with the veal stock.

VIARD AND FOURET
LE CUISINIER ROYAL

## Sour-Cream and Tomato Sauce

### Sos Pomidorowy ze Śmietana

Serve this sauce with boiled beef, pork chops or meat patties.

*To make about 2 cups [½ liter]*

| | | |
|---|---|---|
| 1 cup | sour cream | ¼ liter |
| 5 or 6 | tomatoes, sliced | 5 or 6 |
| 1 tbsp. | butter | 15 ml. |
| ½ cup | veal stock (recipe, page 159) | 125 ml. |
| | salt and pepper | |
| 1½ tsp. | flour | 7 ml. |
| | sugar | |

Melt the butter in a skillet over medium heat and sauté the tomatoes until they are reduced to a paste—about 15 minutes. Press the tomatoes through a sieve into a saucepan, dilute the purée with the stock, and season it to taste with salt and pepper.

Mix the sour cream and flour together. Add the thickened sour cream to the tomato mixture. Sweeten this sauce very sparingly with enough sugar to give it a sweet-and-sour taste. Simmer the sauce until it is smooth and thick—approximately five minutes.

MARJA OCHOROWICZ-MONATOWA
POLISH COOKERY

## Hot Green Sauce

### Sauce Verte Chaude au Séladons

*Lemon balm is a perennial herb that has heart-shaped leaves. The leaves give a lemony flavor to teas, punches and fruit desserts and are a suitable garnish for fish. Dried lemon balm is used in potpourri.*

Serve this sauce with any kind of white or red meat.

*To make 1½ cups [375 ml.]*

| | | |
|---|---|---|
| ¼ lb. | lean boneless veal, in 1 piece | 125 g. |
| ¼ lb. | ham, in 1 piece | 125 g. |
| ⅔ cup | Champagne | 150 ml. |
| 1¼ cups | veal stock (recipe, page 159) | 300 ml. |
| 1 tbsp. each | chopped fresh tarragon, chervil and lemon balm leaves and finely cut fresh chives | 15 ml. each |
| 2 | sprigs fresh parsley | 2 |
| 4 | egg yolks | 4 |
| 1½ tbsp. | fresh lemon juice (optional) | 22½ ml. |

In a saucepan, heat the veal and ham gently until they begin to sweat. Add the Champagne and stock and, stirring occasionally to keep the meat from sticking, continue to cook for 45 minutes. Blanch the herbs in boiling water for 10 seconds, drain them and pound them in a mortar; then squeeze them in a cloth to extract the green juices. Whisk the egg yolks with the juices. Strain the meat cooking liquid into a clean pan; reserve the meat for another use. Whisk a few spoonfuls of the strained liquid into the egg yolks and herb juices, then pour this mixture gradually into the rest of the sauce, whisking constantly. Still whisking, cook the sauce over very low heat until it is thick—about two to three minutes. Add lemon juice to taste, if you like.

LOUIS AUGUSTE DE BOURBON
LE CUISINIER GASCON

## Aromatic Egg-enriched Velouté Sauce

### Sauce Mêlée

*This sauce is a good accompaniment for beef, veal, tongue, brains or sweetbreads.*

*To make about 2 cups [½ liter]*

| | | |
|---|---|---|
| 2 tbsp. | chopped fresh parsley | 30 ml. |
| 2 tbsp. | chopped scallion | 30 ml. |
| ⅓ cup | chopped fresh mushrooms | 75 ml. |
| ½ tsp. | chopped garlic | 2 ml. |
| 2 tbsp. | butter | 30 ml. |
| 1 tsp. | flour | 5 ml. |
| 4 cups | veal stock (recipe, page 159) | 1 liter |
| 2 | sour gherkins, chopped | 2 |
| 3 | egg yolks | 3 |
| | salt and pepper | |

Place the parsley, scallion, mushrooms and garlic in a saucepan with the butter. Cook them for about five minutes, without letting them brown; stir in the flour. Gradually add all but about 3 tablespoons [45 ml.] of the stock. Simmer the sauce for about 45 minutes, or until it is reduced to half its original volume. Add the gherkins to the sauce. Remove the pan from the heat.

Beat the egg yolks lightly with the remaining stock. Stir the yolk mixture gradually into the sauce. Stir the sauce over very low heat for a minute·or two, or until the egg yolks have thickened it slightly. Season the sauce to taste.

MENON
LA CUISINIÈRE BOURGEOISE

## Horseradish Sauce with Apples

### Umak od Hren sa Jabukom

Serve this sauce with cooked beef or ham.

| To make about 1 cup [¼ liter] | | |
|---|---|---|
| 3 to 4 tbsp. | freshly grated horseradish | 45 to 60 ml. |
| 3 | apples, peeled, cored and grated | 3 |
| ½ cup | cold veal stock (recipe, page 159) | 125 ml. |
| 3 tbsp. | fresh lemon juice | 45 ml. |

Combine the horseradish and apples, pour in the veal stock, and immediately add the lemon juice so that the mixture maintains its whiteness.

INGE KRAMARZ
THE BALKAN COOKBOOK

## Red Wine Sauce with Raisins

### Rode Wijnsaus met Rozijnen

This sauce goes well with slices of braised beef tongue. For the most flavor, add the meat before simmering the sauce and cook them gently together.

| To make 2½ cups [625 ml.] | | |
|---|---|---|
| ¾ cup | red wine | 175 ml. |
| ½ cup | raisins, soaked in warm water for 15 minutes and drained | 125 ml. |
| 3 tbsp. | butter | 45 ml. |
| ¼ cup | flour | 50 ml. |
| 2 cups | veal stock (recipe, page 159) | ½ liter |
| 1 | strip lemon peel stuck with 2 whole cloves | 1 |
| 1 | blade mace | 1 |
| | sugar (optional) | |
| | vinegar or fresh lemon juice (optional) | |

In a large saucepan, melt the butter and add the flour. Stirring constantly, cook the mixture until it turns dark yellow. Whisk in the stock gradually and then add the wine. Add the raisins, lemon peel and mace. Let the sauce simmer for about 10 minutes, or until the raisins have puffed up. Remove the spices and lemon peel from the sauce and season, if necessary, with a little sugar and with vinegar or a few drops of fresh lemon juice.

RIA HOLLEMAN
UIT GROOTMOEDERS KEUKEN

## Egg-enriched Velouté Sauce

### Sauce Poulette

*This luxurious sauce is traditionally served with boiled vegetables and poached sweetbreads or brains.*

| To make about 1¼ cups [300 ml.] | | |
|---|---|---|
| 5 tbsp. | butter, 4 tbsp. [60 ml.] cut into small pieces | 75 ml. |
| 1 tbsp. | flour | 15 ml. |
| 2 cups | veal stock (recipe, page 159) | ½ liter |
| | salt and pepper | |
| | freshly grated nutmeg | |
| | bouquet garni | |
| | mushroom peelings or mushroom cooking liquid (optional) | |
| 2 | egg yolks | 2 |
| 1½ tbsp. | fresh lemon juice | 22½ ml. |
| 1 tsp. | chopped fresh parsley | 5 ml. |

In a saucepan, make a pale roux with 1 tablespoon [15 ml.] of the butter and the flour. Whisk in the stock and season the mixture with salt and pepper and a pinch of grated nutmeg. Add the bouquet garni and, if you have any mushroom peelings or mushroom cooking liquid, add it too. Reduce the sauce over very low heat for 30 to 40 minutes, then press it through a fine-meshed sieve into a clean saucepan.

Whisk together the egg yolks and the lemon juice, then stir in 1 to 2 tablespoons [15 to 30 ml.] of the sauce. Gradually whisk this mixture into the sauce, return it to low heat and whisk it as it thickens. Do not allow the sauce to boil. Remove the pan from the heat and whisk in the butter pieces, a handful at a time. Stir in the parsley and serve.

ALOÏDE BONTOU
TRAITÉ DE CUISINE BOURGEOISE BORDELAISE

## Seville Orange Sauce

### Sauce Bigarrade

*This rich sauce is traditionally served with braised or roast duck or goose. Seville oranges—also known as bitter or sour oranges—are tart-flavored fruit obtainable at fruit specialty markets and Latin American markets in the winter. If they are not available, substitute the juices and peels of two sweet oranges and half a lemon. When preparing the peel, make sure that none of the bitter white pith is pared off with it. The julienne should be about half the width of a matchstick.*

| | To make about 2 cups [½ liter] | |
|---|---|---|
| 2 | Seville oranges, the peel thinly pared and cut into very fine julienne, and the juice strained | 2 |
| 3 tbsp. | fresh lemon juice | 45 ml. |
| 4 cups | velouté sauce (recipe, page 162) | 1 liter |

In a heavy saucepan, simmer the velouté sauce until it is reduced to about half its original volume. Meanwhile, parboil the julienne for three minutes, then drain them and dry them with a cloth. Stir the orange and lemon juices into the reduced velouté, then strain the sauce through a sieve into a warmed bowl or sauceboat. Stir in the strips of orange peel.

URBAN DUBOIS AND ÉMILE BERNARD
LA CUISINE CLASSIQUE

# White Sauce from Ibiza

## *Salsa Blanca*

This sauce can be served with either meat or fish.

| | To make about ¾ cup [175 ml.] | |
|---|---|---|
| 2 tbsp. | lard | 30 ml. |
| 1 | onion, finely chopped | 1 |
| 1 | carrot, finely chopped | 1 |
| 1 | turnip, finely chopped | 1 |
| 2 or 3 | sprigs chervil | 2 or 3 |
| 1 tbsp. | chopped celery leaves | 15 ml. |
| 1 | bay leaf | 1 |
| | salt and pepper | |
| 1 tbsp. | potato flour | 15 ml. |
| ⅔ cup | veal stock (recipe, page 159) | 150 ml. |
| ⅓ cup | milk | 75 ml. |
| 1 | egg yolk, lightly beaten | 1 |
| 3 tbsp. | fresh lemon juice | 45 ml. |

Heat the lard in a saucepan. Add the onion, carrot, turnip, chervil, celery leaves, bay leaf, and salt and pepper, and fry them gently. When they begin to brown, stir in the potato flour. Immediately pour in the stock and the milk. Continue to stir until the sauce begins to thicken—about two minutes. Sieve the sauce and return it to the heat to thicken a little more.

Mix together the egg yolk and lemon juice. Stir in a few tablespoons of the sauce, then slowly pour this mixture into the remaining sauce—stirring all the time. Stir everything together briefly over the heat, then serve.

GABRIEL SASTRE RAYÓ AND ANTONIA ORDINAS MARÍ (EDITORS)
LLIBRE DE CUINA DE CA'N CAMES SEQUES

# Savory Egg-based Sauces

## Cambridge Sauce

*This tangy sauce is suitable for cold roasted beef or lamb or for cold poached fish such as salmon.*

The sauce should be kept at about the same degree of thickness as a reduced velouté sauce. Salt must be used in moderation, owing to the anchovies in the composition.

| | To make about 1 cup [¼ liter] | |
|---|---|---|
| 6 | hard-boiled egg yolks | 6 |
| 4 | salt anchovies, soaked, filleted, rinsed and dried | 4 |
| 1 tbsp. | capers, rinsed and drained | 15 ml. |
| 6 | fresh tarragon leaves | 6 |
| 6 | sprigs chervil | 6 |
| 1 tsp. | finely cut chives | 5 ml. |
| 12 | fresh burnet leaves, blanched in boiling water for 1 minute, refreshed in cold water, then drained | 12 |
| 1 tsp. | English mustard | 5 ml. |
| 1 tsp. | French mustard | 5 ml. |
| | salt and pepper | |
| about ⅓ cup | oil | about 75 ml. |
| about 3 tbsp. | tarragon vinegar | about 45 ml. |
| 1 tsp. | finely chopped fresh parsley | 5 ml. |

Take the egg yolks and the anchovy fillets and put them into a large mortar with the capers, tarragon, chervil, chives and burnet. Pound these together with the English and French mustards and some salt and pepper. Moisten the mixture with the oil and tarragon vinegar, taking care that the sauce is kept rather thick.

Having sufficiently moistened the sauce, transfer it from the mortar to a drum sieve placed over a dish and proceed to rub the sauce through the sieve in the same manner as a purée. Pass the back part of a knife along the under part of the sieve, in order to detach any adhesive particles. Collect the sauce in a small bowl and keep it on ice until it is wanted for use. Just before sending the sauce to the table, add some chopped parsley.

CHARLES ELMÉ FRANCATELLI
THE MODERN COOK

# Chive Sauce

## Schnittlauchsauce

*This rich sauce is suitable for vegetable salads, for cold fish, shellfish or poultry, and for poached eggs.*

| | To make about 1 ¼ cups [300 ml.] | |
|---|---|---|
| 2 tbsp. | finely cut fresh chives | 30 ml. |
| 3 | hard-boiled egg yolks | 3 |
| 1 tbsp. | oil | 15 ml. |
| | salt and pepper | |
| 1 cup | heavy cream | ¼ liter |

Press the egg yolks through a sieve, mix them with the oil and season them with salt and pepper. Whisk in the cream, a little at a time, and continue whisking until the mixture is smooth. Stir in the chives just before serving the sauce.

WOLF NEUBER
DIE K.U.K. WIENER KÜCHE

# Gherkin Sauce

## Gurkensosse

This sauce is excellent with boiled beef.

| | To make about 1 ¾ cups [425 ml.] | |
|---|---|---|
| ¾ cup | finely chopped sour gherkins | 175 ml. |
| 2 tbsp. | finely chopped fresh parsley | 30 ml. |
| 1 tbsp. | finely cut fresh dill | 15 ml. |
| 1 | very small onion, finely chopped | 1 |
| 1 | oil-packed flat anchovy fillet, finely chopped | 1 |
| 1 | tomato, peeled, seeded and finely chopped | 1 |
| 2 | hard-boiled eggs, sieved | 2 |
| ½ tsp. | prepared mustard | 2 ml. |
| | salt and freshly ground pepper | |
| | sugar | |
| about 3 tbsp. | olive oil | about 45 ml. |
| about 3 tbsp. | vinegar | about 45 ml. |

Stir the chopped gherkins, parsley, dill, onion, anchovy and tomato into the sieved eggs. Add the mustard, a good pinch of salt, a little pepper and a pinch of sugar. Gradually stir in the olive oil—not quite as gingerly as when making mayonnaise, but with care. Thin the sauce with a little vinegar. Taste, and adjust the seasoning, if necessary.

ROSL PHILPOT
VIENNESE COOKERY

# Cucumber Sauce

## Kurkkukastike

Serve this sauce with cold meats.

| | To make about 4 cups [1 liter] | |
|---|---|---|
| 1 | large cucumber, peeled, halved, seeded and finely chopped (about 2 cups [½ liter]) | 1 |
| 1 cup | mayonnaise (recipe, page 165) | ¼ liter |
| 1 cup | heavy cream, whipped | ¼ liter |
| 1 to 2 tbsp. | fresh lemon juice | 15 to 30 ml. |
| ¼ tsp. | salt | 1 ml. |
| 2 tsp. | finely cut fresh dill | 10 ml. |

Whip the mayonnaise until it is fluffy, then fold in the cream. Stir in the lemon juice and salt. Just before serving the sauce, fold in the cucumber and the dill.

BEATRICE A. OJAKANGAS
THE FINNISH COOKBOOK

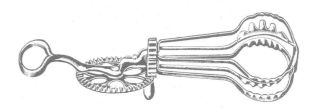

# Frankfurt Green Sauce

## Grüne Sauce

*This piquant sauce is suitable for cold fish, shellfish or poultry, or for cold vegetables or vegetable salads.*

| | To make about 1 ¾ cups [425 ml.] | |
|---|---|---|
| 1 cup | finely chopped mixed fresh parsley, chervil and tarragon leaves | ¼ liter |
| 1 tsp. | finely chopped fresh marjoram leaves | 5 ml. |
| 3 | hard-boiled egg yolks | 3 |
| 1 tsp. | prepared mustard | 5 ml. |
| | salt and pepper | |
| 1 tbsp. | wine vinegar | 15 ml. |
| 1 cup | olive oil | ¼ liter |

Blend the parsley, chervil, tarragon and marjoram with the egg yolks and press the mixture through a fine sieve. Season this purée with the mustard and a little salt and pepper. Mix in the vinegar. Add the olive oil in a thin stream while stirring constantly.

THEODOR BÖTTIGER
SCHALEN UND KRUSTENTIERE

# Garlic and Basil Sauce

## Sauce Pistou à l'Ail

*This sauce is suitable for hot or cold pasta dishes, for grilled strong-flavored fish such as sardines or mackerel, for fish soups, or for crudités.*

To make about 1 1/4 cups [300 ml.]

| | | |
|---|---|---|
| 5 or 6 | garlic cloves, cooked for 10 minutes in boiling water and drained | 5 or 6 |
| 15 | fresh basil leaves | 15 |
| 2 | egg yolks | 2 |
| | salt and white pepper | |
| | fresh lemon juice | |
| 3/4 cup | olive oil | 175 ml. |

Crush the garlic cloves and the basil in a mortar. Add the egg yolks, salt and pepper, and a little lemon juice. Pour in the oil slowly, in a thin stream, pounding it in with the pestle so that the sauce thickens into a mayonnaise.

JEAN AND PAUL MINCHELLI
CRUSTACÉS, POISSONS ET COQUILLAGES

---

# Piedmont Green Sauce

## Bagnet Verd

*This rich sauce goes well with grilled meats and game, cold meats and hot or cold sausages.*

To make 1 cup [1/4 liter]

| | | |
|---|---|---|
| 1/2 cup | fresh parsley leaves | 125 ml. |
| 1 | garlic clove | 1 |
| 2 | hard-boiled egg yolks | 2 |
| 1/2 cup | finely chopped onion | 125 ml. |
| 1/2 cup | fresh white bread crumbs, soaked in 1/4 cup [50 ml.] white wine vinegar and squeezed dry | 125 ml. |
| 1/3 cup | olive oil | 75 ml. |
| 1 tbsp. | vinegar | 15 ml. |
| | salt and pepper | |
| | sugar | |

In a mortar, crush the parsley, garlic, egg yolks, onion and bread crumbs to a coarse paste. Press the mixture through a sieve. Stirring constantly, add the oil, vinegar and a little salt, pepper and sugar.

FELICE CÙNSOLO
LA CUCINA DEL PIEMONTE

---

# A Cold Green Sauce for Fish, Game and Poultry

## Eine Kalte Grüne Sauce zu Fisch, Wildpret, auch zu Geflügel zu Geben

*The traditional herbs for this recipe are a mixture of borage, sorrel, burnet and tarragon.*

To make about 1 1/2 cups [375 ml.]

| | | |
|---|---|---|
| 1/2 lb. | butter, softened | 1/4 kg. |
| 4 | egg yolks | 4 |
| 2 | hard-boiled eggs, chopped | 2 |
| 1 tbsp. | olive oil | 15 ml. |
| 1 tbsp. | vinegar | 15 ml. |
| 1 tsp. | grated lemon peel | 5 ml. |
| 1 tbsp. | prepared German mustard | 15 ml. |
| 1 cup | mixed herb leaves, parboiled for a few seconds, squeezed dry in a towel and finely chopped | 1/4 liter |
| | salt and pepper | |

Cream the butter until it is very smooth. Whisk in the egg yolks one at a time, then incorporate the hard-boiled eggs. Add the oil, vinegar, lemon peel and mustard. Stir in the herbs. Press the sauce through a sieve and season it with salt and pepper to taste.

RATH SCHLOSSER
URGROSSMUTTERS KOCHBUCH

---

# Herring Sauce

## Haringsaus

Serve this sauce with cold meat or with beet salad. The sauce will be milder if chopped hard-boiled egg whites or a spoonful of yogurt or sour cream is added.

To make about 1 1/2 cups [375 ml.]

| | | |
|---|---|---|
| 1 | pickled herring, filleted and skinned | 1 |
| 3 | hard-boiled egg yolks | 3 |
| 1 | onion | 1 |
| about 7 tbsp. | oil | about 105 ml. |
| about 5 tbsp. | vinegar | about 75 ml. |
| | salt and pepper | |

Chop the herring, egg yolks and onion together until fine. Mix in enough oil and vinegar to make a thick sauce. Season it with salt and pepper.

RIA HOLLEMAN
UIT GROOTMOEDERS KEUKEN

## Green Sauce for Beef

### Grüne Sauce zum Ochsenfleisch

*The traditional herbs for this recipe are a mixture of parsley, tarragon, borage and burnet. Both borage and burnet have a cucumber-like taste.*

| | To make ⅔ cup [150 ml.] | |
|---|---|---|
| 3 | hard-boiled egg yolks | 3 |
| | salt and pepper | |
| 1½ tbsp. | oil | 22½ ml. |
| 1 tbsp. | vinegar | 15 ml. |
| ½ tbsp. | prepared German mustard | 7 ml. |
| 3 tbsp. | finely chopped mixed herbs | 45 ml. |
| 3 to 4 tbsp. | sour cream | 45 to 60 ml. |

Mash the egg yolks, season them with salt and pepper, and mix in the oil, vinegar and mustard. Stir in the herbs. Then add enough sour cream to give the sauce the consistency desired. Press the sauce through a sieve before serving it.

RATH SCHLOSSER
URGROSSMUTTERS KOCHBUCH

## Chive Sauce from Vienna

### Schnittlauchsosse

*This piquant sauce is a suitable accompaniment for cold meats, boiled beef or poached sausages.*

| | To make about 1¼ cups [300 ml.] | |
|---|---|---|
| 1 tbsp. | finely cut fresh chives | 15 ml. |
| 2 | slices firm-textured white bread with the crusts removed, soaked in a little milk and squeezed dry | 2 |
| 2 | hard-boiled egg yolks | 2 |
| 1½ tbsp. | fresh lemon juice | 22½ ml. |
| 1 tsp. | sugar | 5 ml. |
| | salt and pepper | |
| | prepared mustard | |
| 3 tbsp. | olive oil | 45 ml. |

Sieve the bread and egg yolks into a bowl. Add the lemon juice, sugar, some salt and pepper, and a little mustard. Stir in the olive oil, at first drop by drop, then pouring it more steadily. Taste the sauce for seasoning and—at the last moment—add the chives.

ROSL PHILPOT
VIENNESE COOKERY

## King Edward VII's Sauce

This sauce was originally invented for His Royal Highness in the year 1861, long before he ascended the throne. It is meant to be served with boiled fish or meats, but also makes a good dressing for salads made with fish, game or poultry.

| | To make about 2 cups [½ liter] | |
|---|---|---|
| 4 | hard-boiled egg yolks | 4 |
| 4 | salt anchovies, soaked, filleted, rinsed and dried | 4 |
| ½ cup | mixed chopped fresh tarragon, chervil, burnet and chives, blanched for a few seconds, drained, then pressed dry in a cloth | 125 ml. |
| 1 tbsp. | capers, rinsed and drained | 15 ml. |
| 1 tbsp. | Dijon mustard | 15 ml. |
| 3 | egg yolks | 3 |
| 1¼ cups | oil | 300 ml. |
| ⅓ cup | tarragon vinegar | 75 ml. |

Place the hard-boiled egg yolks, anchovies, herbs, capers, mustard and raw egg yolks in a mortar and pound them together with a pestle. Then proceed to work in the oil and the vinegar, by degrees. When this is done, rub the sauce through a very fine sieve.

ELIZABETH CRAIG
COURT FAVOURITES

## Butterless Béarnaise Sauce

### Sauce Béarnaise Maigre

*This zesty sauce is suitable for boiled or steamed vegetables, poached or hard-boiled eggs, and grilled beef or fish steaks.*

| | To make 2 cups [½ liter] | |
|---|---|---|
| 2 | shallots, finely chopped | 2 |
| about 6 tbsp. | wine vinegar | about 90 ml. |
| 6 | egg yolks | 6 |
| about ¾ cup | olive oil | about 175 ml. |
| ⅔ cup | tomato purée (recipe, page 159), cooked until reduced to ⅓ cup [75 ml.] and strained | 150 ml. |

Place the shallots and 4 tablespoons [60 ml.] of the vinegar in a small saucepan over low heat and reduce the mixture by simmering it until no more than 1 tablespoon [15 ml.] of the liquid remains. Allow it to cool. Add the egg yolks and whisk them in, then gradually mix in about ½ cup [125 ml.] of the olive oil. Whisk the mixture over very gentle heat until the sauce is thick and frothy, then pass it through a sieve into another saucepan. Whisk in the thickened tomato purée, a little at a time, alternating it with a few more spoonfuls of the olive oil. The sauce should be very thick. Finally, whisk in a little more vinegar to taste in a thin stream.

URBAN DUBOIS AND ÉMILE BERNARD
LA CUISINE CLASSIQUE

## Majorcan Sauce

### Salsa Mallorquina

*To toast the almonds called for in this recipe, bake them in a preheated 350° F. [180° C.] oven for 10 minutes, turning them frequently to brown them evenly. Roll them in a towel to remove their skins.*

This sauce is served with fish, crustaceans and bivalves such as clams or oysters.

*To make 3 cups [¾ liter]*

| | | |
|---|---|---|
| 1 | ripe tomato, lightly oiled | 1 |
| 1 | small sweet apple, lightly oiled | 1 |
| 1 | garlic clove, unpeeled | 1 |
| 8 | almonds, toasted and peeled | 8 |
| ½ tsp. | paprika | 2 ml. |
| 1 tbsp. | anise-flavored liqueur | 15 ml. |
| 1 cup | mayonnaise (recipe, page 165) | ½ liter |
| | veal stock (recipe, page 159) (optional) | |

Roast the tomato, apple and garlic on a baking sheet in a preheated 400° F. [200° C.] oven. Remove the tomato and garlic after 10 minutes, the apple after 20 minutes. Peel and seed the tomato, peel and core the apple, and peel the garlic clove. Pound the garlic in a mortar with the almonds to form a smooth paste. Then add the tomato, the apple pulp and the paprika and pound them well. Mix this paste and the liqueur into the mayonnaise. Thin the sauce with a few spoonfuls of stock if you wish.

ENCICLOPEDIA SALVAT DE LA COCINA: TOMO 8

## Farmer's Wife's Mayonnaise

### Mayonnaise Fermière

This is a cold sauce to be eaten with crudités.

*To make 1¾ cups [425 ml.]*

| | | |
|---|---|---|
| ¾ cup | mayonnaise (recipe, page 165) | 175 ml. |
| 1 cup | farmer cheese or softened cream cheese | ¼ liter |
| 2 or 3 | red peppers, roasted, peeled, halved, seeded, deribbed and chopped | 2 or 3 |
| 2 | small scallions, quartered | 2 |
| | salt and freshly ground black pepper | |
| | cayenne pepper or paprika | |
| | fresh lemon juice | |

Sieve the cheese into a bowl, stir in the red peppers, then work in the mayonnaise, a spoonful at a time. Beat the sauce with a whisk until smooth. Using a garlic press, squeeze the juice of the scallions into the sauce. Season the sauce to taste with salt, black pepper and cayenne pepper or paprika. Mix in a few drops of lemon juice. Transfer the sauce to a sauceboat for serving.

LOUISETTE BERTHOLLE
LA CUISINE DES SAISONS

## Garlic Mayonnaise

### L'Aïoli

Aioli is a triumph of Provençal cooking. It is served with a variety of foods that have been simply cooked in salted water—cod, carrots, turnips, hard-boiled eggs, artichokes and all kinds of Mediterranean seafood.

*To make about 1¾ cups [425 ml.]*

| | | |
|---|---|---|
| 6 | garlic cloves | 6 |
| 3 | egg yolks | 3 |
| ¼ tsp. | salt | 1 ml. |
| 1½ cups | olive oil | 375 ml. |
| 3 tbsp. | fresh lemon juice | 45 ml. |
| 1 tbsp. | boiling water | 15 ml. |

In a mortar, pound the garlic until it is reduced to a paste. Add the egg yolks one at a time, season the mixture with the salt, then proceed as for mayonnaise: Pour a thin thread of oil into the mortar while constantly mixing the ingredients together with the pestle. From time to time, add a few drops of the lemon juice. The finished aioli should be thick and smooth; stir in the boiling water to keep it from separating.

PAUL BOUILLARD
LA GOURMANDISE À BON MARCHÉ

## Provençal Garlic Mayonnaise
### Aïoli

*This pungent sauce is the classic accompaniment for poached salt cod served with such side dishes as boiled potatoes, carrots, green beans, artichokes, chick-peas, beets, hard-boiled eggs, snails and squid stew.*

A good aioli is made with good olive oil. It is traditionally prepared in a marble mortar with a wooden pestle; the weight of the mortar prevents it from slip-sliding around as one turns the pestle with one hand while dribbling the oil with the other. Avoid any garlic cloves that are not firm and crisp or at the heart of which a green germ has begun to form. The oil and the egg yolks should both be at room temperature to discourage the aioli's breaking.

Some people pound a lump of crustless bread, soaked and squeezed dry, into the garlic-and-egg-yolk mixture before beginning to add the oil. A more easily digestible but less silken aioli may be prepared by substituting a small boiled potato—about 3 ounces [90 g.], cooled until only tepid—for the egg yolks.

*To make about 2½ cups [625 ml.]*

| | | |
|---|---|---|
| 3 or 4 | garlic cloves | 3 or 4 |
| | salt | |
| 2 | egg yolks | 2 |
| about 2 cups | olive oil | about ½ liter |
| 3 tbsp. | fresh lemon juice | 45 ml. |
| about 2 tsp. | tepid water | about 10 ml. |

Place the garlic cloves in a mortar and grind them to a paste with a pestle. Add a pinch of salt and the egg yolks and turn them with the pestle until the yellow of the yolks pales. Then start to add the oil, pouring it in a thin thread while turning the mixture with the pestle. Take care to add the oil very slowly and, during this time, never stop turning. You should obtain a thick *pommade*. After having added about 3 to 4 tablespoons [45 to 60 ml.] of the oil, add the lemon juice and a teaspoon [5 ml.] of the tepid water. Continue to add the oil, little by little. When the *pommade* again becomes too thick, add another few drops of water, without which the mixture will fall apart, so to speak—the oil separating from the rest.

If, despite all precautions, this accident should occur, remove everything from the mortar, put another egg yolk and a few drops of lemon juice into the mortar and, little by little, spoonful by spoonful, add the unsuccessful aioli while turning the pestle constantly.

RICHARD OLNEY
SIMPLE FRENCH FOOD

## Tuna Mayonnaise
### Salsa Tonnata

*This sauce accompanies cold poached veal in the classic Italian dish called vitello tonnato.*

*To make about 5 cups [1 ¼ liters]*

| | | |
|---|---|---|
| 1 cup | flaked poached tuna | ¼ liter |
| 2 cups | mayonnaise (recipe, page 165) | ½ liter |
| 1 | celery rib, sliced | 1 |
| 1 | onion, sliced | 1 |
| 2 | salt anchovies, soaked, filleted, rinsed, dried and finely chopped | 2 |
| 2 cups | dry white wine | ½ liter |
| ½ cup | water | 125 ml. |
| 2 tbsp. | butter (optional) | 30 ml. |
| | salt and pepper (optional) | |

Put the tuna, celery, onion and anchovies into a nonreactive saucepan. Moisten them with the wine and the water, bring the liquid to a simmer, and cook the mixture over low heat for 45 minutes. Purée the contents of the pan by pushing them through a sieve. If the purée is very liquid, whisk in the butter while the purée is still hot. Pour the purée into a bowl and let it cool. Before serving, fold in the mayonnaise and add salt and pepper to taste.

ARMIDO FERRANDINI
ONESTÀ IN CUCINA

## Mustard Sauce
### Sauce Moutarde

Serve this sauce with grilled mackerel or herring.

*To make 1 cup [¼ liter]*

| | | |
|---|---|---|
| 2 tbsp. | Dijon mustard | 30 ml. |
| 1 sprig each | parsley, tarragon, chives, chervil and burnet | 1 sprig each |
| 2 | hard-boiled egg yolks | 2 |
| 4 to 5 tbsp. | olive oil | 60 to 75 ml. |
| 2 tbsp. | white wine vinegar | 30 ml. |

Blanch the herbs in boiling water. Drain, freshen them in cold water, then place them in a mortar and pound them with the egg yolks. Then slowly add the olive oil, mustard and vinegar, stirring the mixture all the time.

LA CUISINE LYONNAISE

## Orange Sauce

*Sauce Costelloise*

This sauce has a consistency like that of mayonnaise, and may be used for vegetables—particularly asparagus and broccoli—poached fish and chicken.

*To make 2½ cups [625 ml.]*

| | | |
|---|---|---|
| | peel of 2 oranges, thinly pared and finely chopped | |
| ½ cup | olive oil | 125 ml. |
| ½ cup | peanut oil | 125 ml. |
| ⅓ cup | walnut oil | 75 ml. |
| ⅓ cup | red wine vinegar | 75 ml. |
| ¼ tsp. | coarsely crushed white peppercorns | 1 ml. |
| 3 tbsp. | cold water | 45 ml. |
| 3 | egg yolks | 3 |
| | coarse salt | |

Mix the three oils in a saucepan and warm them slightly over low heat. Do not let them become hot.

Drop the orange peel into a large amount of boiling water and blanch it for five minutes. Drain the peel in a fine sieve, then refresh it in a bowl of cold water and drain it again.

In a heavy 1-quart [1-liter] saucepan, preferably tin-lined copper, reduce the vinegar with the crushed peppercorns over medium heat. When the vinegar barely coats the bottom of the pan, remove it from the stove and add the cold water, followed by the egg yolks. Give the yolks a vigorous stir, using a wire whisk, and set the pan over very low heat. Stirring continuously, incorporate the warm oil in droplets, a few at a time. When all of the oil has been incorporated, mix in the orange peel and add salt to taste.

If the sauce must be prepared in advance, keep it warm in a double boiler over warm, not hot, water.

JEAN AND PIERRE TROISGROS
THE NOUVELLE CUISINE OF JEAN AND PIERRE TROISGROS

## Portobello Sauce

This is a strongly flavored sauce. Its color varies from velvety brown to purplish black—a funereal appearance that is relieved by the last-minute addition of chopped red pepper. The sauce makes an excellent dip for chunks of bread, but its main glory is as an accompaniment to such powerfully flavored fish as skate, conger, tuna and shark or to lend character to squid and octopus.

To serve hot, put the sauce into a double boiler after blending the flavorings with the egg yolks, and stir the mix-

ture over gentle heat until it is warmed through. Garnish it with the red pepper before serving.

*To make 2 cups [½ liter]*

| | | |
|---|---|---|
| 12 | large ripe olives, pitted | 12 |
| 1 | small ripe avocado, halved, pitted and peeled | 1 |
| 2 | garlic cloves | 2 |
| 2 | salt anchovies, soaked, filleted, rinsed and dried | 2 |
| 1½ tbsp. | fresh lemon juice | 22½ ml. |
| ⅔ cup | dry red wine | 150 ml. |
| ⅔ cup | olive oil | 150 ml. |
| 1 tsp. | freshly ground black pepper | 5 ml. |
| 2 | egg yolks, beaten | 2 |
| 1 tbsp. | finely chopped red pepper | 15 ml. |

Pound the olives, avocado, garlic and anchovy fillets to a coarse paste. Add the lemon juice and wine, and purée the mixture in a blender. Place the purée in a small, heavy saucepan, add the olive oil and cook the mixture for seven to eight minutes, stirring frequently. Season with the black pepper. Let the mixture cool completely, then add it to the egg yolks, beating it in gradually with a wooden spoon. Before serving, garnish the sauce with the red pepper.

GEORGE LASSALLE
THE ADVENTUROUS FISH COOK

## Cold Provençal Sauce

*Sauce Provençale Froide*

Serve this sauce with grills, cold meats or fish.

*To make 1¼ cups [300 ml.]*

| | | |
|---|---|---|
| 2 | garlic cloves | 2 |
| 3 | salt anchovies, soaked, filleted, rinsed and dried | 3 |
| 2 | egg yolks | 2 |
| 1 tbsp. | water | 15 ml. |
| | salt | |
| about 1 cup | olive oil | about ¼ liter |
| 3 tbsp. | fresh lemon juice | 45 ml. |

In a mortar, pound the garlic cloves and anchovy fillets together to make a smooth purée. Add the egg yolks, water and a little salt. Pound the mixture vigorously, adding the oil little by little. To finish, add the lemon juice. The sauce should be fairly light in color.

MICHEL BARBEROUSSE
CUISINE PROVENÇALE

## Hot Provençal Sauce

### Sauce Provençale Chaude

*The authors suggest that this sauce can be served plain with fish or poultry, or mixed with a ravigote sauce (recipe, page 163) or just the chopped garnish for a ravigote sauce. They also suggest that you can color the plain mixture green with spinach juice or chopped blanched parsley, depending on the dish you wish it to accompany.*

*To make 1 cup [¼ liter]*

| | | |
|---|---|---|
| 2 | egg yolks | 2 |
| 1 tsp. | egg-yolk-enriched velouté sauce (recipe, page 162) or leftover white sauce (recipe, page 156) (optional) | 5 ml. |
| 1 | garlic clove, pounded to a paste | 1 |
| | cayenne pepper | |
| | salt | |
| ⅓ cup | fresh lemon juice | 75 ml. |
| ⅔ cup | olive oil | 150 ml. |

Put the egg yolks, egg-yolk-enriched velouté sauce or white sauce (if you are using one of them), garlic, a pinch of cayenne pepper, salt and the lemon juice in a small pan. Place the pan in a larger pan of warm water and cook the sauce over medium heat for two to three minutes. As soon as the sauce begins to thicken, remove it from the heat and stir in the oil, a little at a time so the sauce does not curdle. Serve the sauce immediately.

VIARD AND FOURET
LE CUISINIER ROYAL

## Green Goddess Salad Dressing

An excellent accompaniment for all fish and seafood salads.

*To make about 3 cups [¾ liter]*

| | | |
|---|---|---|
| 3 cups | mayonnaise (recipe, page 165), flavored with 2 tbsp. [30 ml.] tarragon vinegar | ¾ liter |
| 1 | scallion, thinly sliced | 1 |
| ½ cup | chopped fresh parsley | 125 ml. |
| 2 tbsp. | chopped fresh tarragon leaves or 2 tsp. [10 ml.] dried tarragon | 30 ml. |
| ¼ cup | finely cut fresh chives | 50 ml. |
| 10 | oil-packed anchovy fillets, rinsed, patted dry and finely chopped | 10 |

Combine all of the ingredients and let the dressing stand for at least one hour to allow the flavors to blend.

JAN MC BRIDE CARLTON
THE OLD-FASHIONED COOKBOOK

## A Salad Sauce

To preserve the crispness of the salad, this mixture should not be poured upon the vegetables; rather, it should be placed in the bottom of the bowl, to be stirred up just before serving. Observe that the liquid ingredients must be proportioned to the quantity of vegetables.

*To make about ⅔ cup [150 ml.]*

| | | |
|---|---|---|
| 2 | hard-boiled egg yolks | 2 |
| 1 tbsp. | freshly grated Parmesan cheese | 15 ml. |
| ½ tsp. | prepared mustard | 2 ml. |
| 1 tbsp. | tarragon vinegar | 15 ml. |
| 1½ tbsp. | mushroom ketchup | 22½ ml. |
| ¼ cup | oil | 50 ml. |
| 1 tbsp. | cider vinegar | 15 ml. |

Mix the egg yolks, Parmesan cheese, mustard, tarragon vinegar and mushroom ketchup together. When they are well blended, add the oil and cider vinegar. Beat the sauce to combine the oil with the other ingredients.

IGNOTUS
CULINA FAMULATRIX MEDICINAE

## Sauce for Cold Fowl or Partridge

*The author suggests that 1 tablespoon [15 ml.] of shallot vinegar can replace the shallot and 1 tablespoon of the wine vinegar. To make shallot vinegar, add four chopped shallots to 2 cups [½ liter] of white wine vinegar. Cover and leave in a warm place for three weeks, then strain the flavored vinegar and bottle it.*

*To make ½ cup [125 ml.]*

| | | |
|---|---|---|
| 2 | hard-boiled egg yolks | 2 |
| 1 | salt anchovy, soaked, filleted, rinsed and dried | 1 |
| 3 tbsp. | white wine vinegar | 45 ml. |
| 1 | shallot, chopped | 1 |
| | cayenne pepper (optional) | |
| 1 tsp. | prepared mustard | 5 ml. |
| 2 tbsp. | oil | 30 ml. |
| | salt | |

Pound the egg yolks in a mortar with the anchovy fillets, vinegar, shallot, cayenne pepper (if you are using it) and mustard. When these are well pounded, add the oil. Strain the sauce and season it with salt to taste.

MRS. RUNDELL
MODERN DOMESTIC COOKERY

# Tyrolean Sauce

## Sauce Tyrolienne

*This piquant sauce is suitable for braised sweetbreads, boiled or steamed vegetables, or fish.*
Make sure that you do not overseason this sauce.

*To make about 3 cups [¾ liter]*

| | | |
|---|---|---|
| ⅔ cup | finely chopped shallots | 150 ml. |
| 2¼ cups | olive oil | 550 ml. |
| 2 | garlic cloves, unpeeled | 2 |
| ⅔ cup | dry white wine | 150 ml. |
| 2 | tomatoes, peeled, seeded and coarsely chopped | 2 |
| 1 | red or green pepper, halved, seeded, deribbed and coarsely chopped | 1 |
| 2 tbsp. | white wine vinegar | 30 ml. |
| 4 | egg yolks | 4 |
| 1 tsp. | Dijon mustard | 5 ml. |
| | salt and pepper | |
| 1 tbsp. each | finely chopped fresh parsley, chervil and tarragon leaves | 15 ml. each |

Fry the shallots gently in ¼ cup [50 ml.] of the olive oil, without letting them brown. Add the garlic and deglaze the pan deposits with the white wine. Add the tomatoes and the red or green pepper, and cook gently for 10 minutes to reduce the mixture. It should not be at all liquid, as this might cause the emulsion to separate.

Meanwhile, reduce the vinegar to half its original volume in a nonreactive pan. Take the pan away from the heat and let it cool slightly before whisking in the egg yolks. Place the pan in a larger pan of gently simmering water and gradually whisk in the remaining olive oil; do not allow the sauce to get hot. Add the mustard and salt and pepper to taste. Finish the sauce by stirring in as much of the tomato mixture as you want. Add the parsley, chervil and tarragon.

LA CUISINE NATURELLE À L'HUILE D'OLIVE

# Auscitaine Sauce

## La Sauce Auscitaine

*This tangy sauce is suitable for grilled or broiled poultry or game birds. Rendered duck or chicken fat may be substituted for the goose fat called for in this recipe. Auch—whence "Auscitaine"—is the capital of the French department of Gers.*

This sauce would be a béarnaise if it were made with butter. Take care not to make scrambled eggs by heating the yolks too much, or to make an unstable sauce by beating the yolks before they are warm enough.

*To make 2 cups [½ liter]*

| | | |
|---|---|---|
| 4 | shallots, finely chopped | 4 |
| 1 | large sprig fresh tarragon, leaves removed and finely chopped | 1 |
| 12 | fresh mint leaves, chopped | 12 |
| ¾ cup | red wine vinegar | 175 ml. |
| | salt | |
| 6 | white peppercorns, coarsely crushed | 6 |
| 1 tbsp. | red wine | 15 ml. |
| 6 | egg yolks | 6 |
| 1 cup | rendered goose fat | ¼ liter |

Place the shallots, tarragon, mint, vinegar, a little salt and the peppercorns in a heavy, nonreactive saucepan. Boil the mixture for 10 minutes, or until it is reduced to a quarter of its original volume. Stir in the wine, remove the saucepan from the heat and let the mixture cool to lukewarm.

Whisk in the egg yolks one at a time. Place the saucepan over very low heat: The pan should not be allowed to become so hot that it burns your hand when you touch it. Whisk the mixture for 30 minutes, or until it is very foamy and tends to collect on the wires of the whisk. Whisk in the melted goose fat little by little to produce a smooth, creamy sauce.

ANDRÉ DAGUIN
LE NOUVEAU CUISINIER GASCON

# Sauce for Chicken or Veal

## Sos Pentru Pui or Vitel

*To make about 1¼ cups [300 ml.]*

| | | |
|---|---|---|
| 6 | egg yolks | 6 |
| 2 tbsp. | flour | 30 ml. |
| 1 tbsp. | finely chopped shallot or fresh chives | 15 ml. |
| 1 tbsp. | butter | 15 ml. |
| ⅔ cup | dry white wine | 150 ml. |
| 3 tbsp. | fresh lemon juice | 45 ml. |

In a small saucepan, mix the egg yolks and flour, then stir in the shallot or chives, butter, wine and lemon juice. Mix them well together and place the saucepan over low heat. Stir the sauce gently until it begins to thicken—about 10 minutes—but do not let it boil. Serve immediately.

ANISOARA STAN
THE ROMANIAN COOK BOOK

## Anchovy Sauce

*La Sauce aux Anchois*

This sauce is to be served with pan-fried veal chops.

*To make about 1 cup [¼ liter]*

| | | |
|---|---|---|
| 5 | salt anchovies, soaked, filleted, rinsed and dried | 5 |
| 8 tbsp. | butter | 120 ml. |
| 2 | shallots, thinly sliced | 2 |
| ⅔ cup | port | 150 ml. |
| 2 | egg yolks | 2 |
| | cayenne pepper | |
| | black pepper | |

Melt the butter in a pan and add the shallots. Cook them over gentle heat for 15 minutes. Add the port and cook to reduce the liquid by about half. Meanwhile, pound the egg yolks and anchovies together to form a paste. Remove the port mixture from the heat and gradually whisk in the anchovy paste. Then place the pan in another pan of boiling water, and whisk the sauce until it is light and frothy. Season the sauce with cayenne and black pepper.

ÉDOUARD DE POMIANE
LE CODE DE LA BONNE CHÈRE

## Bavarian Sauce

*Sauce Bavaroise*

*A sauce for fish.*

*To make 1¼ cups [300 ml.]*

| | | |
|---|---|---|
| ¼ cup | white wine vinegar | 50 ml. |
| 3 or 4 | egg yolks | 3 or 4 |
| 8 tbsp. | butter, cubed | 120 ml. |
| 1-inch | piece fresh horseradish, sliced | 2½-cm. |
| | salt | |
| | freshly grated nutmeg | |
| 7 tbsp. | crayfish butter *(recipe, page 157)* | 105 ml. |

Place the vinegar in a nonreactive saucepan and boil it until it is reduced to half its original volume. Remove the saucepan from the heat, let the vinegar cool, then add three or four egg yolks—depending on the strength of the vinegar—2 tablespoons [30 ml.] of the butter and the horseradish. Beat them all together, add a little salt and nutmeg, and stir the sauce over low heat until it thickens slightly. Sieve the sauce into a clean saucepan, add the remaining butter, set over low heat and beat the sauce until it is foamy. Do not allow it to boil. Finally, beat in the crayfish butter.

ALEXANDRE DUMAS
LE GRAND DICTIONNAIRE DE CUISINE

## Béarnaise Sauce

*Sauce Béarnaise*

*This tangy sauce is suitable for grilled meats or fish and for grilled or braised artichoke bottoms.*

Should the sauce curdle while the pieces of butter are being blended into it, here is a method of rescuing it: Put half a teaspoon [2 ml.] of cold fresh lemon juice into a chilled bowl, then pour the sauce very slowly into the bowl while stirring and beating it constantly with a wooden spoon. The sauce should regain its emulsified consistency.

*To make 1¼ cups [300 ml.]*

| | | |
|---|---|---|
| 1 cup | white wine vinegar | ¼ liter |
| 5 or 6 | shallots, very finely chopped | 5 or 6 |
| 1 tbsp. | coarsely chopped fresh tarragon | 15 ml. |
| 1 tbsp. | coarsely chopped mixed fresh parsley, chervil and chives | 15 ml. |
| 4 | egg yolks | 4 |
| ½ lb. | butter, cut into small pieces | ¼ kg. |

Boil the vinegar, shallots, tarragon and mixed herbs in a small saucepan until the liquid has reduced to about 3 tablespoons [45 ml.]. Strain the liquid through a fine-meshed sieve set over a small pan. Stir the egg yolks into the strained liquid and place the pan in a larger pan of warm water set over gentle heat. Stir the mixture with a wooden spoon. Add the pieces of butter, a few at a time, stirring constantly in the same direction. After all the butter has been blended in, remove the sauce from the heat, pour it into a warmed sauceboat and serve it.

IRÈNE LABARRE
LA CUISINE DES TROIS B

## Egg Sauce

This sauce is an agreeable accompaniment to roasted poultry or salted fish.

*To make 1½ cups [375 ml.]*

| | | |
|---|---|---|
| 3 | eggs | 3 |
| 1¼ cups | mock hollandaise sauce *(recipe, page 166)* | 300 ml. |

Put the eggs into boiling water and boil them for about 12 minutes, when they will be hard. Put them into cold water until you want them. This will make the yolks firmer and prevent the whites from darkening, and you will be able to cut them neatly.

Use only two of the whites; cut the whites into very small dice and all the yolks into bits about ¼ inch [6 mm.] square. Put them into a sauceboat, pour the mock hollandaise sauce on them and stir them together.

DR. KITCHINER
THE COOK'S ORACLE

# Fried Lamb Pieces with Mint and Shallot Sauce

## Goujonnettes d'Agneau

You can substitute softened butter for the clarified butter. Other herbs can be used instead of mint.

To serve 4

| 1 lb. | boneless leg of lamb, sliced ¼ inch [6 mm.] thick and cut into strips 2½ inches [6 cm.] long and ¼ inch wide | ½ kg. |
|---|---|---|
| | salt and pepper | |
| 1 | egg | 1 |
| 1 tbsp. | cold water | 15 ml. |
| 1½ cups | fresh white bread crumbs | 375 ml. |
| | peanut oil for deep frying | |

**Mint and shallot sauce**

| 10 | fresh mint leaves, washed and dried, half finely chopped, half coarsely chopped | 10 |
|---|---|---|
| 2 | shallots, finely chopped | 2 |
| 9 tbsp. | butter | 135 ml. |
| 10 | peppercorns, coarsely crushed | 10 |
| ¼ cup | sherry vinegar | 50 ml. |
| ¼ cup | dry white wine | 50 ml. |
| 2 | egg yolks | 2 |

Season the lamb with salt and pepper. Break the egg into a shallow dish, season the egg, add the cold water and beat the mixture well. Put the bread crumbs in another shallow dish. Dip each piece of lamb into the beaten egg mixture, then roll the piece in the bread crumbs, shaking any excess bread crumbs back into the second dish. When the lamb pieces have been coated, set them aside in a single layer.

To make the sauce, first melt 8 tablespoons [120 ml.] of the butter in a heavy pan over very low heat. When the butter starts to foam, use a spoon to skim off the scum; continue skimming until no more scum rises—about eight minutes. Set the clarified butter aside.

Melt the remaining butter in a heavy, nonreactive pan over low heat and use a wooden spoon to stir in the finely chopped mint and the shallots. Cook them for five minutes, until the shallots are translucent but not brown. Add the crushed peppercorns, sherry vinegar and white wine; stir the mixture together well and reduce it for about five minutes, until only about 3 tablespoons [45 ml.] of liquid are left. Remove the pan from the heat and let the liquid cool.

Put the two egg yolks into a heavy pan and beat them together well. When the reduced mint mixture is cold, strain it through a fine-meshed sieve into the pan containing the egg yolks. Whisk well. Place the pan over low heat and whisk the egg-yolk mixture constantly for four minutes; use a circular motion, making figure 8s with the whisk so that all the mixture is beaten. Do not let the mixture boil.

When the mixture has increased in volume and is thick and foamy, remove the pan from the heat and whisk in the clarified butter—a little at a time—until the sauce is very smooth. Add the coarsely chopped mint, season the sauce with salt and pepper, pour it into a heated sauceboat and set it aside. The sauce is meant to be served warm and must not be reheated.

Pour peanut oil into a deep fryer to a depth of at least ¾ inch [2 cm.] and set it over medium heat. When the oil reaches 375° F. [190° C.], fry the lamb pieces in it for one to two minutes. The meat should be pink and rare inside its coating of browned bread crumbs. Remove the cooked lamb pieces from the deep fryer and let them drain on a paper towel for one to two minutes. Place the meat on a warmed serving dish. Whisk the sauce and serve it with the lamb.

ALAIN AND EVENTHIA SENDERENS
LA CUISINE RÉUSSIE

# Heavenly Sauce from Metz

## Divine Sauce Messine

This sauce should accompany a fine fish cooked in a court bouillon. It is very important that you should not start to heat the sauce until just before you want to serve it.

To make about 2½ cups [625 ml.]

| 2 cups | heavy cream | ½ liter |
|---|---|---|
| 1 tbsp. | butter, mashed with 1 tbsp. [15 ml.] flour | 15 ml. |
| 2 | egg yolks, beaten | 2 |
| ½ tsp. | Dijon mustard | 2 ml. |
| 1 tbsp. | finely chopped fresh chervil leaves | 15 ml. |
| 2 tbsp. | finely chopped fresh parsley | 30 ml. |
| 1½ tsp. | finely chopped fresh tarragon leaves | 7 ml. |
| 1 | shallot, finely chopped | 1 |
| 1 tsp. | grated lemon peel | 5 ml. |
| 3 tbsp. | fresh lemon juice | 45 ml. |

Place all of the ingredients except the lemon juice together in a pan over very low heat. Cook the sauce, whisking it all the time, for about 15 minutes, until the sauce is almost boiling, but on no account should you let it boil. Stir in the lemon juice and serve.

E. AURICOSTE DE LAZARQUE
CUISINE MESSINE

## Dijon Mustard Sauce
### *La Mousseline Dijonnaise*

This sauce admirably complements all poached or grilled fish, as well as fried or soft-boiled eggs.

*To make about ¾ cup [175 ml.]*

| | | |
|---|---|---|
| 1½ tbsp. | Dijon mustard | 22½ ml. |
| 3 | egg yolks | 3 |
| 3 tbsp. | fresh lemon juice | 45 ml. |
| 1 tsp. | cold water | 5 ml. |
| | salt and pepper | |
| 8 tbsp. | butter, diced and chilled | 120 ml. |

Put the egg yolks, lemon juice, water, salt, a pinch of pepper and the butter into a medium-sized saucepan. Put the pan in a larger pan containing some boiling water. With a whisk, stir the egg yolks and butter together briskly. The sauce will very quickly become foamy and lightly thickened. At this stage the sauce is ready: Add the Dijon mustard, adjust the seasoning, if necessary, and serve.

PAUL BOUILLARD
LA GOURMANDISE À BON MARCHÉ

## Cooked Sour-Cream Dressing

An excellent sauce for potato, vegetable or meat salads.

*To make 1¾ cups [425 ml.]*

| | | |
|---|---|---|
| 1 cup | sour cream | ¼ liter |
| ¼ cup | sugar | 50 ml. |
| 2 tbsp. | flour | 30 ml. |
| 1 tsp. | dry mustard | 5 ml. |
| ⅛ tsp. | salt | ½ ml. |
| ½ cup | vinegar | 125 ml. |
| 2 | eggs, beaten | 2 |

Combine the sugar, flour, mustard and salt in a heavy saucepan. Stir in the vinegar. Stirring constantly, cook the mixture until it comes to a boil and thickens slightly. Remove the mixture from the heat. Gradually add a small amount of the hot mixture to the eggs, beating constantly, then stir them into the hot mixture. Cool, stirring the dressing frequently. Finally, fold in the sour cream.

JAN MC BRIDE CARLTON
THE OLD-FASHIONED COOKBOOK

## Fish with a Royal Gray Sauce
### *Ryba w Szarym Sosie po Krolewsku*

This unusual sauce is customarily served with carp, but will lend interest to most fish, especially the richer ones. In these instructions, it is assumed that you have prepared separately enough fish for four people, preferably by poaching it.

*To make 1¼ cups [300 ml.]*

| | | |
|---|---|---|
| 2 | egg yolks, lightly beaten | 2 |
| ¼ cup | finely crumbled gingerbread, or substitute 1 tbsp. [15 ml.] cornstarch mixed with 1 tsp. [5 ml.] ground ginger | 50 ml. |
| ½ tsp. | ground white pepper | 2 ml. |
| ½ tsp. | ground cinnamon | 2 ml. |
| ⅔ cup | dry red wine | 150 ml. |
| 1 tbsp. | fresh lemon juice | 15 ml. |
| 2 tbsp. | sugar or 1 tbsp. [15 ml.] honey | 30 ml. |
| 1 tsp. | grated lemon peel (optional) | 5 ml. |
| ⅓ cup | seedless white raisins | 75 ml. |
| ¼ cup | almonds, blanched, peeled and finely slivered | 50 ml. |
| ¼ cup | pitted green olives, finely chopped | 50 ml. |

Combine the egg yolks with the gingerbread. Add the pepper and cinnamon, followed by the wine, lemon juice, sugar or honey and the lemon peel, if you are using it. Mix them well and heat them slowly until the mixture comes to a boil. Then remove the sauce from the heat and add the raisins, almonds and olives. Let the sauce rest for at least two minutes, then pour it over the fish.

ALAN DAVIDSON
NORTH ATLANTIC SEAFOOD

## Sea Urchin Hollandaise
### *Sauce à la Crème d'Oursins*

*This sauce is suitable for hot or cold fish or shellfish. To open a sea urchin, cut a circular piece from the dimpled underside with scissors. Shake the urchin to empty out the viscera; discard them. Scoop out the pink roe with a spoon.*

*To make 1¼ cups [300 ml.]*

| | | |
|---|---|---|
| 4 or 5 | sea urchins, roe removed and sieved (about ⅓ cup [75 ml.]) | 4 or 5 |
| ¾ cup | thick hollandaise sauce (recipe, page 166) | 175 ml. |

Whisk the sea urchin purée into the warm hollandaise sauce. Serve the flavored hollandaise immediately.

MICHEL BARBEROUSSE
CUISINE PROVENÇALE

## Fish Liver and Garlic Sauce

### Rouille

*This sauce is served with bouillabaisse and fish soups. For the sauce, use the liver of a monkfish or mullet, and use the fish itself as one of the ingredients of the fish soup. The livers are obtainable from fish dealers if specially ordered.*

*To make about 1 ¼ cups [300 ml.]*

| | | |
|---|---|---|
| 1 | fish liver, poached in court bouillon (recipe, page 164) for about 1 minute, or until slightly firm | 1 |
| 2 | garlic cloves | 2 |
| | salt | |
| 1 | egg yolk | 1 |
| 1 tsp. | cayenne pepper | 5 ml. |
| ⅔ cup | olive oil | 150 ml. |
| 1 tbsp. | fish stock (recipe, page 164) | 15 ml. |
| | powdered saffron | |

Crush the garlic cloves in a mortar with a pinch of salt. Add the egg yolk, the fish liver and the cayenne pepper and stir them all together well. Pour in the olive oil a little at a time, in a thin trickle, stirring the mixture all the time with the pestle. Finally, stir in the fish stock and a pinch of saffron.

LUCETTE REY-BILLETON
LES BONNES RECETTES DU SOLEIL

---

## Good Mustard Sauce

### Feine Senfsauce

This sauce is appropriate for fish, game or boiled beef.

*To make 2 ½ cups [625 ml.]*

| | | |
|---|---|---|
| ⅓ cup | Dijon mustard | 75 ml. |
| 6 tbsp. | butter | 90 ml. |
| 6 | egg yolks, beaten until smooth | 6 |
| 1 cup | beef stock (recipe, page 159) | ¼ liter |
| | salt | |
| 1 ½ tbsp. | fresh lemon juice | 22 ½ ml. |
| 1 tbsp. | red currant jelly | 15 ml. |

Combine the mustard, butter, egg yolks and stock in the top of a double boiler set above hot, but not boiling, water. Over low heat, whisk the mixture until it is thick — about 10 minutes. Do not let it boil. Blend in a pinch of salt, the lemon juice and the currant jelly.

WOLF NEUBER
DIE K.U.K. WIENER KÜCHE

---

# Integral Sauces

## Beef Pot Roast, Marseilles-Style

### Boeuf à la Mode Marseillaise

*The technique of larding is demonstrated on page 80.*

*To serve 8*

| | | |
|---|---|---|
| 4 lb. | boneless beef sirloin roast | 2 kg. |
| 1 lb. | salt pork with the rind removed | ½ kg. |
| 1 cup | dry blackberry brandy | ¼ liter |
| | coarse salt | |
| | freshly ground black pepper | |
| 2 | onions, coarsely chopped | 2 |
| 3 to 4 | garlic cloves, finely chopped | 3 to 4 |
| 3 | bay leaves | 3 |
| 12 | sprigs fresh parsley | 12 |
| 2 to 3 tsp. | dried thyme leaves | 10 to 15 ml. |
| 3 tbsp. | tomato paste | 45 ml. |
| | beef stock (recipe, page 159) | |
| 2 cups | green Mediterranean-style olives | ½ liter |
| 2 cups | black Mediterranean-style olives | ½ liter |
| 2 tbsp. | butter | 30 ml. |

Cut 12 long larding strips from the salt pork and soak them in the brandy. Cut the rest of the pork into cubes and fry them until crisp. Drain them on paper towels. Pour 3 tablespoons [45 ml.] of the pork fat into a large, heavy casserole.

Lard the beef roast, reserving the brandy. Sprinkle the beef with the salt and pepper, and brown it quickly on all sides in the hot pork fat. Remove the beef; add the onions and garlic and sauté them lightly. Place the browned beef on this vegetable bed and add the bay leaves, parsley and thyme. Stir the tomato paste into the reserved brandy, and pour it over the beef along with enough stock to just cover the roast. Bring the liquid to a boil over high heat, cover the casserole, and place it in a preheated 350° F. [180° C.] oven for about two hours, depending on how well done you like the meat.

Lift out the beef and keep it warm. Skim off the fat from the liquid remaining in the casserole and boil the vegetables for five minutes to draw out the final juices. Strain the liquid into a smaller pot and continue boiling to reduce and concentrate the flavors. Taste for seasoning. Sauté the olives in the butter for two minutes. Slice the meat diagonally, cover it with the sauce, and garnish it with the olives and pork cubes.

JUDITH ETS-HOKIN
THE SAN FRANCISCO DINNER PARTY COOKBOOK

## Beef Brisket in Red Wine Sauce

### Gedünstete Rinderbrust

*For the soup greens, use a mixture of celery, onion, carrot and leek. A very little chopped lovage leaf may be added to them. Serve this dish with dumplings, potatoes or pasta.*

| | To serve 4 | |
|---|---|---|
| 2 lb. | beef brisket, rinsed under cold running water | 1 kg. |
| | salt and pepper | |
| 1 tbsp. | lard | 15 ml. |
| 1 cup | chopped soup greens | ¼ liter |
| 1 | bay leaf | 1 |
| 1 tbsp. | chopped fresh thyme leaves | 15 ml. |
| 1 tbsp. | chopped fresh marjoram leaves | 15 ml. |
| 2 oz. | salt pork rind, in 1 piece | 60 g. |
| 1 cup | veal stock *(recipe, page 159)* | ¼ liter |
| 1 tbsp. | flour | 15 ml. |
| ½ cup | dry red wine | 125 ml. |
| 2 | tomatoes, peeled and quartered | 2 |

Salt and pepper the beef on all sides. In a heavy pot, brown the meat quickly in the lard. Add the soup greens, bay leaf, thyme, marjoram, salt pork and ¼ cup [50 ml.] of the stock. Cover the pot and cook the mixture gently, until the vegetables are lightly browned and the stock has almost completely cooked away—about 12 minutes.

Stir in the flour and let it soak in for two minutes. Pour in the remaining stock and the red wine, add the quartered tomatoes, cover, and cook the brisket slowly until tender—about one and one half hours. Transfer the meat to a warmed serving dish; sieve the sauce and serve it with the meat.

HANS GUSTL KERNMAYR
SO KOCHTE MEINE MUTTER

## Steaks with Shallot Sauce

| | To serve 8 | |
|---|---|---|
| 8 | rib-eye steaks, cut ½ inch [1 cm.] thick | 8 |
| 12 | shallots, finely chopped | 12 |
| | salt and freshly ground black pepper | |
| 6 tbsp. | butter | 90 ml. |
| ¼ cup | finely chopped fresh parsley | 50 ml. |
| 1 tbsp. | dried oregano leaves | 15 ml. |

Sprinkle the steaks with salt and pepper. In a heavy skillet over high heat, fry them quickly in 2 tablespoons [30 ml.] of the butter to the desired degree of doneness—one half min-

ute on each side for rare. Remove the steaks from the pan to a warmed serving platter. Over medium heat, add the remaining butter to the pan juices, and sauté the shallots, parsley and oregano. Continue cooking this sauce gently until most of the liquid has cooked away. Coat each steak thickly with the sauce and serve at once.

JUDITH ETS-HOKIN
THE SAN FRANCISCO DINNER PARTY COOKBOOK

## Halfway House Yankee Pot Roast

*This pot roast can be accompanied by carrots and homemade dumplings. The carrots should be added for the last 30 minutes of cooking; the dumplings, the last 15 minutes.*

| | To serve 6 to 8 | |
|---|---|---|
| 3 to 4 lb. | beef chuck arm or tip roast | 1½ to 2 kg. |
| 2 | garlic cloves, crushed to a paste | 2 |
| 4 tbsp. | butter | 60 ml. |
| | salt | |
| | flour | |
| 1 | large onion, thinly sliced | 1 |
| 12 | peppercorns | 12 |
| 12 | whole allspice | 12 |
| 1 | bay leaf, crumbled | 1 |
| 1 tbsp. | freshly grated horseradish | 15 ml. |
| ½ cup | rum or dry red wine | 125 ml. |
| ½ cup | water | 125 ml. |
| | finely cut fresh dill | |

In a large saucepan, sauté the garlic in the butter. Rub the meat with salt and flour, and brown it well on all sides in the butter. Place the onion slices in a large Dutch oven or other heavy pot with a tight-fitting lid, and put the meat on top of the onions. Add the butter from the saucepan, the peppercorns, allspice, bay leaf and horseradish, and pour the rum or wine over the meat. Cover the pot tightly and simmer for three to four hours, or until the roast is tender. This may be done either in the oven or on the back of the stove. (A good pot roast will supply most of its own juices, but as it cooks add the water to ensure an ample supply of gravy.)

When the pot roast is done, transfer it to a warmed round platter. Stir the gravy until it is smooth, correcting the seasoning if necessary. Pour the gravy over the roast; garnish it with fresh dill.

SARA B. B. STAMM AND THE LADY EDITORS OF YANKEE MAGAZINE
YANKEE MAGAZINE'S FAVORITE NEW ENGLAND RECIPES

## Meat Sauce for Pasta

### Il Sugo di Carne

*To make about 3 cups [¾ liter]*

| ¼ lb. | lean ground beef | 125 g. |
|---|---|---|
| ⅓ cup | olive oil | 75 ml. |
| 1 | onion, chopped | 1 |
| | salt | |
| 3 | medium-sized tomatoes, peeled, seeded and coarsely chopped | 3 |
| 1½ tbsp. | pine nuts, pounded to a paste | 22½ ml. |
| ½ tsp. | chopped dried mushrooms, soaked in warm water for 30 minutes and drained | 2 ml. |
| 1 | sprig rosemary, tied with 1 bay leaf | 1 |

Heat the oil in a pan, add the onion and cook over medium heat until the onion is golden—about 10 minutes. Add the meat, season with salt and cook for five minutes, or until the meat loses all traces of pink. Add the tomatoes, pine nuts, mushrooms, and rosemary and bay leaf. Cook over low heat for 30 minutes, stirring often.

LUCETTO RAMELLA
RICETTE TRADIZIONALI DELLA LIGURIA

---

## Bolognese Meat Sauce

### Ragù alla Bolognese

*To make about 4 cups [1 liter]*

| 10 oz. | lean ground beef | 300 g. |
|---|---|---|
| 7 tbsp. | butter | 105 ml. |
| ¼ cup | finely chopped onion | 50 ml. |
| 1 | carrot, finely chopped | 1 |
| ¼ cup | chopped prosciutto or lean ham (optional) | 50 ml. |
| 1 | strip lemon peel | 1 |
| | freshly grated nutmeg | |
| 1 tbsp. | tomato purée (recipe, page 159) | 15 ml. |
| about 1¼ cups | veal stock (recipe, page 159) | about 300 ml. |
| | salt | |
| 2 tbsp. | heavy cream | 30 ml. |

Melt the butter in a heavy casserole. Add the onion and carrot, and fry them gently in the butter until they are soft but not browned. Add the ground beef and cook it, stirring,

until it loses all traces of pink. Then stir in the chopped prosciutto or ham, if you are using it, and add the lemon peel and a pinch of grated nutmeg. Stir in the tomato purée and pour in enough stock to cover the meat. Add salt to taste, then cover the casserole and simmer the sauce gently for at least one hour.

A few minutes before the end of the cooking time, remove the lemon peel from the sauce and stir in the cream.

GIUSEPPE OBEROSLER
IL TESORETTO DELLA CUCINA ITALIANA

## Pecos River Bowl of Red

*The author suggests serving this lively version of chili con carne with pinto beans.*

*To serve 6*

| 2 tbsp. | lard or rendered bacon fat | 30 ml. |
|---|---|---|
| 1 | large onion, coarsely chopped | 1 |
| 3 lb. | lean boneless beef chuck, coarsely ground in a food grinder | 1½ kg. |
| 3 | medium-sized garlic cloves, finely chopped | 3 |
| 4 tbsp. | ground hot red chili | 60 ml. |
| 4 tbsp. | ground mild red chili | 60 ml. |
| 2 tsp. | ground cumin | 10 ml. |
| 3 cups | water | ¾ liter |
| 1½ tsp. | salt | 7 ml. |

Melt the lard or bacon fat in a large, heavy pot over medium heat. Add the onions and cook them until they are translucent. Combine the meat with the garlic, ground chili and cumin. Add this meat-and-spice mixture to the pot. Break up any lumps with a fork and cook, stirring occasionally, until the meat loses all traces of pink. Stir in the water and salt. Bring the mixture to a boil, then reduce the heat. Stirring occasionally and adding more water if necessary, simmer the mixture uncovered until the meat is very tender and the flavors are well blended—two and one half to three hours. Taste and adjust the seasonings.

JANE BUTEL
CHILI MADNESS

## Curried Lamb

### *Shahi Korma*

*The ghee called for in this recipe may be obtained at Indian food stores. The volatile oils in chilies may irritate your skin. Wear rubber gloves when handling them or wash your hands immediately afterward.*

| | To serve 4 | |
|---|---|---|
| 2 lb. | lamb shoulder, boned, excess fat removed, cubed | 1 kg. |
| ¼ cup | ghee | 50 ml. |
| 1½ cups | farmer cheese | 375 ml. |
| | salt | |
| about 2 cups | water | about ½ liter |
| 2 | cinnamon sticks | 2 |
| 1 | bay leaf | 1 |
| 2 | whole cloves | 2 |
| 2 | whole cardamoms, seeds removed and separated | 2 |
| 10 | almonds, blanched, peeled and halved | 10 |
| | **Masala** | |
| 3 | medium-sized onions, chopped | 3 |
| 1-inch | piece fresh ginger, peeled and sliced | 2½-cm. |
| 3 | garlic cloves | 3 |
| 4 | dried hot chilies, stemmed and seeded | 4 |
| 1½ tbsp. | poppy seeds | 22½ ml. |
| 1 tsp. | ground coriander | 5 ml. |

Grind together all of the *masala* ingredients to make a smooth paste. In a saucepan over low heat, melt the *ghee.* Add the *masala,* stir the mixture well and cook it until the *ghee* separates. Add the farmer cheese and, stirring constantly, cook the mixture until it is well blended—about five minutes. Add the lamb and salt to taste. Stir in ¼ cup [50 ml.] of water, the cinnamon, bay leaf, cloves and cardamom seeds. Cook over low heat, adding a little more water from time to time, until the lamb becomes a rich brown color. Then add 1¼ cups [300 ml.] of water, cover the pan and cook the lamb until it is tender and the gravy is a rich brown— about one and one half hours. Just before serving the lamb, add the almonds.

VIMLA PATIL (EDITOR)
KASHMIR TO KANYAKUMARI

## Royal Roast Leg of Lamb with Saffron Raisin Sauce

### *Shahi Raan*

To bone the leg of lamb, hold it with the top side down on a chopping board. With a sharp boning knife held at the tip of the hip bone, cut the leg all the way down from the butt end to the shank end, thus opening the leg and exposing the bones. Remove the bones with the knife, scraping and pushing the meat away from them. Form the leg into a cylinder, making sure to tuck in the meat at the shank tip. Secure the leg by tying it with string at several places.

| | To serve 8 to 12 | |
|---|---|---|
| 7 to 9 lb. | leg of lamb, all fat removed, boned, rolled and tied with strings | 3½ to 4½ kg. |
| 2 tsp. | saffron threads, crushed to a powder and steeped in 2 tbsp. [30 ml.] hot water for 15 minutes | 10 ml. |
| 2 tbsp. | flour or cornstarch, mixed with 3 tbsp. [45 ml.] water | 30 ml. |
| | **Spicy marinade** | |
| 1 tbsp. | chopped garlic | 15 ml. |
| 2 tbsp. | chopped fresh ginger | 30 ml. |
| 1 tsp. | black or white cumin seeds | 5 ml. |
| about 1 tsp. | cayenne pepper | about 5 ml. |
| 1½ tsp. | Mughal garam masala | 7 ml. |
| 4 tsp. | coarse salt | 20 ml. |
| ¾ cup | seedless white raisins | 175 ml. |
| ½ cup | pistachios or walnuts | 125 ml. |
| ¼ cup | fresh lemon juice | 50 ml. |
| ¼ cup | light brown sugar | 50 ml. |
| ¾ cup | yogurt | 175 ml. |
| ¼ cup | sour cream | 50 ml. |

Prick the top of the lamb with a fork or thin skewer, and place the lamb in a large, fireproof, nonmetal 5-quart [5-liter] casserole that will hold it snugly. Set it aside.

Put all of the ingredients for the marinade into the container of a food processor or electric blender, and blend the ingredients until they are reduced to a fine, thick paste. If the machine begins to clog, add 2 to 3 tablespoons [30 to 45 ml.] of water. Pour the marinade all over the lamb and spread it to coat the lamb thoroughly. Cover the lamb and let it marinate in the refrigerator for three days. Remove the casserole from the refrigerator about one hour before cooking (or four hours before serving).

Sprinkle the dissolved saffron over the lamb. Place the casserole over medium heat and bring the contents to a boil.

Pour 1 cup [¼ liter] of boiling water down the sides of the casserole. Place a piece of aluminum foil on top of the casserole and cover it tightly with its lid. Cook the lamb in the middle of a preheated 350° F. [180° C.] oven for one and one half hours. Reduce the heat to 225° F. [110° C.] and continue cooking the lamb for another 45 minutes. Turn off the heat and let the casserole remain in the oven, with the door shut, for another 45 minutes. The cooking process is now finished, but keep the casserole in the oven until you are ready to serve. The lamb will stay warm for 45 minutes in the oven.

To serve, take the casserole from the oven, uncover it and carefully place the lamb on a carving board. Cut off and discard the trussing strings. Heat the contents of the casserole to a gentle simmer over low heat, skimming off the fat floating on the surface. Add the flour or cornstarch paste and, stirring rapidly, cook for one to two minutes, until the sauce is thickened. Check for salt.

Carve the meat into slices ⅛ to ¼ inch [3 to 6 mm.] thick and arrange them on a warmed serving platter. Spoon some sauce over the slices and serve the rest of it in a heated bowl or a gravy boat.

JULIE SAHNI
CLASSIC INDIAN COOKING

———————————◆———————————

# Sweetbreads with Creamed Snow Peas

*Ris de Veau à la Crème de Pois Gourmands*

You can replace the snow peas with green beans, the ginger with lime and the sweetbreads with brains.

*To serve 4*

| | | |
|---|---|---|
| 1½ lb. | veal sweetbreads, soaked in cold water for 1½ hours, parboiled for 10 minutes, drained and the membrane removed | ¾ kg. |
| ½ lb. | snow peas, strings removed | ¼ kg. |
| 7 tbsp. | butter | 105 ml. |
| | salt and pepper | |
| 1 tbsp. | oil | 15 ml. |
| ¼ cup | chopped shallots | 50 ml. |
| 1 tbsp. | finely chopped fresh ginger | 15 ml. |
| 2 tbsp. | sherry vinegar | 30 ml. |
| 2 tbsp. | brandy | 30 ml. |
| 2 tbsp. | dry white wine | 30 ml. |
| 1 cup | *crème fraîche (recipe, page 158)* or heavy cream | ¼ liter |
| 1 | medium-sized tomato, peeled, seeded and cut into cubes | 1 |

Set half of the snow peas aside. Purée the rest to a fine pulp in a blender or food processor. Blend in 4 tablespoons [60 ml.] of the butter. When this mixture is smooth, sieve it, pressing the mixture through the mesh with a spoon. Stir the snow-pea purée and chill it.

Season the sweetbreads with salt and pepper. Heat the oil in a skillet and, when it is hot, add 1 tablespoon [15 ml.] of the remaining butter. When the butter melts, quickly sauté the sweetbreads until they are lightly browned on all sides—about six minutes. Then transfer them to paper towels to drain.

Pour off the fat remaining in the skillet. Over low heat, melt another tablespoon of butter in the skillet. Add the shallots and ginger. Sauté them, without letting them brown, for about 10 minutes. Add the sherry vinegar and boil the mixture over high heat for three to four minutes. Then stir in the brandy and the white wine. Boil for another four to five minutes, then reduce the heat to low and add the *crème fraîche* or heavy cream. Stir the sauce, bring it slowly to a boil and season it with salt and pepper. As soon as the cream starts to bubble, return the sweetbreads to the skillet; cover the skillet and simmer the sweetbreads for eight minutes. Remove the sweetbreads from the skillet and keep them warm. Set the skillet aside, off the heat.

Bring 2 quarts [2 liters] of salted water to a boil in a large pan. Drop the reserved whole snow peas into the pan and boil them for five minutes. Drain them, rinse them under cold water and drain them again.

Strain the sweetbread sauce through a conical sieve set over a saucepan. Bring the sauce to a boil over medium heat, add the whole snow peas and simmer them for five minutes. Meanwhile, melt the remaining butter in another saucepan. When it is hot, add the tomatoes and season them with salt and pepper. Stirring constantly, sauté the tomatoes for three minutes. Add the tomatoes to the sauce and remove the pan from the heat. Whisk the snow-pea purée into the sauce and continue to whisk until the sauce is smooth and creamy.

Adjust the seasoning of the sweetbreads and arrange them on a serving dish. Pour the sauce over them, garnish the dish with the whole snow peas and serve immediately.

ALAIN AND EVENTHIA SENDERENS
LA CUISINE RÉUSSIE

## Chicken in Onion Tomato Gravy

### *Murgh Masala*

To serve 8

| two 3 lb. | chickens, each cut into 8 to 10 pieces, the wing tips discarded | two 1½ kg. |
|---|---|---|
| ⅔ cup | light vegetable oil | 150 ml. |
| 6 cups | thinly sliced onions | 1½ liters |
| 2 tbsp. | finely chopped garlic | 30 ml. |
| 3 tbsp. | finely chopped fresh ginger | 45 ml. |
| two 3-inch | cinnamon sticks | two 8-cm. |
| 4 | black or 8 green whole cardamoms | 4 |
| 1 tbsp. | turmeric | 15 ml. |
| 1 tsp. | cayenne pepper | 5 ml. |
| 2 | medium-sized ripe tomatoes, peeled, seeded and puréed | 2 |
| 1 tbsp. | coarse salt | 15 ml. |
| 2 cups | boiling water | ½ liter |
| 1½ tbsp. | cumin seeds, toasted in a dry pan for a few minutes, then finely ground | 22½ ml. |
| 3 to 4 tbsp. | chopped fresh coriander leaves or 2 tbsp. [30 ml.] dried coriander | 45 to 60 ml. |

Pull away the skin from the chicken pieces, using paper towels to get a better grip. Place 2 tablespoons [30 ml.] of the oil in a 5-quart [5-liter] heavy-bottomed pan, preferably one with a nonstick surface. Heat the oil over high heat. When the oil is very hot, add a few of the chicken pieces and sear them until they lose their pink color and are nicely browned on all sides—about three to four minutes. Remove them with a slotted spoon and reserve them in a bowl. Repeat with the rest of the chicken pieces until all of them are seared.

Add the remaining oil to the pan, along with the onions. Reduce the heat to medium and fry the onions until they turn light brown—about 30 minutes—stirring them constantly to keep them from burning. Add the garlic and the ginger, and fry them for five minutes. Add the cinnamon and the cardamoms, and continue frying for about two minutes more, until the spices are slightly puffed and are beginning to turn brown.

Add the turmeric and the cayenne pepper, and stir the mixture rapidly for 10 to 15 seconds. Add the puréed tomatoes, the chicken pieces, the salt and the boiling water. Stir to mix, reduce the heat, cover and simmer until the chicken is cooked and very tender and the gravy is thick and pulpy—about 45 minutes.

Check the mixture frequently to ensure that the gravy is not burning. If the liquid evaporates too fast, add a little water. If the gravy, on the other hand, has not thickened adequately after 45 minutes, increase the heat and boil the mixture rapidly, uncovered, until the gravy thickens.

Turn off the heat and let the dish rest, covered, for at least one hour, preferably two hours. When ready to serve, heat the chicken thoroughly, fold in the ground cumin and chopped coriander, check for salt and serve.

JULIE SAHNI
CLASSIC INDIAN COOKING

## Chicken in Red Wine Sauce

### *Poulet Sauté au Brouilly*

*The author suggests serving this dish with a gratin of noodles and cheese and a salad. Brouilly is a Beaujolais wine.*

To serve 4

| one 2½ to 3 lb. | chicken, cut into serving pieces, including the back, neck, gizzard and liver | one 1¼ to 1½ kg. |
|---|---|---|
| | salt and freshly ground pepper | |
| 2 tbsp. | butter | 30 ml. |
| ¼ lb. | mushrooms, left whole if very small, otherwise halved, quartered or sliced | 125 g. |
| ¼ cup | chopped shallots | 50 ml. |
| 1 tsp. | finely chopped garlic | 5 ml. |
| 2 tbsp. | flour | 30 ml. |
| 1½ cups | dry red wine, preferably a Brouilly | 375 ml. |
| ⅔ cup | chicken stock (recipe, page 159) | 150 ml. |
| 1 | bay leaf | 1 |
| 1 | sprig fresh parsley | 1 |
| 2 | sprigs fresh thyme or ¼ tsp. [1 ml.] dried thyme leaves | 2 |

Sprinkle the chicken pieces, including the back, neck, gizzard and liver, with salt and pepper. Heat the butter in a skillet large enough to hold the chicken pieces in one layer without crowding. Add the chicken pieces, skin side down, and cook them over moderately high heat until they are golden brown—about six to seven minutes. Turn them and cook for about five minutes longer.

Stir in the mushrooms, shallots and garlic, and cook this mixture for about one minute before sprinkling flour over it evenly. Add the wine and ½ cup [125 ml.] of the stock, and bring the wine to a boil. Add the bay leaf, parsley and thyme; season the mixture with salt and pepper to taste. Cover and cook this sauce for 15 to 20 minutes.

Using a slotted spoon, transfer the chicken serving pieces to a heatproof casserole, leaving the back, neck, gizzard and liver in the skillet. Add the mushrooms to the casserole. Strain the sauce over the casserole, pressing the sauce with a wooden spoon to extract the liquid. Add the remaining stock to the skillet and swirl it around. Strain this over the chicken. Reheat the chicken thoroughly before serving.

PIERRE FRANEY
THE NEW YORK TIMES 60-MINUTE GOURMET

# Circassian Chicken

## Çerkes Tavuğu

*To remove the slightly bitter brown skin from shelled walnuts, blanch them in a little boiling water for two to three minutes, then peel off the loosened skin. The walnuts can be ground in a food processor.*

To serve 6 to 8

| | | |
|---|---|---|
| one 3½ lb. | chicken | one 1¾ kg. |
| 1 | thick slice firm-textured white bread with the crust removed | 1 |
| ½ lb. | shelled walnuts, blanched, peeled and ground to a paste | ¼ kg. |
| 1 | garlic clove, crushed to a paste | 1 |
| 1 tbsp. | walnut oil | 15 ml. |
| 2 tbsp. | paprika | 30 ml. |
| | pitted ripe black olives, preferably Mediterranean-style black olives (optional) | |

### Turkish court bouillon

| | | |
|---|---|---|
| 1 | sprig fresh parsley | 1 |
| 1 | bay leaf | 1 |
| 1 | strip lemon peel | 1 |
| 1 | carrot, sliced | 1 |
| 1 | onion, sliced | 1 |
| 1 | celery rib, sliced | 1 |
| | salt and pepper | |
| about 2 quarts | water | about 2 liters |

Make your court bouillon with the parsley, bay leaf, lemon peel, carrot, onion, celery, salt and pepper, and just enough water to cover the chicken. Poach the chicken in this for about one hour, or until it is tender, then allow it to cool in the liquid. Lift out the chicken, remove the skin and as many bones as possible, and lay the meat in neat pieces, slightly heaped, in a large dish. Strain the stock.

Soak the bread in some of the chicken stock, squeeze the bread and add it to the walnut paste with the crushed garlic. Blend in a food processor until the mixture forms a smooth paste. Now add to the paste as much of the stock as is necessary to make a thick, creamy sauce, blend it well and pour it over the chicken, covering the pieces completely.

In a small pan, heat very gently the walnut oil and paprika, until the oil becomes a red color. Remove it from the heat to cool and let the pepper settle to the bottom of the pan. Carefully pour off the colored oil. Indent a pattern in the surface of the walnut sauce with your finger—traditionally a big curly S and a couple of smaller wiggles at the side—and pour as much as you need of the oil into the pattern.

Serve the chicken lukewarm if possible. If it has been refrigerated, bring it to room temperature before serving. Garnish the chicken, if you like, with a few black olives.

DOROTHY BROWN (EDITOR)
SYMPOSIUM FARE

# Chicken Makhni

*Edible silver leaf is obtainable at Indian food stores.*

To serve 4

| | | |
|---|---|---|
| 1 | small chicken | 1 |
| 2 tbsp. | vinegar | 30 ml. |
| | salt | |
| 1 cup | farmer cheese | ¼ liter |
| ½ | papaya, peeled, seeded and chopped | ½ |
| 1 tsp. | cayenne pepper | 5 ml. |
| 3 tbsp. | tomato purée (recipe, page 159) | 45 ml. |
| 2 | large onions, finely chopped | 2 |
| 2 tbsp. | butter | 30 ml. |
| ¼ tsp. | turmeric | 1 ml. |
| ¼ tsp. | garam masala | 1 ml. |
| 4 | tomatoes, peeled, seeded and chopped | 4 |
| ¼ cup | heavy cream, lightly whipped | 50 ml. |
| ½ cup | water | 125 ml. |
| 2 tbsp. | cashews | 30 ml. |
| 2 tbsp. | pistachios | 30 ml. |
| 3 tbsp. | raisins, soaked in warm water for 15 minutes and drained | 45 ml. |
| 1 | sheet edible silver leaf (optional) | 1 |

Make deep cuts all over the chicken. Marinate it for 15 minutes in the vinegar with 2 teaspoons [10 ml.] of salt.

Mix together half of the farmer cheese, the papaya, ½ teaspoon [2 ml.] of the cayenne pepper and 2 tablespoons [30 ml.] of the tomato purée. Rub this mixture into the chicken and leave it for two hours.

Roast the chicken in a preheated 400° F. [200° C.] oven for 45 minutes. Meanwhile, in a large saucepan, fry the onions in the butter until they start to brown. Stir in the turmeric, the remaining cayenne pepper, the *garam masala* and the chopped tomatoes. Simmer uncovered for about five minutes, then add the cream, the remaining farmer cheese and tomato purée, and the water. Season with salt.

Add the chicken to the pan and spoon the sauce over it. Cover the pan and cook over medium heat for 10 minutes. Serve the chicken garnished with the nuts and raisins, and the silver leaf, if used.

VIMLA PATIL (EDITOR)
KASHMIR TO KANYAKUMARI

# Ducks with Lemon and Whiskey Sauce

### Canards au Citron et Whiskey

To serve 6

| | | |
|---|---|---:|
| three 4 lb. | ducks, excess fat removed, the necks, gizzards and hearts reserved | three 2 kg. |
| 3 | lemons, the peel thinly pared, cut into fine julienne and blanched, and the juice strained | 3 |
| ⅔ cup | bourbon | 150 ml. |
| ½ cup | peanut oil | 125 ml. |
| 2 | medium-sized carrots, sliced | 2 |
| 2 | medium-sized onions, sliced | 2 |
| 2 tbsp. | flour | 30 ml. |
| 3 cups | dry vermouth | ¾ liter |
| 3 quarts | water | 3 liters |
| 1 | bouquet garni | 1 |
| ¼ cup | sugar | 50 ml. |
| 3 tbsp. | wine vinegar | 45 ml. |
| 1½ tsp. | salt | 7 ml. |
| | freshly ground pepper | |
| 4 tbsp. | butter | 60 ml. |
| | watercress sprigs | |

Cut up the ducks, removing each drumstick and thigh in one piece and keeping the breasts whole. Refrigerate the legs and breasts until you are ready to prepare them.

Make a brown sauce by first heating 3 tablespoons [45 ml.] of the oil in a heavy casserole. Add the duck wings, necks, backs, gizzards and hearts, and the carrots and onions. Set the casserole in a preheated 450° F. [230° C.] oven. Stirring the contents from time to time, bake them for 30 to 40 minutes, or until nicely browned. Sprinkle in the flour and return the casserole to the oven for five to 10 minutes—stirring the contents once or twice to help the flour brown evenly. Set the casserole on top of the stove, stir in the vermouth and water and add the bouquet garni. Over medium heat, bring the liquid to a boil, stirring and scraping the bottom of the casserole to deglaze it thoroughly. Simmer the mixture over low heat for two to three hours, skimming it occasionally of fat and scum; add water if needed to cover the ingredients. Strain the contents of the casserole through a colander, pressing the vegetables with a wooden spoon to extract all of their juices. Refrigerate the sauce for a few hours and spoon away the fat from the surface when it has congealed. Once degreased, the sauce can wait in the refrigerator for a day or two.

Pat the duck legs dry with a paper towel. In the casserole, heat the remaining oil and brown the duck legs on all sides—in two lots if necessary—taking care not to crowd them. When the meat is all browned, remove the legs from the casserole and pour off the fat. Return the duck legs to the casserole, add about half of the brown sauce, and season it lightly. Bring the mixture to a boil over high heat. Lay a piece of wax or parchment paper over the duck, cover the casserole and braise the duck in a preheated 400° F. [200° C.] oven for 40 to 45 minutes, turning the pieces once. The duck is done when the meat begins to shrink slightly from the bone and the juices run clear when a thigh is pricked.

Meanwhile, in a large saucepan, warm the bourbon over low heat. Set it alight and let it flame gently for two or three minutes. Pour in the remaining brown sauce and add all but a few strands of the blanched lemon julienne.

While the sauce simmers slowly, combine the sugar and vinegar in a small saucepan. Bring them to a boil, without stirring, and cook the mixture until it forms a rich brown caramel. Remove the pan from the heat and add first drops and then several tablespoons of the simmering sauce, watching out for splatters. Return the caramel briefly to high heat, swirling to dissolve it thoroughly, then pour the liquid into the sauce, which can simmer gently until the duck is ready.

When the legs are done, pour off the braising liquid and set the legs aside in the covered casserole. Degrease the liquid thoroughly and add it to the simmering sauce. Boil the sauce rapidly, with the pan set slightly to one side of the burner, and skim away the fat and scum that will accumulate on the surface of the sauce. Cook the sauce until it is reduced to about 2 cups [½ liter]. Season it with salt and pepper and add the lemon juice—a tablespoon [15 ml.] at a time; the sauce should taste slightly tart. Pour the sauce back over the duck legs, which may now wait at room temperature for an hour or two, or overnight in the refrigerator if returned to room temperature before rewarming.

Thirty minutes before serving, bring the duck legs in their sauce to a simmer on top of the stove. Preheat the oven to 450° F. [230° C.] and roast the duck breasts in a shallow pan for 15 to 18 minutes; the meat should just be medium rare. Set the breasts aside briefly until they are cool enough to handle, then remove and discard the skin. Bone the breast meat, carve it into thin slices and season them to taste with salt and pepper.

Separate the duck legs and thighs and arrange them on a warmed platter. Remove the sauce from the heat, add the butter and correct the seasoning. Place the slices of the breast meat over each piece of leg or thigh, pour on a bit of the sauce, and garnish the platter with the watercress sprigs and the reserved lemon peel. Present the remaining sauce in a sauceboat.

SIMONE BECK
NEW MENUS FROM SIMCA'S CUISINE

## Burgundian Roast Hare

*Le Lièvre Rôti à la Bourguignonne*

*To make this sauce, you will need a freshly killed, skinned hare. Slit the hare's belly, draw out the innards and discard all but the liver, cutting it free of the gall bladder. To release the blood, hold the animal over a bowl containing 1 tablespoon [15 ml.] of vinegar and slit open the animal's diaphragm. Pour the blood from the chest cavity into the vinegar, which will prevent clotting. The technique for larding meat is shown on page 80.*

*To serve 2*

| | | |
|---|---|---:|
| 1 | hare, forequarters and hind legs removed, liver and blood reserved | 1 |
| 2 oz. | pork fat, cut into strips | 60 g. |
| 4 tbsp. | butter, melted | 60 ml. |
| | salt | |
| ½ cup | game stock *(recipe, page 159)* | 125 ml. |
| ¼ cup | dry white wine | 50 ml. |
| ¼ cup | meat glaze *(recipe, page 160)* | 50 ml. |
| 1½ tbsp. | fresh lemon juice | 22½ ml. |
| 1 | shallot, chopped | 1 |
| 2 or 3 | small sour gherkins, chopped | 2 or 3 |

Lard the saddle of hare with the pork fat and place it on a spit. Place a drip pan underneath the meat. After five minutes of cooking, baste it with the melted butter and season with salt. Season the meat again with salt 15 minutes later. In the drip pan, place half of the stock, the wine, the meat glaze and the lemon juice. Baste the hare with this mixture and continue to cook it for a total of about one hour.

Pour the sauce from the drip pan into a small saucepan. Add the hare's liver pounded to a purée with the blood and the remaining stock. Heat the sauce gently, without boiling, to thicken it slightly.

Sieve the sauce into a sauceboat containing the shallot and gherkins. Serve this with the hare.

PAUL MÉGNIN
250 MANIÈRES DE CUIRE ET ACCOMMODER LE GIBIER

---

## Stewed Rabbit with Tarragon and Garlic

*Fricassée de Lapin à l'Estragon et à l'Ail*

Instead of straining the sauce into a sauceboat, it can be poured directly over the rabbit. You can substitute any kind of poultry or veal for the rabbit. Shallots can be used instead of garlic, and basil, fennel, curry powder or paprika can be substituted for tarragon.

*To serve 4*

| | | |
|---|---|---:|
| one 2 lb. | rabbit, cut into serving pieces | one 1 kg. |
| | salt and pepper | |
| 1 tbsp. | peanut oil | 15 ml. |
| 2 tbsp. | butter | 30 ml. |
| 3 tbsp. | tarragon vinegar | 45 ml. |
| 2 | small tomatoes, peeled, seeded and chopped | 2 |
| 12 | sprigs tarragon, leaves removed and reserved, stems tied in a bunch | 12 |
| 2 cups | *crème fraîche (recipe, page 158)* or heavy cream | ½ liter |
| 12 to 14 | garlic cloves, unpeeled | 12 to 14 |
| 1 cup | milk | ¼ liter |
| | sugar | |

Season each rabbit piece with salt and pepper. In a cast-iron skillet, heat the oil and sauté the rabbit pieces on all sides for about 15 minutes, turning them occasionally with a fork. Add half of the butter to the pan. When the rabbit pieces are well browned, put them on a plate and keep them warm.

Pour off the fat remaining in the skillet and blot up any traces of fat with paper towels. Return the skillet to the heat and add the tarragon vinegar. Scrape the bottom of the skillet with a wooden spoon to dislodge the caramelized juices. Let the liquid reduce for two to three minutes, then add the tomatoes and the bunch of tarragon stems and simmer the mixture for four minutes.

Pour the *crème fraîche* or heavy cream into the skillet. Season this sauce mixture with salt and pepper. Bring it to just below the boiling point, then add the rabbit. Turn the pieces to coat them with the sauce. Cover the skillet and simmer over low heat for 15 minutes. Meanwhile, combine the garlic cloves and milk in a saucepan. Bring the milk to a boil and simmer the cloves for four minutes, then drain the cloves and peel them. Discard the milk.

Put the remaining butter into a clean saucepan and melt it over low heat. Add the garlic cloves, salt, pepper and a pinch of sugar. Cook the garlic over low heat for about 15 minutes, stirring the cloves gently from time to time so that they color evenly.

When the rabbit is tender, arrange the pieces on a warm serving dish. Taste the sauce and adjust the seasoning. Whisk the sauce, then strain it into a warmed sauceboat. Sprinkle the rabbit with the tarragon leaves and arrange the caramelized garlic cloves around it. Serve immediately.

ALAIN AND EVENTHIA SENDERENS
LA CUISINE RÉUSSIE

# Burbot in Leek, Coriander and Saffron Sauce

## Lotte aux Blancs de Poireaux, Coriandre Frais et Safran

The burbot can be replaced by any white fish of your choice, the leeks by cucumbers, the coriander by fresh mint leaves, and the sauce flavored with curry powder instead of saffron.

| To serve 4 | | |
|---|---|---|
| 1¼ lb. | burbot, cleaned, cut into 4 equal pieces and trimmed | 600 g. |
| 4 | leeks, white parts only, each cut crosswise into 3 pieces | 4 |
| 2 | sprigs fresh coriander, leaves plucked | 2 |
| | powdered saffron | |
| ½ lb. plus 2 tbsp. | butter | ¼ kg. plus 30 ml. |
| 2 | shallots, finely chopped | 2 |
| ¼ cup | finely chopped fresh mushrooms | 50 ml. |
| | salt and pepper | |
| ⅔ cup | dry white wine | 150 ml. |
| 1½ cups | crème fraîche (recipe, page 158) or heavy cream | 375 ml. |

Put the coriander in a heavy pan with a pinch of saffron and set the pan aside. Melt the butter in a large, wide, ovenproof pan over medium heat; add the shallots, stirring them well with a wooden spoon. Cook the shallots for about one minute without letting them brown. Stir in the mushrooms. Salt and pepper the fish pieces on both sides, then place them on the shallot mixture, making sure that the pieces do not overlap. Add the wine, bring the mixture to a boil and bake in a preheated 425° F. [220° C.] oven for six minutes.

Meanwhile parboil the leeks in lightly salted boiling water for five minutes. Drain the leeks on paper towels.

Take the fish out of the oven and drain the fish pieces on paper towels. Over high heat, reduce the liquid in which the fish was cooked to about 2 tablespoons [30 ml.]. Whisk in the cream, then bring the mixture to a boil. Decrease the heat and let this sauce simmer for several minutes to thicken to a smooth, creamy consistency. Season with salt and pepper.

Add the leeks to the pan containing the coriander and the saffron; set a very-fine-meshed sieve over this pan and strain the sauce into it, pushing the sauce through with a wooden spoon. Place the pan on the heat and simmer the sauce gently for three to four minutes, or until it has thickened slightly.

Place a slice of fish on each of four heated plates and put the plates in the oven—with the door slightly ajar—until the sauce is cooked. Coat the fish with the sauce and arrange the leek slices around the fish. Serve immediately.

ALAIN AND EVENTHIA SENDERENS
LA CUISINE RÉUSSIE

# Cod in Garlic and Chili Sauce

## Rumesco

*The volatile oils in chilies may irritate your skin. Wear rubber gloves when handling them or wash your hands afterward.*

| To serve 4 | | |
|---|---|---|
| 2 lb. | salt cod, cut into serving pieces, soaked in water for 36 hours and drained | 1 kg. |
| 6 | garlic cloves | 6 |
| 4 | dried hot chilies, stemmed, seeded and soaked in hot water for 2 hours | 4 |
| 2 | slices firm-textured white bread with the crusts removed | 2 |
| 1 cup | olive oil | ¼ liter |
| 1 | red pepper, roasted, peeled, halved, seeded, deribbed and chopped | 1 |
| 2 | tomatoes, peeled, seeded and chopped | 2 |
| ¼ cup | almonds, blanched and peeled | 50 ml. |
| 2⅓ cups | water | 575 ml. |
| 1 tbsp. | flour | 15 ml. |

In a heavy casserole, fry the bread and garlic in the oil until golden. Transfer the bread and garlic to a mortar—setting the casserole aside—and pound them to a paste with the chilies, red pepper, tomatoes and almonds. Mix in ⅓ cup [75 ml.] of water and the flour. Pour the paste into the reserved casserole and add the cod. Cook over medium heat for a minute or two, then stir in the remaining water and simmer over low heat for 15 minutes.

COCINA REGIONAL ESPAÑOLA

# Cod with Green Sauce

## Småtorsk med Grønn Saus

| To serve 6 | | |
|---|---|---|
| one 4 lb. | cod, cleaned, head and fins removed | one 2 kg. |
| 6 cups | fish stock (recipe, page 164) | 1½ liters |
| 2 tbsp. | butter | 30 ml. |
| 3 tbsp. | flour | 45 ml. |
| 4 | tomatoes, peeled, seeded and chopped | 4 |
| 2 | hard-boiled eggs, chopped | 2 |
| 1 tbsp. | finely cut fresh dill | 15 ml. |
| 1 tbsp. | finely cut fresh chives | 15 ml. |
| | salt and pepper | |
| ⅓ cup | grated cheese | 75 ml. |

Poach the fish in the fish stock for 20 minutes, or until a skewer inserted behind the gills meets no resistance. Transfer the fish to an ovenproof dish. Strain and reserve 2½ cups [625 ml.] of the cooking liquid. Melt the butter in a saucepan, add the flour and cook it gently for a few minutes. Whisk in the reserved cooking liquid, bring the mixture to a boil and cook it gently for two minutes. Stir in the tomatoes, hard-boiled eggs and herbs. Season with salt and pepper.

Pour the sauce over the fish, sprinkle with the grated cheese and bake in a preheated 375° F. [190° C.] oven for five to six minutes to allow the flavors to mingle.

HROAR DEGE
FRA NEPTUNS GAFFEL

## Creole Court Bouillon

*Use firm-fleshed fish such as redfish or red snapper to make the following dish.*

To serve 6

| | | |
|---|---|---|
| 3 lb. | fish, cleaned and cut into slices | 1½ kg. |
| 1 tbsp. | lard | 15 ml. |
| 2 tbsp. | flour | 30 ml. |
| 12 | whole allspice, crushed | 12 |
| 2 tsp. | finely chopped fresh parsley | 10 ml. |
| 1 tsp. | chopped fresh thyme leaves | 5 ml. |
| 1 | bay leaf | 1 |
| 1 tbsp. | chopped fresh marjoram leaves | 15 ml. |
| 1 | garlic clove, crushed to a paste | 1 |
| 1 | onion, finely chopped | 1 |
| 4 | tomatoes, peeled, seeded and chopped | 4 |
| ¾ cup | red wine | 175 ml. |
| 4 cups | water | 1 liter |
| | salt | |
| | cayenne pepper | |
| 3 tbsp. | fresh lemon juice | 45 ml. |

Melt the lard in a large pot, stir in the flour gradually, then add the allspice, parsley, thyme, bay leaf, marjoram, garlic and onion. Mix them well, then add the tomatoes, wine and water. Bring the mixture to a boil and cook it for seven to eight minutes, then season it with salt and cayenne pepper. Continue to cook and taste the court bouillon until the flavor is right, then add the fish slices, one at a time. Add the lemon juice and poach the slices gently for 10 minutes. Serve the fish in the court bouillon.

CORA, ROSE AND BOB BROWN
SOUPS, SAUCES AND GRAVIES

## Lucien's Mussels

*Moules, Façon Lucien*

*The technique for cleaning mussels is shown on page 10.*

To serve 4

| | | |
|---|---|---|
| 3 dozen | live mussels, scrubbed and debearded | 3 dozen |
| 1 | onion, finely chopped | 1 |
| 1 | shallot, finely chopped | 1 |
| 6 | sprigs fresh parsley, finely chopped | 6 |
| ½ cup | dry white wine | 125 ml. |
| 1 tbsp. | heavy cream | 15 ml. |
| 3 | tomatoes, peeled, seeded and coarsely chopped | 3 |
| ¾ cup | hollandaise sauce (recipe, page 166) | 175 ml. |
| 3 tbsp. | fresh lemon juice | 45 ml. |
| | freshly ground pepper | |
| 1 tbsp. | fines herbes | 15 ml. |

Place the mussels in a large, nonreactive pan. Add the onion, shallot, parsley sprigs and the wine. Cover the pan tightly and set it over high heat. After two minutes, shake the pan vigorously. Do this three more times during cooking, which should take only five to six minutes in all. The mussels should then be cooked and their shells wide open. Lift out the mussels and keep them hot.

Strain the mussel cooking liquid through a fine-meshed sieve. Rinse out the pan and return the strained liquid to it; heat it and pour in the cream. Bring the mixture to a boil gently, whisk it, and boil until the mixture is reduced to half its original volume. Heat the tomatoes in a small pan to evaporate their water—for about five minutes—then add them to the reduced cream mixture. Remove the pan from the heat and pour in the hollandaise sauce. Reheat, but be careful that the sauce does not boil; otherwise it will separate. Add the lemon juice and a pinch of pepper.

Remove the upper shell from each of the mussels and place the mussels flat on four warmed plates. Pour the sauce over the mussels and sprinkle them with the fines herbes Serve them at once.

ALEXANDER WATT
PARIS BISTRO COOKERY

# Mussel and Zucchini Gratin

*Gratin de Moules aux Courgettes*

*To serve 6*

| | | |
|---|---|---|
| 4 dozen | live mussels, scrubbed and debearded | 4 dozen |
| 8 | medium-sized zucchini, cut into ⅛-inch [3-mm.] slices | 8 |
| 1 | bay leaf | 1 |
| ⅓ cup | peanut oil | 75 ml. |
| | salt and pepper | |
| 1 tbsp. | butter | 15 ml. |
| 1 tbsp. | flour | 15 ml. |
| 2 | egg yolks | 2 |
| 2 tbsp. | *crème fraîche (recipe, page 158)* or heavy cream | 30 ml. |
| ½ cup | grated Gruyère cheese | 125 ml. |

Place the mussels in a large, heavy-bottomed casserole over high heat. Add the bay leaf and cover the casserole. After about five minutes, steam will start to pour out from under the lid of the casserole, indicating that the mussels have opened. Place a large sieve lined with cheesecloth or muslin over a large mixing bowl and strain the mussels into this. In this way, you can drain the mussels without losing any of their liquor, which you will need to make the sauce.

Heat the peanut oil in a large skillet over high heat. When the oil is hot, add the zucchini slices and a little salt and pepper. Cook them for about six minutes, turning them from time to time with a skimmer. Meanwhile, shuck the mussels and reserve them on a plate.

When the zucchini slices are cooked, take them from the pan with the skimmer and drain them of as much oil as possible. Distribute them evenly over the bottom of a shallow gratin dish. Scatter the mussels over the bed of zucchini.

Melt the butter in a small saucepan over gentle heat. When the butter begins to foam, add the flour, stir it in and let it cook for one minute. Then add the mussels' cooking liquor and salt and pepper to taste. Turn the heat to high and whisk this sauce mixture continuously until it thickens— about three minutes. Take the pan from the heat.

Place the egg yolks in a bowl and add the *crème fraîche* or heavy cream. Mix them together and then pour this mixture into the thickened sauce, whisking all the time.

Pour the sauce evenly over the mussels in the gratin dish, then sprinkle the grated cheese over the top. Bake the assembly in a preheated 475° F. [250° C.] oven for five minutes, then place it under a hot broiler for a further five minutes to form an even, crisp crust over the mussels.

MICHEL OLIVER
MES RECETTES À LA TÉLÉ

# Trout with Leeks

*Truites aux Poireaux*

*To serve 6*

| | | |
|---|---|---|
| 6 | trout, cleaned, each split down the back to within ½ inch [1 cm.] of either end of the spine, the spine broken and removed | 6 |
| 3 | large leeks, white parts only | 3 |
| 4 | shallots, finely chopped | 4 |
| 1 cup | dry white wine | ¼ liter |
| ½ lb. | butter | ¼ kg. |
| 3 tbsp. | cream | 45 ml. |
| | salt and pepper | |
| **Whiting stuffing** | | |
| 3 | whole whiting, cleaned, filleted and skinned | 3 |
| 3 | egg yolks | 3 |
| 3 tbsp. | heavy cream | 45 ml. |
| 2 tbsp. | finely chopped onion | 30 ml. |
| | freshly grated nutmeg | |
| 2 tbsp. | butter | 30 ml. |

First prepare the stuffing. Pound the whiting fillets in a mortar, add the egg yolks, cream, onion and a pinch of nutmeg, and mix them well. Melt the butter and gently heat the stuffing in it. Stuff the bellies of the trout.

Blanch the leeks in boiling salted water for 15 minutes. Separate the leaves, select the tender inner ones and wrap them, in ribbon fashion, around each of the trout.

Make a bed of the shallots on the bottom of a shallow nonreactive pan. Pour in the wine and place the trout on top of the shallots. Cover the pan with a piece of buttered parchment paper, and poach the trout in a preheated 350° F. [180° C.] oven for 15 minutes, or until they are tender. Remove the trout and arrange them on a hot, heatproof serving dish. Pour the juices from the pan into a saucepan, and reduce them quickly until there is about ⅓ cup [75 ml.] of liquid left. Remove the liquid from the heat and whisk in the butter and the cream, a little at a time. Adjust the seasoning. Pour the sauce over the fish and brown the fish under a preheated broiler. Be careful that the sauce does not boil; otherwise it will separate.

ALEXANDER WATT
PARIS BISTRO COOKERY

# Dessert Sauces

## Molded Tapioca Pudding with Apricot Sauce

*Pudding Moulé au Tapioca, Sauce aux Abricots*

*If you wish to serve the tapioca pudding hot or warm, heat the apricot sauce until it is warmed through, remove it from the heat and stir in 1 tablespoon [15 ml.] of butter. If the pudding is to be served cold, a fresh raspberry purée can be substituted for the apricot sauce.*

| | To serve 4 | |
|---|---|---|
| ½ cup | tapioca | 125 ml. |
| 2 cups | milk | ½ liter |
| ¼ cup | sugar | 50 ml. |
| | salt | |
| ½ | vanilla bean or ½ tsp. [2 ml.] vanilla extract | ½ |
| 6 tbsp. | butter | 90 ml. |
| 3 | eggs, the yolks separated from the whites, and the whites stiffly beaten | 3 |
| | **Apricot sauce** | |
| 12 | ripe apricots (about 1 lb. [½ kg.]), halved and pitted | 12 |
| ⅓ cup | Madeira or port (optional) | 75 ml. |
| ⅔ cup | sugar syrup (recipe, page 167) | 150 ml. |

To make the tapioca pudding, first combine the milk, sugar, a small pinch of salt, the vanilla and 3 tablespoons [45 ml.] of the butter in an ovenproof saucepan. Stirring constantly, bring to a boil and slowly pour in the tapioca. Stir the mixture over direct heat for one minute, then cover the saucepan and bake the mixture in a preheated 300° F. [150° C.] oven for 20 minutes. Transfer the mixture to a mixing bowl and remove the vanilla bean, if you used it. Stir in the rest of the butter and the egg yolks. Gently fold in the stiffly beaten egg whites. Butter a 4-cup [1-liter] mold generously and sprinkle the inside lightly with dry tapioca. Pour the mixture into the mold and put the mold in a pan partly filled with hot, but not boiling, water. Bake the pudding in a preheated 325° to 350° F. [160° to 180° C.] oven for about 30 minutes, or until the center springs back when prodded lightly. Remove the mold from the hot water and let the pudding settle for about 10 minutes before unmolding it. If the pudding is to be served chilled, leave the mold over it until just before serving to protect the surface from the air.

To make the sauce, put the apricots in a nonreactive pan with the Madeira or port, if you are using it. Add the syrup. Poach the apricots for five minutes, or until they are tender. Transfer the apricots to a nonreactive sieve set over a bowl; reserve the poaching liquid. Rub the apricots through the sieve and discard the skins. If you wish, add a little of the poaching liquid to this sauce to thin it.

Coat the pudding with some of the sauce and send the rest of the sauce to the table in a separate dish.

RICHARD OLNEY
THE FRENCH MENU COOKBOOK

## Apricot Jam Sauce

*This fragrant sauce goes well with puddings and cakes.*

| | To make about 2 cups [½ liter] | |
|---|---|---|
| 1 lb. | apricot jam, sieved (about 1½ cups [375 ml.]) | ½ kg. |
| 3 tbsp. | fresh lemon juice | 45 ml. |
| ¾ cup | sherry | 175 ml. |
| 2 tbsp. | sugar syrup (recipe, page 167) | 30 ml. |

Stir the lemon juice, sherry and syrup into the sieved apricot jam. Bring to a boil, stirring constantly, and serve hot.

MASSEY AND SON'S COMPREHENSIVE PUDDING BOOK

## Apricot Butter with Rum

*The author suggests that this sauce should be served with Christmas pudding and mince pie. It will keep for up to one month in the refrigerator.*

| | To make about 2 cups [½ liter] | |
|---|---|---|
| ¾ cup | dried apricots, soaked in water overnight, drained and cut into eighths with scissors | 175 ml. |
| ½ lb. | butter, softened | ¼ kg. |
| 1 tbsp. | rum | 15 ml. |
| ¼ cup | almonds, blanched, peeled and ground | 50 ml. |
| 1 tsp. | grated lemon peel | 5 ml. |
| ½ tsp. | vanilla extract | 2 ml. |

Combine the apricots with all of the other ingredients in a small, deep bowl or in the container of a blender. Mash the apricot mixture with a fork or blend it at low speed until it forms a smooth paste. Pack the flavored butter into small pots, cover them with plastic wrap or foil, and put them in the refrigerator.

PATRICIA HOLDEN WHITE
FOOD AS PRESENTS

## Almond Custard

### Mandelsauce

*This rich sauce is a suitable topping for baked or steamed puddings or sweet dumplings. The original version of the recipe calls for two bitter almonds, which are not obtainable in America; almond extract makes a suitable substitute.*

*To make about 3 cups [¾ liter]*

| | | |
|---|---|---|
| ¼ cup | almonds, blanched, peeled and chopped | 50 ml. |
| 1 | vanilla bean | 1 |
| ⅔ cup | milk | 150 ml. |
| 2 cups | heavy cream | ½ liter |
| 2 tsp. | flour | 10 ml. |
| 2 tsp. | sugar | 10 ml. |
| 3 | egg yolks, beaten | 3 |
| ⅛ tsp. | almond extract | ½ ml. |

Simmer the almonds and the vanilla bean in the milk for 15 minutes. Remove the vanilla bean and press the almond milk through a sieve into a heavy saucepan; whisk in the cream, flour and sugar. Stirring constantly, cook the mixture over very low heat until it is very thick—about 10 minutes. Then slowly whisk in the egg yolks and almond extract, and cook the custard for a few minutes more.

HENRIETTE DAVIDIS
PRAKTISCHES KOCHBUCH

---

## Almond Cream Sauce

*The egg white in this recipe prevents the almonds from becoming oily when they are pounded.*
Serve this sauce as hot as possible with any hot pudding.

*To make about 1 ½ cups [375 ml.]*

| | | |
|---|---|---|
| ¼ cup | almonds, blanched and peeled | 50 ml. |
| ¼ tsp. | almond extract | 1 ml. |
| ½ cup | heavy cream | 125 ml. |
| 2 | eggs, the yolks separated from the whites, the whites lightly beaten, the yolks well beaten | 2 |
| ½ cup | sugar | 125 ml. |
| 1 tbsp. | orange-flower water | 15 ml. |

Pound the almonds in a mortar (or put them twice through a food grinder, using the finest disk), adding alternately the almond sxtract, a little of the egg white, the sugar and the orange-flower water. Put this mixture in a heavy saucepan (or the top of a double boiler set over hot water).

Mix the beaten egg yolks with the cream. Pour the cream into the almond mixture and beat with a whisk over very low heat until the mixture is smooth, thick and frothy.

LOUIS P. DE GOUY
THE GOLD COOK BOOK

## Aniseed Cream Sauce

### Sauce Crème à l'Anisette

This sauce is served with cold or frozen desserts. By replacing the aniseed with cumin seeds or chopped ginger, coffee extract, a vanilla bean, crushed fresh rose or violet petals, grated chocolate, etc., you can produce endless variations on this exquisite cream. To flavor it with fruit, add puréed fruit with the cream when the preparation is on the ice.

*To make about 4 cups [1 liter]*

| | | |
|---|---|---|
| 2 tsp. | aniseed | 10 ml. |
| 1 cup | heavy cream, whipped | ¼ liter |
| 2 cups | milk | ½ liter |
| ¼ cup | sugar | 50 ml. |
| 8 | egg yolks, lightly beaten | 8 |
| ⅓ cup | kirsch | 75 ml. |

In a heavy saucepan, simmer the milk, sugar and aniseed together for 10 minutes. Remove the pan from the heat and let the mixture cool slightly. Whisking constantly, pour the flavored milk into the egg yolks, a little at a time. Then pour the mixture into the saucepan, place it over low heat and continue to whisk the mixture until it thickens—about one minute. Do not let this custard boil. Press the custard through a sieve into a clean pan, then add the kirsch. Set the pan on ice and stir the custard until it is cool. Finally, fold in the whipped cream.

JOSEPH FAVRE
DICTIONNAIRE UNIVERSEL DE CUISINE PRATIQUE

## Merton Sauce

*This rich sauce is suitable for steamed or baked puddings or for baked apples or pears.*

*To make about 1 ½ cups [375 ml.]*

| | | |
|---|---|---|
| 8 tbsp. | butter, softened | 120 ml. |
| ½ cup | sugar | 125 ml. |
| ⅓ cup | sherry | 75 ml. |
| ⅓ cup | brandy | 75 ml. |

Work the butter with a wooden spoon to a cream, adding first the sugar and then the sherry and the brandy by degrees.

MASSEY AND SON'S COMPREHENSIVE PUDDING BOOK

## Sauce for His Serene Highness's Puddings

*This recipe is from the author's family recipe book. She suggests that "His Serene Highness" must have been Prince Edward of Saxe-Weimar, a noted gourmet. The sauce complements most puddings, especially steamed puddings.*

*To make about 1 cup [¼ liter]*

| | | |
|---|---|---|
| 8 tbsp. | butter | 120 ml. |
| 1 cup | confectioners' sugar | ¼ liter |
| 2 tbsp. | brandy | 30 ml. |
| 1 tbsp. | sherry | 15 ml. |

Beat the butter and sugar together until they are quite white and very light; this takes time. Then very slowly add the brandy and sherry by degrees, and beat the sauce until the ingredients are thoroughly mixed.

LADY MURIEL BECKWITH
SAUCES, SWEET AND SAVOURY

## Foamy Sauce

*This sauce is traditionally served with steamed pudding.*

*To make about 2 cups [½ liter]*

| | | |
|---|---|---|
| 8 tbsp. | butter, softened | 120 ml. |
| 1 cup | confectioners' sugar | ¼ liter |
| 1 | egg, beaten | 1 |
| 2 tbsp. | brandy or sherry | 30 ml. |
| ½ cup | heavy cream, whipped | 125 ml. |

Cream the butter and gradually add the sugar. Add the beaten egg. Place the mixture in the top part of a double boiler set over boiling water, and add the brandy or sherry. Beat the mixture constantly with a whisk until it thickens and becomes hot and foamy—about 10 minutes. Remove the mixture from the heat and fold in the whipped cream. Place the sauce in a serving bowl and serve it at once while it is warm.

JUNE PLATT
JUNE PLATT'S NEW ENGLAND COOK BOOK

## Butterscotch Sauce

*This rich sauce is suitable as a topping for cakes, profiteroles or éclairs as well as for ice cream.*
The sauce is good either hot or cold.

*To make about 3 cups [¾ liter]*

| | | |
|---|---|---|
| 1 ½ cups | brown sugar | 375 ml. |
| ⅔ cup | light corn syrup | 150 ml. |
| ⅓ cup | water | 75 ml. |
| 4 tbsp. | butter | 60 ml. |
| ½ tsp. | vanilla extract | 2 ml. |
| 6 tbsp. | heavy cream | 90 ml. |

In a saucepan, combine the brown sugar, corn syrup, water and butter, and cook until the mixture has the consistency of heavy cream. Cool, then add the vanilla extract and the cream. If the sauce is too thick, add a little more cream.

THE WOMAN'S AUXILIARY OF OLIVET EPISCOPAL CHURCH
VIRGINIA COOKERY—PAST AND PRESENT

## Champagne Sabayon Sauce

*Sabayon au Champagne*

*This delicate sauce can be served over ice cream, sherbet, fresh fruit or cold pudding.*

This sauce is fragile, and must be made no more than 30 minutes before being served. It is always served at room temperature, never chilled.

*To make about 3¾ cups [925 ml.]*

| | | |
|---|---|---|
| 1 cup | white or pink Champagne | ¼ liter |
| 5 | egg yolks | 5 |
| ¾ cup | sugar | 175 ml. |

Place the egg yolks and Champagne in the top of a double boiler or in a heatproof bowl and set it over simmering—not boiling—water. The water should not touch the vessel containing the ingredients.

Whisk the egg yolks and Champagne gently for eight to 10 minutes; the mixture should not expand and its temperature should be kept at 115° F. [45° C.]. Use a cooking thermometer to check it.

Pour the mixture into a bowl and add the sugar. Using an electric mixer set at medium speed, beat the mixture for five minutes; then beat it at low speed or with a whisk for an additional five minutes.

GASTON LENÔTRE
LENÔTRE'S ICE CREAMS AND CANDIES

## Cherry Sauce in the French Style

### Sauce de Cerise à la Française

This is served warm with hot desserts and cooled—flavored with a little kirsch—to accompany cold desserts. If you use black cherries, substitute red wine for the white, and vanilla extract for the cinnamon and lemon peel.

*To make 2 cups [ ½ liter]*

| | | |
|---|---|---|
| 1 lb. | red cherries, pitted | ½ kg. |
| ⅔ cup | water | 150 ml. |
| ⅓ cup | dry white wine | 75 ml. |
| ¼ cup | sugar | 50 ml. |
| ½ tsp. | ground cinnamon | 2 ml. |
| 1 tsp. | grated lemon peel | 5 ml. |

Cook the cherries with the water, wine, sugar, cinnamon and lemon peel for about 15 minutes. When the cherries are soft, press them through a very fine sieve into another pan. Continue to cook the purée until it has a thick consistency and a perfect flavor—about 10 minutes more.

JOSEPH FAVRE
DICTIONNAIRE UNIVERSEL DE CUISINE PRATIQUE

## Chocolate Cream

### Crème au Chocolat

*This rich sauce is suitable for spongecake or angel food cake, profiteroles or éclairs.*

*To make about 6 cups [1 ½ liters]*

| | | |
|---|---|---|
| 1 ½ oz. | semisweet chocolate | 45 g. |
| ¼ cup | water | 50 ml. |
| 4 cups | milk | 1 liter |
| ½ cup | sugar | 125 ml. |
| 4 | eggs | 4 |
| 5 | egg yolks | 5 |

Melt the chocolate in the water over very gentle heat, stirring it all the time. Stir in the milk and sugar, bring the mixture to a boil, then let it cool.

Beat the eggs and the egg yolks together, then pour in the chocolate-flavored milk. Put the mixture in a saucepan over very low heat and cook it, stirring vigorously as it thickens. When the custard is thick enough to coat the spoon, strain it through a fine-meshed sieve into a large bowl and let it cool.

ALFRED CONTOUR
LE CUISINIER BOURGUIGNON

## Fluffy Chocolate-Nut Sauce

*Serve this sauce with ice cream.*

*To make about 2 cups [ ½ liter]*

| | | |
|---|---|---|
| 6 oz. | semisweet chocolate, cut into pieces | 175 g. |
| 1 cup | heavy cream | ¼ liter |
| ½ cup | chopped nuts | 125 ml. |

In a small saucepan, combine the chocolate pieces and ½ cup [125 ml.] of the cream. Heat the mixture gently, stirring constantly until the chocolate melts and the mixture is smooth. Cool the sauce and refrigerate it until it is thoroughly chilled. Whip the remaining cream, then fold it into the chocolate mixture along with the nuts.

PAUL DICKSON
THE GREAT AMERICAN ICE CREAM BOOK

## Hot Lemon Sauce

Serve the sauce hot or warm over puddings and cakes.

*To make about 1 ½ cups [375 ml.]*

| | | |
|---|---|---|
| 3 tbsp. | fresh lemon juice | 45 ml. |
| 1 ½ tsp. | grated lemon peel | 7 ml. |
| ½ cup | sugar | 125 ml. |
| 2 tbsp. | cornstarch | 30 ml. |
| ¼ tsp. | salt | 1 ml. |
| 1 cup | water | ¼ liter |
| 1 ½ tbsp. | butter | 22 ½ ml. |

In a saucepan, combine the sugar, cornstarch and salt. Stir in the water. Stirring constantly, cook over low heat until the mixture thickens and becomes clear. Add the lemon juice, lemon peel and butter.

JAN MC BRIDE CARLTON
THE OLD-FASHIONED COOKBOOK

## Peanut-Butter Fudge Sauce

Serve this sauce hot or cold over your favorite ice cream.

*To make about 2 ½ cups [625 ml.]*

| | | |
|---|---|---|
| ¾ cup | smooth peanut butter | 175 ml. |
| 8 oz. | semisweet chocolate | 250 g. |
| 4 oz. | unsweetened chocolate | 125 g. |
| ½ cup | sugar | 125 ml. |
| ½ cup | light cream | 125 ml. |
| ½ cup | water | 125 ml. |

In a heavy saucepan, combine the semisweet and unsweetened chocolates, the sugar, cream and water. Stir the mixture over low heat until the chocolate is melted. Add the peanut butter and stir until the sauce is smooth.

DOROTHY C. FRANK
THE PEANUT COOKBOOK

---

## Peach-Leaf Custard

### Crème à la Feuille de Pêcher

*This delicately flavored sauce will complement hot or cold poached fruits. Scented geranium leaves can be substituted for the peach leaves.*

To make about 4 cups [1 liter]

| | | |
|---|---|---|
| 6 | peach leaves | 6 |
| 3 cups | milk | ¾ liter |
| 5 | egg yolks | 5 |
| 1 cup | superfine sugar | ¼ liter |
| | cornstarch | |

In a heavy saucepan, bring the milk to a boil with the peach leaves, then set the mixture aside to infuse for 15 minutes. In a large bowl, beat the egg yolks and sugar together until the yolks are very pale and light. Stir in a pinch of cornstarch.

Bring the milk to a boil again. Stirring constantly, pour it into the egg yolks a little at a time. Pour this custard mixture into the saucepan and place it over low heat. Cook the custard for about three minutes, stirring it all the time with a wooden spoon. As soon as the custard thickens, remove it from the heat. Discard the peach leaves and let the custard cool.

ANNICK MARIE
LE GRAND LIVRE DE LA CUISINE BOURGUIGNONNE

---

## Raspberry Sauce

### Coulis de Framboises

*Classically, this sauce is served with fresh strawberries or raspberries. It also goes well with poached fruit, angel food cake or poundcake, and ice cream or sherbet.*

To ensure that this sauce has a fresh taste, it is very important to use only the freshest and ripest raspberries.

To make about 1 cup [¼ liter]

| | | |
|---|---|---|
| 1½ cups | ripe raspberries | 375 ml. |
| ¼ cup | superfine sugar | 50 ml. |
| 3 tbsp. | fresh lemon juice | 45 ml. |
| 1 tbsp. | raspberry liqueur | 15 ml. |

Purée the raspberries in a blender. Stir in the sugar. Flavor with the lemon juice and the raspberry liqueur. Strain the purée through a fine-meshed sieve to remove the seeds.

ANTON MOSIMANN
CUISINE À LA CARTE

---

## Orange Dessert Sauce

*This sauce is suitable for angel food cake.*

To make 1 cup [¼ liter]

| | | |
|---|---|---|
| 1 cup | fresh orange juice | ¼ liter |
| 2 tbsp. | grated orange peel | 30 ml. |
| 2 tbsp. | cornstarch | 30 ml. |
| 1 tbsp. | sugar | 15 ml. |
| 1 | egg yolk | 1 |

In a heavy, nonaluminum pot, stir the orange peel, cornstarch and sugar together. Gradually pour in the orange juice while stirring with a whisk to keep the mixture smooth. Over medium heat, stir the sauce for three or four minutes, until it thickens. Place the egg yolk in a small bowl and beat it as you slowly pour in the hot sauce. Scrape in all the sauce from the pot, then transfer the contents of the bowl to the pot. Return the sauce to the heat for half a minute while continuing to beat it. Cool, then chill before serving.

CAROL CUTLER
THE WOMAN'S DAY LOW-CALORIE DESSERT COOKBOOK

---

## Rhubarb Sauce

### Rhabarber-Sauce

This sauce is served with puddings and fruit dumplings.

To make 3 cups [¾ liter]

| | | |
|---|---|---|
| 1 lb. | rhubarb, trimmed and cut into 2-inch [5-cm.] lengths (about 4 cups [1 liter]) | ¼ kg. |
| 1 cup | water | ¼ liter |
| 2 tbsp. | potato flour | 30 ml. |
| 1¼ cups | sweet white wine | 300 ml. |
| ½ cup | dried currants | 125 ml. |
| 2-inch | cinnamon stick | 5-cm. |
| 2 | strips thinly pared lemon peel | 2 |
| about ½ cup | sugar | about 125 ml. |

Boil the rhubarb in ½ cup [125 ml.] of the water until it is soft—about 20 minutes. Press it through a sieve into a non-reactive pan. Whisk the potato flour with half of the wine, stir this into the rhubarb purée and add the remaining wine. Stirring continuously, bring the mixture to a boil over low heat and simmer it until thick—about five minutes.

Meanwhile, boil the currants with the cinnamon and lemon peel in the remaining water until the currants are plump—about 10 minutes. Remove the cinnamon and lemon peel, then add the currants—with their cooking liquid—to the rhubarb mixture. Add sugar to taste.

LOUISE RICHTER AND SOPHIE CHARLOTTE HOMMER
ILLUSTRIRTES HAMBURGER KOCHBUCH

## Vanilla Cream

*Crème à la Vanille*

*This thick sauce is a suitable topping for baked or steamed pudding and for baked or poached fruit.*

*To make about 6 cups [1 ½ liters]*

| | | |
|---|---|---|
| 1 | vanilla bean | 1 |
| 4 cups | milk | 1 liter |
| ½ cup | sugar | 125 ml. |
| 4 | eggs | 4 |
| 5 | egg yolks | 5 |

Bring the milk to a boil with the sugar and the vanilla bean, then cover it and let it cool. Remove the vanilla bean.

Beat the eggs and the egg yolks together and gradually stir in the milk. Put the mixture in a heavy saucepan or in the top part of a double boiler set over hot water. Stirring vigorously, cook the mixture over very low heat for about five minutes. When the custard is thick enough to coat the spoon, strain it through a fine sieve into a large bowl. Let this sauce cool before serving it.

ALFRED CONTOUR
LE CUISINIER BOURGUIGNON

## Foamy Vanilla Sauce

*Sauce Mousseuse à la Vanille*

*This delicate sauce is suitable to serve with dessert waffles, pancakes or omelets.*

*To make 1 ¾ cups [425 ml.]*

| | | |
|---|---|---|
| ½ | vanilla bean | ½ |
| ½ cup | sugar | 125 ml. |
| ⅓ cup | water | 75 ml. |
| 7 | egg yolks, lightly beaten | 7 |
| | heavy cream, whipped | |

In a saucepan over low heat, dissolve the sugar in the water, then bring it to a boil and cook the syrup for one minute. Add the half vanilla bean and set the syrup aside for 20 minutes to allow the vanilla flavor to infuse.

Remove the vanilla bean from the syrup and pour the syrup into the egg yolks, stirring constantly. Strain the egg-and-syrup mixture into a heavy pan. Place the pan over very low heat, and whisk the mixture until it is very thick and frothy. Remove the pan from the heat and continue to whisk the mixture while it cools. When it is cold, fold in several spoonfuls of whipped cream.

URBAIN DUBOIS AND ÉMILE BERNARD
LA CUISINE CLASSIQUE

## Tea Sauce

*This zesty sauce is suitable for hot or cold puddings.*

*To make 2 cups [½ liter]*

| | | |
|---|---|---|
| ⅓ cup | strong black tea | 75 ml. |
| 3 tbsp. | brandy | 45 ml. |
| | sugar | |
| | **Custard** | |
| 4 | egg yolks | 4 |
| 2 tbsp. | milk | 30 ml. |
| 1 ¼ cups | cream | 300 ml. |

First prepare the custard. Mix the egg yolks with the milk. In a saucepan, stir the cream over gentle heat until it comes to a boil. Remove the saucepan from the heat and quickly stir in the egg mixture.

Pour the tea and the brandy into a bowl and stir in the custard. Sweeten the sauce with sugar to taste.

MASSEY AND SON'S COMPREHENSIVE PUDDING BOOK

# Standard Preparations

## White Sauce

*Sauce Béchamel*

*To make about 1 ½ cups [375 ml.]*

| | | |
|---|---|---|
| 2 tbsp. | butter | 30 ml. |
| 2 tbsp. | flour | 30 ml. |
| 2 cups | milk | ½ liter |
| | salt and pepper | |
| | freshly grated nutmeg (optional) | |

Melt the butter in a heavy saucepan. Stir in the flour and cook, stirring, over low heat for two to three minutes. Pour in all of the milk, whisking constantly to blend the mixture smooth. Increase the heat and continue whisking while the sauce comes to a boil. Season with a very little salt. Reduce the heat and simmer for at least 45 minutes, stirring occasionally to prevent the sauce from sticking to the bottom of the pan. When the sauce thickens to the desired consistency, add pepper, and a pinch of nutmeg if you like; taste for seasoning and correct it if necessary.

*Crème (Cream sauce).* Whisk up to 1 cup [¼ liter] of heavy cream into 1 ½ cups [375 ml.] of white sauce. Yield: about 2 cups [½ liter].

*Bohémienne (Tangy enriched white sauce).* Stir ¾ cup [175 ml.] of white sauce until it is cold. Whisk in two egg yolks and 2 tablespoons [30 ml.] of tarragon vinegar. Season with salt and pepper to taste. Whisk in ¾ cup of olive oil in a light trickle, as for mayonnaise. Finish the sauce with more tarragon vinegar to taste. Serve the sauce with cold meats or hot or cold vegetables. Yield: about 2 cups [½ liter].

*Cardinal (Truffle-and-lobster-flavored white sauce).* Mix 1½ cups [375 ml.] of white sauce with ⅓ cup [75 ml.] of fish stock *(recipe, page 164)* and 2 to 3 tablespoons [30 to 45 ml.] of liquid from preserved truffles. Boil the mixture until it has reduced to about 1½ cups. Remove the pan from the heat, stir in 2 tablespoons of cream, 2 tablespoons of lobster-butter pieces *(recipe, page 157)* and a little cayenne pepper. Serve the sauce with lobster or fish. Yield: about 2 cups [½ liter].

*Mornay (Cheese sauce).* Make 2 cups [½ liter] of cream sauce and stir in about ⅓ cup [75 ml.] of heavy cream. Add about 3 tablespoons [45 ml.] each of grated Gruyère and Parmesan cheeses, stirring until the cheeses have melted. Remove the pan from the heat and finish the sauce with 1 tablespoon [15 ml.] of butter, added in pieces. Serve the sauce with fish or cooked vegetables. Yield: about 2½ cups [625 ml.]. If the sauce is to be used for a gratin, stir in an additional ⅓ cup of cream in place of the butter. Yield: about 2½ cups.

*Nantua (Crayfish-flavored white sauce).* Make 1½ cups [375 ml.] of sauce and stir in ⅓ cup [75 ml.] of cream. Remove the pan from the heat, then stir in 3 tablespoons [45 ml.] of crayfish-butter pieces *(recipe, page 157)* and, if you like, add a garnish of crayfish tails. Serve the sauce with poached white fish or use it to make a gratin of crayfish tails. Yield: about 2 cups [½ liter].

*Soubise (Onion sauce).* Make 1½ cups [375 ml.] of white sauce and 1½ cups of onion purée *(pages 38-39)*. Combine the white sauce and the onion purée. Reheat and stir in ½ cup [125 ml.] of cream. Serve this sauce with lamb. Yield: about 3 cups [¾ liter].

---

## Compound Butter

*To make about 10 ounces [300 g.]*

| ½ lb. | unsalted butter | ¼ kg. |
|---|---|---|
| 8 | salt anchovies, soaked, filleted, rinsed and dried | 8 |

Soften the butter to room temperature or beat it to make it pliable. In a large mortar or heavy bowl, pound the anchovies with a pestle until they form a coarse paste. Using a pestle or wooden spoon, work the butter into the anchovy paste. Press the flavored butter through a very fine-meshed drum sieve with a flexible scraper. Use the butter immediately or cover and refrigerate it.

*Crayfish butter.* Poach ½ pound [¼ kg.] of live crayfish in a court bouillon *(recipe, page 164)* for five to 10 minutes. Let the crayfish cool in their cooking liquid. Pull off the tail of each crayfish, remove its shell and reserve the tail meat for a garnish or main dish. Place the shells and heads in a mortar and pound them to a creamy paste. Pass this paste through the medium or coarse disk of a food mill to remove fragments of shell, then pass this purée through a fine sieve into a heavy bowl. Work in ½ pound of softened butter. Sieve the butter again if necessary.

*Herb butter.* Remove the stems from 2 cups [½ liter] of mixed fresh parsley, chives, tarragon and chervil. Blanch the leaves in boiling water for one minute, drain them and press them dry in a towel. Blanch two finely chopped shallots for one minute, then drain and dry them. Place the herbs and shallots in a mortar, add a little coarse salt and pound them to a fine purée. Work in ½ pound [¼ kg.] of softened butter. Press the compound butter through a fine sieve.

*Lobster butter.* Plunge a live 1-pound [½-kg.] female lobster into a large pot half-full of simmering water. Return the water to a simmer and simmer the lobster, uncovered, for 25 minutes. Remove the lobster and drain it. Twist off the claws, tail and legs and use their meat for a main dish. Place the tail and leg shells in a mortar and pound them to a creamy paste. Pass this paste through the medium or coarse disk of a food mill to remove fragments of shell, then pass this purée through a fine sieve into a heavy bowl. Break open the body of the lobster, extract the tomalley and roe, and mash them along with the shell purée with ½ pound [¼ kg.] of softened butter. Pound the mixture until it is smooth and sieve it again if necessary.

*Shallot butter.* Blanch three finely chopped shallots for one to two minutes, then drain them. Pound the shallots in a mortar with ½ pound [¼ kg.] of softened butter. Rub the purée through a fine sieve. Remove and discard any fibers that remain in the sieve.

---

## Whipped Butter Sauce

### Beurre Blanc

For a creamier, more delicately flavored sauce, increase the butter to ¾ pound [350 g.].

*To make about 1½ cups [375 ml.]*

| ½ lb. | cold butter, cut into small cubes | ¼ kg. |
|---|---|---|
| ¼ cup | dry white wine | 50 ml. |
| ¼ cup | white wine vinegar | 50 ml. |
| 2 | shallots, finely chopped | 2 |
| | salt and pepper | |

In a heavy stainless-steel, enameled or tin-lined pan, simmer the wine and the vinegar with the shallots over low heat until only enough liquid remains to moisten the shallots. Remove the pan from the heat, season the mixture with salt and pepper, and allow it to cool for a few minutes. Place the pan on a heat-diffusing pad over very low heat and whisk in the butter cubes, a handful at a time, adding more after the preceding batch begins to disappear. Remove the pan from the heat as soon as all the butter has been incorporated and the sauce has the consistency of light cream.

## Bread Sauce

To make the sauce thicker, whisk in more bread crumbs after removing the onion and seasonings. If a thinner consistency is preferred, add more cream.

*To make about 2 cups [ ½ liter]*

| | | |
|---|---|---|
| 4 | slices stale homemade-style white bread, crumbled | 4 |
| 2 cups | milk | ½ liter |
| 1 | onion, stuck with 2 whole cloves | 1 |
| 1 | bay leaf | 1 |
| 1 or 2 | blades mace | 1 or 2 |
| | salt | |
| ½ cup | heavy cream | 125 ml. |
| 2 tbsp. | cold butter, cut into small cubes | 30 ml. |

Pour the milk into a heavy saucepan. Add the onion, bay leaf, mace and a pinch of salt, and bring the milk to a boil. Stir in the bread crumbs, then reduce the heat to low. Stirring occasionally, simmer the milk for about 20 minutes. Remove the onion and herbs with a slotted spoon, and whisk the cream into the sauce. Off the heat, whisk in the butter.

## Vinaigrette

The proportion of vinegar to oil may be varied according to taste, but one part vinegar to four parts oil is a good ratio. Fresh lemon juice may replace the vinegar.

*To make about ½ cup [125 ml.]*

| | | |
|---|---|---|
| 1 tsp. | salt | 5 ml. |
| ¼ tsp. | freshly ground black pepper | 1 ml. |
| 2 tbsp. | wine vinegar | 30 ml. |
| ½ cup | oil | 125 ml. |

Put the salt and pepper into a small bowl. Add the vinegar and stir until the salt dissolves. Then stir in the oil.

*Garlic vinaigrette.* Pound half a garlic clove to a purée with the salt and pepper before adding the vinegar.

*Green vinaigrette.* Soak, fillet, rinse and dry two salt anchovies, and pound them in a mortar with a garlic clove, 1 teaspoon [5 ml.] of coarse salt and some freshly ground pepper. When the mixture forms a smooth paste, stir in the vinegar, then about ⅓ cup [75 ml.] of oil. Stir in 2 tablespoons [30 ml.] of parboiled, squeezed and finely chopped spinach, together with 1 tablespoon [15 ml.] of chopped capers and 2 tablespoons of chopped mixed fresh parsley, chives, tarragon, basil and chervil leaves.

*Mustard vinaigrette.* Mix 1 teaspoon [5 ml.] of Dijon mustard with the salt and pepper. Add the vinegar and stir until the mustard is dissolved before adding the oil.

*Ravigote sauce.* Make ½ cup [125 ml.] of vinaigrette. Stir in 1 tablespoon [15 ml.] of chopped capers, 1 tablespoon of finely chopped onion and 2 tablespoons [30 ml.] of finely chopped mixed fresh chives, parsley, chervil and tarragon.

*Tomato vinaigrette.* Peel and halve one large, ripe tomato; squeeze out the seeds and juice and press the flesh through a sieve. Stir together the salt and pepper and vinegar, then mix in the puréed tomato. Gradually stir in ½ cup [125 ml.] of oil.

*Vinaigrette with egg.* Before adding the oil, stir in the yolk of a soft-boiled egg. If desired, chop the cooked part of the egg white and add it to the prepared vinaigrette. Fines herbes and chopped shallot may also be added to taste.

## Lemon and Cream Sauce

To flavor the sauce with mint, lightly crush six to eight mint leaves, and macerate them in the lemon juice for 15 minutes. For this sauce, use the pasteurized—but not ultrapasteurized—heavy cream obtainable at health-food stores.

*To make about 1 ½ cups [375 ml.]*

| | | |
|---|---|---|
| 3 tbsp. | fresh lemon juice | 45 ml. |
| | salt and pepper | |
| 1 ¼ cups | heavy cream | 300 ml. |

Put the lemon juice in a bowl and add salt and pepper. Stir the mixture until the salt dissolves. Stirring constantly, add the cream in a thin stream.

*Red pepper and cream sauce.* Dissolve salt and pepper in 1 ½ tablespoons [22½ ml.] of lemon juice, then stir in 2 to 3 tablespoons [30 to 45 ml.] of puréed red pepper. Stirring all the time, gradually incorporate light cream—1 to 1½ cups [250 to 375 ml.]—until the sauce has achieved the consistency and color required.

## Crème Fraîche

For best results, use the pasteurized—but not ultrapasteurized—heavy cream obtainable at health-food stores.

*To make about 2 cups [ ½ liter]*

| | | |
|---|---|---|
| 2 cups | heavy cream | ½ liter |
| 1 tbsp. | cultured buttermilk | 15 ml. |

In a small, heavy enameled saucepan, stir the cream and buttermilk together until well blended. Set the pan over low heat and insert a meat-and-yeast thermometer into the cream mixture. Stirring gently but constantly, warm the mixture until the thermometer registers 85° F. [30° C.]

Immediately remove the pan from the heat and pour the cream mixture into a 1-quart [1-liter] jar that has been scalded by filling it with boiling water, then pouring out the water. Cover the jar loosely with foil or wax paper. Set the cream mixture aside at a room temperature of 60° to 85° F. [15° to 30° C.] for eight to 24 hours, or until it reaches the consistency of whipped cream.

Cover the jar tightly. Refrigerated, the cream will keep for about a week.

## Carrot Sauce

*To make 4 cups [1 liter]*

| | | |
|---|---|---|
| about 10 | carrots, peeled and trimmed | about 10 |
| 7 tbsp. | butter, 4 tbsp. [60 ml.] cut into small cubes | 105 ml. |
| about 1 tbsp. | sugar | about 15 ml. |
| | salt | |
| about 1¼ cups | heavy cream | about 300 ml. |

In a saucepan, combine the carrots, 3 tablespoons [45 ml.] of the butter, sugar to taste, a little salt and enough water to cover the carrots halfway. Bring the water to a boil, then partially cover the pan and simmer the carrots, shaking the pan occasionally, until they are very tender—40 to 45 minutes. Remove the lid and reduce the cooking liquid over high heat until it becomes a thick glaze—five to 10 minutes.

Purée the carrots and their glaze in a food processor. Return the purée to the pan and reheat it over high heat, stirring continuously. Whisk in enough cream to give the sauce a pouring consistency. Finally, remove the pan from the heat and whisk in the cubed butter, a little at a time.

## Tomato Purée

When fresh, ripe tomatoes are not available, use canned plum tomatoes. The sauce can be flavored with various herbs: Parsley, basil, oregano and marjoram are all suitable.

*To make about 1¼ cups [300 ml.]*

| | | |
|---|---|---|
| 5 | medium-sized very ripe tomatoes, chopped | 5 |
| 1 | onion, finely chopped | 1 |
| 2 | garlic cloves, chopped | 2 |
| 1 tbsp. | olive oil | 15 ml. |
| 3 or 4 | sprigs fresh thyme or 1 tsp. [5 ml.] dried thyme leaves | 3 or 4 |
| 1 | bay leaf | 1 |
| 1 to 2 tsp. | sugar (optional) | 5 to 10 ml. |
| | salt and freshly ground black pepper | |

In a large enameled, stainless-steel or tin-lined pan, gently fry the onion and garlic in the oil until they are soft but not brown. Add the tomatoes, thyme, bay leaf and sugar if you are using it. Simmer the mixture gently, uncovered, for about 30 minutes, stirring it occasionally with a wooden spoon. When the tomatoes have been reduced to a thick pulp, press the mixture through a sieve with a wooden pestle.

Return the purée to the pan and, stirring frequently, cook it over low heat for about 30 minutes. Season the purée with salt and pepper to taste just before serving.

## Veal Stock

To produce a very gelatinous stock suitable for use as aspic, add two split, blanched calf's feet to the ingredients. Then reduce the finished stock briefly after removing all of the fat so that the stock will set to a firm jelly.

*To make about 3 quarts [3 liters]*

| | | |
|---|---|---|
| 2 lb. | veal shank | 1 kg. |
| 2 lb. | beef shin | 1 kg. |
| 2 lb. | chicken backs, necks and wing tips | 1 kg. |
| about 5 quarts | water | about 5 liters |
| 1 | bouquet garni, including leek and celery | 1 |
| 1 | garlic bulb | 1 |
| 2 | medium-sized onions, 1 stuck with 2 whole cloves | 2 |
| 4 | large carrots | 4 |

Place a round wire rack in the bottom of a large stockpot to prevent the ingredients from sticking. Fit all of the meat, bones and chicken pieces into the pot and add enough water to cover them by about 1½ inches [4 cm.]. Bring the water very slowly to a boil while using a spoon to skim off the scum that rises. Keep skimming, occasionally adding a glass of cold water, until no more scum rises—after about 10 to 15 minutes. Add the bouquet garni, garlic, onions and carrots, and skim once more as the liquid returns to a boil. Reduce the heat to very low, cover the pot with the lid ajar and simmer for at least five and preferably seven hours. From time to time, skim off any fat that rises to the surface.

Strain the stock into a large bowl, then strain it again through a colander lined with dampened muslin or cheesecloth. Let the stock cool, then refrigerate it. When the stock has set to a jelly, scrape off the solid layer of fat and discard it. Remove any remaining traces of fat by pressing a paper towel gently onto the surface of the stock.

*Beef stock.* Substitute 4 pounds [2 kg.] of beef tail, shank or chuck for the veal shank and the chicken pieces, and simmer the stock for five hours.

*Chicken stock.* Omit the veal and beef, and substitute about 5 pounds [2½ kg.] of chicken carcasses, necks, feet, wings, gizzards and hearts. Simmer the chicken stock for about two hours.

*Game stock.* Add 2 pounds [1 kg.] of game carcasses and trimmings to the veal stock ingredients.

*Lamb or pork stock.* Use 7 pounds [3½ kg.] of meaty bones and trimmings of the appropriate meat instead of the veal, beef and chicken; lamb and pork stock are only used in dishes made with their respective meats.

## Meat Glaze

### Glace de Viande

Prepare veal stock (recipe, page 159). When all of the fat has been removed, put the stock into a saucepan just large enough to hold it and bring it to a boil. Set the pan half off the heat and let the stock boil gently. From time to time, skim off the skin of impurities that collects on the cooler side of the pan. When the stock has reduced by about a third—after one hour or so—strain it through a fine-meshed sieve into a smaller pan. Skimming occasionally, continue to simmer the stock gently for another hour, or until it again is reduced by about a third. Strain it once more into a smaller pan and let it reduce for another hour. The liquid will be thick and syrupy. Pour it into a bowl, let it cool, then refrigerate it. The glaze will keep in the refrigerator almost indefinitely. Yield: about 1½ cups [375 ml.].

## Enriched Veal Stock

### Coulis

*To make about 3 cups [¾ liter]*

| | | |
|---|---|---|
| 2 tbsp. | olive oil | 30 ml. |
| 4 lb. | veal shank | 2 kg. |
| 1 | meaty ham knucklebone, preferably from salt-cured ham | 1 |
| 2 | carrots, coarsely chopped | 2 |
| 2 | onions, coarsely chopped | 2 |
| 1¼ cups | dry white wine | 300 ml. |
| 2 quarts | veal stock (recipe, page 159) | 2 liters |
| 1 | bouquet garni | 1 |

Heat the olive oil in a heavy pot just broad enough to hold all the meats in one layer. Add the meats and the vegetables. Cover and cook them over low heat, turning them occasionally, until the juices exuded from the meats form caramelized deposits in the bottom of the pot—about 45 minutes. Pour in about half of the wine and scrape the pot vigorously with a spatula to incorporate the deposits into the liquid. Increase the heat and let the liquid evaporate. When the liquid starts to caramelize, pour in the rest of the wine; deglaze the pot again and reduce the liquid once more.

Add enough of the veal stock to cover the meats and vegetables. Bring to a simmer, repeatedly skimming off the scum that rises to the surface. When no more scum rises, add the bouquet garni. Set the lid slightly ajar over the pot and cook the mixture over very low heat for about four hours.

Remove the pieces of meat from the pan and discard them. Take out the bouquet garni, place it in a sieve set over a large bowl, press out all the juices and discard it. Then strain the *coulis* through the sieve—a ladleful at a time—and press out all the juices from the vegetables.

Pour the strained *coulis* into a heavy pan and set half of the pan over low heat. Simmer the *coulis* gently, occasional-ly removing the skin of impurities that collects on the cooler side of the pan. When the liquid has reduced by half—after an hour—remove the pan from the heat and pour the *coulis* through a fine-meshed sieve into a bowl. Let the *coulis* cool, stirring continuously, then refrigerate it.

## Concentrated Brown Sauce

### Demi-glace

With the addition of a little tomato purée (recipe, page 159), brown sauce becomes *sauce espagnole*, or Spanish brown sauce. Plain brown sauce may be used in any recipe that calls for *sauce espagnole*.

Brown game sauce is made by substituting the bones and trimmings from game birds, rabbit, hare and/or venison for the beef and veal, and by using either game stock or veal stock to moisten the meats. About ⅓ cup [75 ml.] of wine vinegar can be used along with the white wine for deglazing the roasting pan, and four or five juniper berries can be added with the stock.

*To make about 2 cups [½ liter]*

| | | |
|---|---|---|
| 1 lb. | beef shank, cut up | ½ kg. |
| 1 | veal knucklebone, broken up | 1 |
| 2 lb. | boneless lean stewing veal, cubed | 1 kg. |
| 1 lb. | chicken wing tips, backs and necks | ½ kg. |
| 1 | 8-by-6-inch [20-by-15-cm.] piece of pork rind, parboiled for 2 to 3 minutes, refreshed in cold water, drained and coarsely chopped | 1 |
| 2 | carrots, coarsely chopped | 2 |
| 2 | leeks, coarsely chopped | 2 |
| 2 | onions, coarsely chopped | 2 |
| 1 | celery rib, coarsely chopped | 1 |
| 4 or 5 | garlic cloves, crushed to a paste | 4 or 5 |
| 2 | sprigs thyme | 2 |
| 1 | bay leaf | 1 |
| about ¼ cup | oil | about 50 ml. |
| ¼ cup | flour | 50 ml. |
| 3 cups | dry white wine | ¾ liter |
| about 2 quarts | veal stock (recipe, page 159) or water | about 2 liters |
| | salt | |

In a large, shallow roasting pan, distribute the meats, chopped vegetables, garlic and herbs. Toss all of the ingredients with the oil until they are evenly coated. Cook the meats in a preheated 450° F. [230° C.] oven until they are well browned—about 30 minutes; stir the meats about halfway through. Sprinkle in the flour, stir, and return the pan to the oven for about 10 minutes to brown the flour.

Set the pan over medium heat. To deglaze the pan, pour in the white wine and scrape the caramelized deposits on the bottom of the pan into the wine. Stirring constantly, cook the deglazing mixture until most of the liquid has evaporated—about 10 minutes.

Transfer the contents of the pan to a stockpot and add enough veal stock or water to cover the meats. Partially cover the pot, bring the mixture to a boil, then simmer it very gently for at least three hours, preferably for five to six.

Ladle the meats and vegetables—a small batch at a time—into a sieve set over a deep bowl. Discard the bones. Using a pestle, press the juices from the meats and vegetables through the sieve. Strain the liquid remaining in the pot. Let the sauce cool, then remove the fat from its surface.

Ladle the sauce through a fine-meshed sieve into a pan. Set the pan to one side of medium heat and let the sauce simmer and reduce for about one hour. From time to time, skim off the skin that forms on the cooler side of the pan. Toward the end of the cooking, adjust the seasoning.

*Bordelaise (Red-wine-flavored brown sauce).* Boil 4 cups [1 liter] of red wine until it is reduced to 2 cups [½ liter]. Add the reduced red wine to 2 cups of brown sauce. Simmer over medium heat until the mixture has reduced to about 2 cups. Stir in 1 tablespoon [15 ml.] of meat glaze *(recipe, page 160)* and a little lemon juice. This sauce is served with grilled meats. Yield: about 2 cups.

*Moelle (Brown sauce with marrow).* Dice ¼ pound [125 g.] of beef marrow and poach it in salted water for three minutes. Add the marrow to 2 cups [½ liter] of *sauce bordelaise* made—if you like—with reduced white rather than red wine. A little chopped fresh parsley may be stirred in. This sauce is served with grilled beef. Yield: about 2 cups.

*Chasseur (Brown sauce with mushrooms and tomato).* Sauté 1 cup [¼ liter] of finely chopped fresh mushrooms in 1 tablespoon [15 ml.] of butter until they are golden. Add 1 tablespoon of chopped shallots, one or two halved, seeded and chopped tomatoes and 1 cup of dry white wine. Simmer until the mixture is reduced to half its original volume. Add 1 cup of brown sauce and return the mixture to a boil. Garnish the sauce with 1 teaspoon [5 ml.] of chopped fresh parsley. This sauce is served with sautéed chicken, rabbit or veal; the sauté pan can be deglazed with stock and the deglazing juices added to the sauce. Yield: about 2 cups [½ liter].

*Chateaubriand (Brown sauce with herbs and mushrooms).* Place ¼ cup [50 ml.] of chopped shallots, a sprig of thyme, a bay leaf, ¼ cup of finely chopped fresh mushrooms and ½ cup [125 ml.] of dry white wine in a pan and simmer them until the liquid is reduced to ⅓ cup [75 ml.]. Add 1 cup [¼ liter] of brown sauce. Sieve the mixture and return it to a boil. Remove the pan from the heat, swirl in 4 tablespoons [60 ml.] of chilled butter pieces and a little fresh tarragon and chopped fresh parsley. This sauce can also be made using 1 cup of velouté *(recipe, page 162)* instead of brown sauce. *Sauce Chateaubriand* is served with grilled beef. Yield: about 2½ cups. [625 ml.].

*Lyonnaise (Onion-flavored brown sauce).* Cook ¼ cup [50 ml.] of thinly sliced onion in 1 tablespoon [15 ml.] of butter until soft and yellow. Add ½ cup [125 ml.] each of dry white wine and wine vinegar, and simmer until the liquid is reduced to ⅓ cup [75 ml.]. Add 2 cups [½ liter] of brown sauce and reheat. This sauce is served with grilled meats. Yield: about 2½ cups [625 ml.].

*Madère (Madeira sauce).* Boil 2 cups [½ liter] of brown sauce, stirring it all the time, until it is reduced to about 1½ cups [375 ml.]. Add 2 to 3 tablespoons [30 to 45 ml.] of Madeira, or enough Madeira to bring it back to its original consistency. This sauce is served with braised ham and tongue. Yield: about 2 cups.

*Périgueux (Madeira sauce with truffles).* Add 1 tablespoon [15 ml.] of liquid from preserved truffles to 1½ cups [375 ml.] of *sauce madère.* Garnish with ⅓ cup [75 ml.] of diced truffle. (When the garnish is sliced truffle, this sauce is sometimes known as *périgourdine.)* The sauce is usually served with grilled beef or with poached white meats. Yield: about 2 cups [½ liter].

*Poivrade ordinaire (Pepper sauce).* Prepare 2 cups [½ liter] of brown sauce, substituting red wine vinegar for ½ cup [125 ml.] of the white wine. After the sauce has been reduced, wrap 10 crushed black peppercorns in cheesecloth and drop the bag into the sauce. Cook the sauce for five to 10 minutes, then discard the bag of peppercorns. This sauce is served with game or hot meat patés. Yield: about 2 cups.

*Poivrade gibier (Pepper sauce for game).* Prepare *sauce poivrade ordinaire,* using a brown game sauce. Yield: about 2 cups [½ liter].

*Chevreuil (Red-wine-flavored pepper sauce).* Prepare a *sauce bordelaise,* substituting *sauce poivrade gibier* for the brown sauce. Finish with a little cayenne pepper. This sauce is served with game. Yield: about 2 cups [½ liter].

*Diane (Creamed pepper sauce).* Make 2 cups [½ liter] of *sauce poivrade gibier* and finish it by stirring in ½ cup [125 ml.] of heavy cream (or more, to taste). This sauce is served with game and grilled meats. Yield: about 2¼ cups [550 ml.].

*Grand-veneur (Pepper sauce with currants and cream).* Make 2 cups [½ liter] of *sauce poivrade gibier.* Melt 1 tablespoon [15 ml.] of currant jelly over low heat and stir in ½ cup [125 ml.] of heavy cream. Remove the pan from the heat and stir this mixture into the sauce. This sauce is served with roast or broiled venison. Yield: about 2½ cups [625 ml.].

*Romaine (Sweet-and-sour brown sauce).* Cook 2 tablespoons [30 ml.] of sugar until it caramelizes. Add ¼ cup [50 ml.] of vinegar and stir until the caramel dissolves. Add 2 cups [½ liter] of brown game sauce or *sauce poivrade.* Cook until the mixture is reduced to about 1½ cups [375 ml.]. Garnish with 2 tablespoons [30 ml.] of toasted pine nuts and with 2 tablespoons each of seedless white raisins and dried currants, plumped by soaking in warm water. This sauce is served with roast or broiled venison. Yield: about 2 cups.

*Zingara.* Mix 1 cup [¼ liter] of tomato purée *(recipe, page 159)* with 2 cups [½ liter] of brown sauce. Add 2 tablespoons [30 ml.] of Madeira and a little cayenne pepper. Garnish the sauce with 2 tablespoons each of julienned mushrooms, ham and tongue and a small truffle cut into julienne. This sauce is served with broiled chicken or roast veal. Yield: about 3 cups [¾ liter].

# Velouté Sauce

For a very fine and concentrated velouté, the sauce should be simmered and reduced over low heat for several hours—with occasional skimming as it cooks. To produce 2 cups [½ liter] of such a sauce, you will need to start with three times the quantities of ingredients given here.

| To make about 2 cups [½ liter] | | |
|---|---|---|
| 4 tbsp. | butter | 60 ml. |
| ¼ cup | flour | 50 ml. |
| 4 cups | veal, chicken or game stock *(recipe, page 159)* or fish stock *(recipe, page 164)* | 1 liter |
| | heavy cream | |

Melt the butter in a heavy saucepan over low heat. With a whisk, stir in the flour to make a roux. Still stirring, cook for a minute or two. Pour the stock into the pan, whisking constantly. Increase the heat and continue to whisk until the sauce comes to a boil. Reduce the heat to low and move the pan half off the heat so that the liquid simmers on only one side. A skin of impurities will form on the surface of the still side. Remove this skin periodically with a spoon. Cook the sauce for at least 45 minutes to reduce it to about half its original volume. Stir in enough cream to give the sauce the required consistency.

*Aurore (Tomato-flavored velouté)*. Make 2 cups [½ liter] of velouté using veal, chicken or fish stock. Add ⅓ cup [75 ml.] of tomato purée *(recipe, page 159)*. Remove the pan from the heat and whisk in 4 tablespoons [60 ml.] of butter pieces, a handful at a time. This sauce is served with vegetables, chicken or fish. Yield: about 2½ cups [625 ml.].

*Bercy (Wine-flavored fish velouté)*. Make 2 cups [½ liter] of velouté using fish stock. Sauté ¼ cup [50 ml.] of chopped shallots in a little butter, add 1 cup [¼ liter] of dry white wine, and boil the mixture until it has reduced to about a third of its original volume. Strain the reduced liquid and mix it with the fish velouté; reduce the sauce to a coating consistency. Remove the pan from the heat, stir in a little

fresh lemon juice, 4 tablespoons [60 ml.] of butter pieces and some chopped fresh parsley. This sauce is served with poached fish. Yield: about 2½ cups [625 ml.].

*Marinière (Mussel-flavored fish velouté)*. Make 2½ cups [625 ml.] of *sauce Bercy*. Poach 12 to 18 mussels *(page 10)*. Shuck them and strain their cooking liquid. Add ⅔ cup [150 ml.] of the liquid to the sauce. Reduce the sauce to its original quantity and then garnish with the mussels. This sauce is served with fish. Yield: about 2½ cups.

*Bonnefoy (White-wine-and-shallot veal velouté)*. Make 2 cups [½ liter] of velouté using veal stock. Boil 1 cup [¼ liter] of dry white wine with ½ cup [125 ml.] of chopped shallots until only a little liquid remains. Mix the reduction with the velouté and simmer for 20 minutes. Sieve, reheat, then garnish the sauce with a little chopped fresh parsley and tarragon leaves. This sauce is served with fish and white meats. Yield: about 2 cups.

*Bretonne (Aromatic fish velouté)*. Make 2 cups [½ liter] of velouté using fish stock. Combine ¼ cup [50 ml.] each of leek, celery, scallion and mushroom julienne with a little butter, and sweat the aromatics in the butter until they are soft. Mix the julienne with the fish velouté. This sauce is served with poached fish. Yield: about 2½ cups [625 ml.].

*Chivry (Herb-flavored chicken velouté)*. Make 2 cups [½ liter] of velouté using part of the chicken's poaching liquid. Put ¼ cup [50 ml.] of fines herbes and a pinch of chopped fresh burnet, if available, into 1 cup [¼ liter] of dry white wine. Cover and let the flavors infuse for at least 10 minutes. Strain, then add to the chicken velouté. Boil until the mixture has reduced to about 2 cups. Remove the pan from the heat, and stir in 4 tablespoons [60 ml.] of herb butter *(recipe, page 157)* that has been cut into pieces. This sauce is served with poached chicken. Yield: about 2¼ cups [550 ml.].

*Normande (White-wine fish velouté)*. This sauce, sometimes known as *sauce vin blanc,* usually accompanies sole poached in fish stock and mushroom cooking liquid. The poaching liquid is added to the sauce and, classically, the dish is garnished with poached oysters, mussels, shrimp and mushrooms and—in many cases—with sliced truffle and whole crayfish. The poaching liquid of the garnishes is often added to the sauce; the sauce may be finished with crayfish butter *(recipe, page 157)* or another flavored butter. A simpler garnish of mushrooms and mussels alone will suit today's tastes better. Any delicately flavored fish can be prepared in this way—turbot or flounder, for instance.

Make 2 cups [½ liter] of velouté with fish stock. Add ⅔ cup [150 ml.] of the fish's poaching liquid and ⅓ cup [75 ml.] of mussel cooking liquid. Reduce the mixture to 2 cups. Mix 2 tablespoons [30 ml.] of the velouté with four egg yolks and 3 tablespoons [45 ml.] of heavy cream, then gradually stir this mixture into the velouté. Stirring continuously, cook the sauce over gentle heat until it begins to thicken. Remove the pan from the heat and stir in 4 tablespoons [60 ml.] of butter pieces. Yield: about 3 cups [¾ liter].

*Poulette (Egg-yolk-enriched velouté)*. This sauce—also known as *sauce allemande* or *sauce blanquette*—is made in the same way as *sauce normande,* except that the velouté is based on veal or chicken stock or poaching liquid from the meats to be sauced. If mushrooms are included in the sauce's garnish, their cooking liquid is added to the sauce.

Make 2 cups [½ liter] of velouté using veal or chicken stock. Mix 2 to 3 tablespoons [30 to 45 ml.] of the velouté with four egg yolks, 3 tablespoons of heavy cream and 1½ tablespoons [22½ ml.] of fresh lemon juice. Remove the pan from the heat and slowly stir this mixture into the velouté. Return the pan to low heat and stir until the sauce is lightly thickened, but do not let it boil. To finish the sauce, remove the pan from the heat and stir in 4 tablespoons [60 ml.] of butter pieces. This sauce is served with poached white and variety meats. Yield: about 3 cups [¾ liter].

*Ravigote (Tangy wine-flavored veal velouté).* Make 2 cups [½ liter] of velouté using veal stock. Mix ½ cup [125 ml.] of white wine with 2 tablespoons [30 ml.] of white wine vinegar. Boil the wine-and-vinegar mixture until it has reduced to about half of its original volume. Add the reduced liquid to the velouté. Remove the pan from the heat, stir in 2 tablespoons of shallot-butter pieces *(recipe, page 157),* and a little chopped chervil, tarragon and chives. This sauce is served with white meats. Yield: about 2½ cups [625 ml.].

*Suprême (Cream-enriched chicken velouté).* This sauce accompanies poached chicken, and the chicken's poaching liquid is used to make the sauce. The richest sauce is made by poaching the chicken in veal stock, but the chicken also may be poached in chicken stock or water. If mushrooms garnish the dish, their cooking liquid is added to the sauce. The sauce can be finished with a flavored butter.

Make 2 cups [½ liter] of velouté with some of the chicken's poaching liquid. Add ¾ cup [375 ml.] of heavy cream, a little at a time, and reduce the mixture to 2 cups over fairly high heat. Strain the sauce through a fine-meshed sieve. Remove the pan from the heat and stir in 2 to 3 more tablespoons [30 to 45 ml.] of cream and 2 tablespoons of butter pieces. Yield: about 2½ cups [625 ml.].

*Crème aurore (Tomato-flavored cream velouté).* Incorporate about ½ cup [125 ml.] of tomato purée *(recipe, page 159)* into the finished *sauce suprême* to make it pink. This sauce is served with white meats. Yield: about 3 cups [¾ liter].

*Hongroise (Paprika-flavored cream velouté).* Sweat one chopped onion seasoned with a large pinch of paprika in butter until it is soft but not browned. Add ⅓ cup [75 ml.] of dry white wine and a small bouquet garni. Boil the liquid until it has reduced to about a third of its original volume, then add it to the finished *sauce suprême.* Skimming frequently, simmer the sauce gently for about 10 minutes, then strain it. This sauce is served with fried meats. Yield: about 2½ cups [625 ml.].

*Ivoire (Glazed cream velouté).* Stir 2 tablespoons [30 ml.] of meat glaze *(recipe, page 160)* into the finished *sauce suprême.* If this sauce is finished with red-pepper butter or if a red-pepper purée is added, it becomes *sauce Albufera,* or red-pepper-flavored cream velouté. This sauce is served with roasted or grilled meats. Yield: about 2 cups [½ liter].

*Vénitienne (Tangy fish velouté).* Make 2 cups [½ liter] of velouté using fish stock. Boil 1 tablespoon [15 ml.] of chopped shallots with ¼ cup [50 ml.] each of tarragon vinegar and dry white wine until only a little liquid remains.

Strain the reduction and add the liquid to the velouté. Remove the pan from the heat, stir in 4 tablespoons [60 ml.] of herb butter *(recipe, page 157)*—a few pieces at a time—and a little chopped fresh chervil and tarragon. This sauce is served with poached fish. Yield: about 2½ cups [625 ml.].

---

## White Aspic Cream
### *Chaud-Froid Blanc*

To make a brown aspic cream—a *chaud-froid brun*—substitute ½ cup [125 ml.] of concentrated brown sauce *(recipe, page 160)* for the heavy cream and reduce the mixture only by about one third. Red aspic cream, or *chaud-froid rouge,* is made by stirring enough tomato or red-pepper purée into the finished white sauce to give it the intensity of color required. A yellow sauce can be made by adding powdered saffron that has been dissolved in hot water, and a green sauce by adding spinach that has been parboiled, squeezed dry and puréed.

To make fish aspic cream, first stir 3 tablespoons [45 ml.] of powdered gelatin—softened in 6 tablespoons [90 ml.] of warm water—into 1 quart [1 liter] of warm fish stock *(recipe, page 164).* Test the consistency of the stock by chilling a spoonful; if it does not set, add another tablespoon [15 ml.] of softened gelatin. Make fish velouté sauce *(recipe, page 162)* with the gelatinous fish stock, and proceed as for white aspic cream, omitting the addition of meat glaze.

| To make about 1½ cups [375 ml.] | | |
|---|---|---|
| 2 cups | velouté sauce *(recipe, page 162)* | ½ liter |
| 2 tbsp. | meat glaze or enriched veal stock *(recipes, page 160)* | 30 ml. |
| 1 cup | heavy cream | ¼ liter |

Over low heat, stir the meat glaze or enriched veal stock into the velouté sauce and bring the mixture to a simmer. Gradually stir in the cream and simmer the mixture until it is reduced to about one half of its original volume. Then pour the sauce into a metal bowl and stir it over ice until it cools and starts to thicken.

# Pan Gravy

*To make about 2 cups [½ liter]*

| | | |
|---|---|---|
| 2 tbsp. | flour | 30 ml. |
| 2 cups | veal or chicken stock *(recipe, page 159)*, heated | ½ liter |

Remove the meat or bird from the roasting pan. Spoon off all but about 2 tablespoons [30 ml.] from the fat remaining in the pan. Over low heat, scrape the bottom of the pan to dislodge clinging brown particles. Stir in the flour and—stirring constantly—cook the mixture for three minutes. Then gradually stir in the heated stock. Continue stirring over low heat until the gravy thickens—about five minutes.

# Court Bouillon

This is an all-purpose poaching liquid for tender white variety meats such as brains and for all kinds of fish and shellfish. The amount of wine can be increased or decreased according to taste. For brains, omit the fennel and garlic. For crayfish, substitute two sprigs of dill for the fennel.

*To make about 2 quarts [2 liters]*

| | | |
|---|---|---|
| 1 | large onion, sliced | 1 |
| 1 | large carrot, sliced | 1 |
| 1 | large leek, sliced | 1 |
| 1 | celery rib, diced | 1 |
| 12 | sprigs fresh parsley | 12 |
| 2 | sprigs thyme | 2 |
| 2 | fennel stalks (optional) | 2 |
| 1 | garlic clove (optional) | 1 |
| 1 | bay leaf | 1 |
| 6 cups | water | 1½ liters |
| | salt | |
| 2 cups | dry red or white wine | ½ liter |
| 5 or 6 | peppercorns | 5 or 6 |

Put the vegetables, herbs and water into a large, nonreactive pan, and season them with a pinch of salt. Bring them to a boil, then reduce the heat, cover and simmer the mixture for about 15 minutes. Pour in the wine and simmer the court bouillon for 15 minutes—adding the peppercorns for the last few minutes of cooking. Strain the court bouillon through a sieve into a bowl or a clean pan before using it.

# Fish Stock

*Fumet de Poisson*

*To make about 2 quarts [2 liters]*

| | | |
|---|---|---|
| 2 lb. | fish heads, bones and trimmings, rinsed and broken into pieces | 1 kg. |
| 1 | onion, sliced | 1 |
| 1 | carrot, sliced | 1 |
| 1 | leek, sliced | 1 |
| 1 | celery rib, cut into pieces | 1 |
| 1 | bay leaf | 1 |
| 2 | sprigs thyme | 2 |
| 2 | sprigs fresh parsley | 2 |
| 2 cups | dry red or white wine | ½ liter |
| about 2 quarts | water | about 2 liters |

Place the fish, vegetables and herbs in a large, nonreactive pot. Add the wine and enough water to cover the fish. Bring it to a boil over low heat. With a large spoon, skim off the scum that rises to the surface as the liquid reaches a simmer. Keep skimming until no more scum rises, then simmer the stock, uncovered, for 30 minutes. Strain the stock through a colander lined with dampened cheesecloth or muslin.

# Mousseline

To color mousseline with spinach, remove the coarse stems from 1 pound [½ kg.] of spinach. Boil the leaves in salted water for one to two minutes, then refresh them in cold water, drain them well and squeeze them dry. Press the spinach through a fine sieve or purée it in a food processor. Stir enough of the purée into the mousseline to produce the desired color.

*To make about 2½ cups [625 ml.]*

| | | |
|---|---|---|
| ½ lb. | whiting, pike, salmon, hake or monkfish fillets, skinned and chopped | ¼ kg. |
| | salt and pepper | |
| | freshly grated nutmeg (optional) | |
| | cayenne pepper (optional) | |
| 1 | egg white | 1 |
| 1 cup | heavy cream | ¼ liter |

Work the fish to a smooth purée by pounding it in a mortar or blending it in a food processor. Season the purée with salt and pepper and add nutmeg and cayenne pepper, if you wish. Add the egg white, pounding or blending until it is completely incorporated. Rub the purée—a little at a time—through a fine-meshed sieve, using a plastic scraper for a drum sieve, but a wooden pestle for other sieves. Pack the purée into a glass or metal bowl and press plastic wrap against the surface. Place the bowl of purée in a larger bowl containing crushed ice and refrigerate it for at least one hour.

Remove the bowls from the refrigerator. Using a wooden spoon, work a little of the cream into the purée. Return the bowls to the refrigerator for 15 minutes. Continue beating in small quantities of cream, refrigerating the mixture for 15 minutes after each addition. Replenish the crushed ice in the larger bowl when necessary.

As soon as the mixture becomes soft enough, beat it vigorously. When about half of the cream has been incorporated, refrigerate the mixture for a few minutes. Lightly whip the remaining cream and fold it in. Cover the mousseline with plastic wrap and refrigerate it until you are ready to use it. The mousseline can be kept safely for two days.

❦

## Mayonnaise

To prevent curdling, all of the ingredients should be at room temperature and the oil should be added very gradually at first. In a covered container, the mayonnaise can be safely refrigerated for three days; stir it well before use. For a tangier mayonnaise, 1 to 2 teaspoons [5 to 10 ml.] of Dijon mustard may be mixed in with the vinegar or lemon juice.

*To make about 2 cups [½ liter]*

| | | |
|---|---|---|
| 2 | egg yolks | 2 |
| | salt and pepper | |
| 1 tbsp. | wine vinegar or fresh lemon juice | 15 ml. |
| 2 cups | oil | ½ liter |

Put the egg yolks in a bowl. Season them with salt and pepper and whisk them until they are smooth. Add the vinegar or lemon juice and mix thoroughly. Whisking constantly, add the oil, drop by drop to begin with. When the sauce starts to thicken, pour the remaining oil in a thin, steady stream, whisking rhythmically. If the mayonnaise becomes too thick, thin it with a little more vinegar or lemon juice or with warm water.

*Andalouse (Tomato-flavored mayonnaise).* Make 2 cups [½ liter] of mayonnaise. Stir in 2 to 3 tablespoons [30 to 45 ml.] of tomato purée *(recipe, page 159)*. Garnish the mayonnaise with a red pepper that has been roasted, seeded, peeled and julienned. This sauce is served with cold meats or fish.

*Chantilly (Cream-enriched mayonnaise).* Make 2 cups [½ liter] of mayonnaise using lemon juice. Beat 3 tablespoons [45 ml.] of heavy cream until foamy but not stiff. Fold the cream into the mayonnaise just before serving. This sauce is served with poached fish and boiled vegetables.

*Mousquétaire (Shallot-flavored mayonnaise).* Make 2 cups [½ liter] of mayonnaise. Boil two or three finely chopped shallots in ½ cup [125 ml.] of dry white wine until virtually no liquid remains. Cool the shallots and then stir them into the mayonnaise. Garnish the mayonnaise with 1 tablespoon [15 ml.] of finely cut fresh chives and a little cayenne pepper. This sauce is served with grilled meats.

*Rémoulade (Pickle-and-herb-flavored mayonnaise).* Prepare 2 cups [½ liter] of mayonnaise, adding 1 tablespoon [15 ml.] of prepared mustard. Stir in 1 tablespoon each of chopped sour gherkins and whole capers, 1 tablespoon of chopped mixed fresh parsley, chervil and tarragon, and two or three finely chopped anchovy fillets. This sauce is served with cold lobster, meat or poultry.

*Suédoise (Apple-and-horseradish mayonnaise).* Make 2 cups [½ liter] of mayonnaise. Stir in 4 tablespoons [60 ml.] of unsweetened apple purée and 1 tablespoon [15 ml.] of freshly grated horseradish. This sauce is served with cold beef.

*Tartare (Pungent mayonnaise).* Make 2 cups [½ liter] of mayonnaise using hard-boiled egg yolks and one raw yolk, as for *sauce gribiche (recipe, page 165)*. Stir in ⅓ cup [75 ml.] of finely chopped onion and 1 tablespoon [15 ml.] of finely cut fresh chives. This sauce is served with fish. Alternatively, make 2 cups of mayonnaise. Stir in finely chopped sour gherkins, capers and fines herbes—varying the proportions according to taste. This is also served with fish.

*Verte (Green mayonnaise).* Make 2 cups [½ liter] of mayonnaise. Blanch ¼ cup [50 ml.] each of fresh parsley, chervil, tarragon, chives and watercress and ½ cup [125 ml.] of spinach leaves separately in boiling water for about two minutes each. Drain and refresh each herb in cold water, then squeeze it dry in a towel. Pound the blanched herbs to a paste, then pass the paste through a sieve. Stir the sieved paste into the mayonnaise. This sauce is served with fried fish and cold vegetables.

❦

## Tangy Mayonnaise

### Sauce Gribiche

This mayonnaise may be used to accompany cold fish and cold variety meats.

*To make about 2½ cups [625 ml.]*

| | | |
|---|---|---|
| 6 | eggs | 6 |
| 1 tsp. | Dijon mustard | 5 ml. |
| 1 tbsp. | fresh lemon juice | 15 ml. |
| 2 cups | oil | ½ liter |
| 1 tbsp. | mixed chopped fresh tarragon, parsley and chervil leaves | 15 ml. |
| 1 tbsp. | mixed chopped sour gherkins and capers | 15 ml. |

Hard-boil five of the eggs. Separate the yolks from the whites. Cut the whites into julienne and set them aside. Mash the hard-boiled yolks with the remaining raw egg yolk and the mustard to form a smooth paste. Add the lemon juice and mix thoroughly. Whisking constantly, add the oil, drop by drop to begin with, then in a steady stream as the sauce begins to thicken. Stir in the chopped fresh herbs and the mixed sour gherkins and capers. Garnish the mayonnaise with the julienned egg whites.

# Hollandaise Sauce

To make a smoother sauce, ⅔ cup [150 ml.] of melted clarified butter can be substituted for the cubed butter. Pour the melted butter, a small ladleful at a time, into the pan, whisking constantly. Do not add more butter until the previous addition has been completely incorporated. If the finished sauce is too thick, thin it by whisking in warm water, 1 tablespoon [15 ml.] at a time, or a little extra lemon juice.

When whisking the butter cubes into the egg-yolk mixture, remove the pan from the water bath if the butter is melting too fast. The side of the saucepan should never be too hot to be comfortably touched by the palm of your hand.

*To make about 1 ½ cups [375 ml.]*

| 3 | egg yolks | 3 |
|---|---|---|
| 1 tbsp. | cold water | 15 ml. |
| | salt and pepper | |
| ½ lb. | cold butter, cut into small cubes | ¼ kg. |
| 1 tbsp. | strained fresh lemon juice | 15 ml. |

To make a water bath, pour water to a depth of about 1 inch [2½ cm.] into a large pan. Place a metal rack or trivet inside the pan. Bring the water to a simmer, then reduce the heat to low. In a smaller heavy saucepan, combine the egg yolks, cold water and a little salt and pepper. Set the saucepan in the water bath and whisk the egg yolks until the mixture is smooth. Whisk a handful of butter cubes into the yolks and, when the butter is absorbed, add more. Repeat until all the butter is incorporated. Whisk the sauce until it becomes thick and creamy. Finally, whisk in the lemon juice.

*Béarnaise (Shallot-and-tarragon-flavored hollandaise).* Combine ⅔ cup [150 ml.] of dry white wine, ¼ cup [50 ml.] of wine vinegar, two finely chopped shallots and ¼ cup each of chopped fresh tarragon and chervil leaves in an enameled or stainless-steel saucepan. Boil until about 2 tablespoons [30 ml.] of syrupy liquid remain. Strain the reduction, discarding the solids, let it cool and return it to the saucepan. Gradually whisk in three egg yolks. Place the pan in a water bath and whisk the mixture until it thickens slightly. Whisk in ½ pound [¼ kg.] of butter or 1 cup [¼ liter] of oil. Thin with water or lemon juice, if necessary. Stir in 1 teaspoon [5 ml.] each of finely chopped tarragon and chervil. This sauce is served with grilled meats. Yield: about 1½ cups [375 ml.].

*Choron (Tomato-flavored hollandaise).* Prepare 1½ cups [375 ml.] of béarnaise sauce; if you prefer, omit the final addition of chopped tarragon and chervil. Stir in 2 tablespoons [30 ml.] of tomato purée *(recipe, page 159)*. This sauce is served with poached or grilled fish. Yield: about 1½ cups.

*Foyot (Hollandaise with meat glaze).* Make 1½ cups [375 ml.] of béarnaise sauce. Whisk in 2 tablespoons [30 ml.] of melted meat glaze *(recipe, page 160)*. This sauce, which is also known as *valois,* is usually served with grilled beef. Yield: about 1½ cups.

*Paloise (Mint-flavored hollandaise).* Make 1½ cups [375 ml.] of béarnaise sauce, using mint in place of the tarragon.

This sauce is served with grilled or roasted meats. Yield: about 1½ cups.

*Maltaise (Orange-flavored hollandaise).* Make 1½ cups [375 ml.] of hollandaise sauce. Instead of the final addition of lemon juice, whisk in ⅓ cup [75 ml.] juice of blood oranges. If blood oranges are not available, regular oranges may be used. The sauce will have the same flavor but the color will be less intense. This sauce is served with vegetables, especially asparagus. Yield: about 1¾ cups [425 ml.].

*Noisette (Brown-butter-flavored hollandaise).* Make 1½ cups [375 ml.] of hollandaise sauce. Heat 4 tablespoons [60 ml.] of butter until it foams. As it begins to turn brown, it will give off a characteristic hazelnut odor; remove it from the heat. Let the melted butter stand for a while to allow the solids to settle before pouring it into a sieve that is lined with dampened cheesecloth or muslin and set over a bowl. Discard any solids that cling to the dampened cloth. Stir the strained clarified butter into the hollandaise sauce. This sauce is usually served with boiled fish, especially salmon and trout. Yield: about 1½ cups.

# Mock Hollandaise Sauce
## Sauce Bâtarde

*To make about 2 cups [½ liter]*

| 2 | egg yolks | 2 |
|---|---|---|
| 1 tbsp. | cold water or heavy cream | 15 ml. |
| 16 tbsp. | butter, 12 tbsp. [180 ml.] cut into small pieces | 240 ml. |
| 3 tbsp. | flour | 45 ml. |
| 2 cups | warm water, lightly salted | ½ liter |
| 1 tbsp. | strained fresh lemon juice | 15 ml. |
| | salt and pepper | |

In a bowl, beat the egg yolks with the cold water until they are smooth. Set the egg yolks aside.

Over low heat, melt 4 tablespoons [60 ml.] of the butter in a heavy saucepan, add the flour, and stir the mixture with a whisk until it begins to bubble. Whisk in the lightly salted warm water and whisk the mixture rapidly until it boils. Remove the mixture from the heat, let it cool for at least one minute, then gradually whisk in the beaten egg yolks. Return the pan to low heat and whisk until the sauce thickens slightly. Do not let it boil.

Remove the pan from the heat and whisk in the lemon juice. Add the butter pieces—a handful at a time—whisking steadily until the butter has been amalgamated. Adjust the seasoning and serve the sauce immediately.

*Câpres (Caper sauce).* Make 2 cups [½ liter] of mock hollandaise. Stir in 2 tablespoons [30 ml.] of rinsed capers. This sauce is usually served with poached fish.

## Savory Sabayon Sauce

*To make about 1 ¼ cups [300 ml.]*

| 1 ¼ cups | fish stock (recipe, page 164) | 300 ml. |
|---|---|---|
| 3 | egg yolks | 3 |
| 12 to 16 tbsp. | cold butter, cut into small cubes | 180 to 240 ml. |

In a small saucepan, boil the fish stock until it has been reduced to about ⅓ cup [75 ml.]. Let it cool, then add the egg yolks. Place the pan in a larger one set over low heat and partly filled with water that is very hot but not simmering; the smaller pan's bottom should not touch the water. Whisk the egg yolks and the stock together and continue whisking them until the mixture is thick—about 10 minutes. Then whisk in the butter cubes, a handful at a time, making sure that each addition is completely incorporated into the sauce before the next is added. When enough butter has been incorporated to make a thick, foamy sauce, transfer the sauce to a warmed sauceboat and serve it.

## Sugar Syrup

The amounts given below produce a light sugar syrup that is a suitable poaching medium for fruit.

*To make about 5 cups [1 ¼ liters]*

| 2 cups | sugar | ½ liter |
|---|---|---|
| 4 cups | water | 1 liter |

Place the sugar and water in a saucepan and set the pan over medium heat. Stir gently until the sugar has dissolved. Brush down the sides of the pan from time to time with a pastry brush dipped in water to dissolve any sugar crystals that may have stuck to the sides. When the sugar has dissolved, stop stirring and increase the heat to bring the syrup to a boil. Boil rapidly for a minute or two.

*Caramel sauce.* Reduce the quantity of water to 1 cup [¼ liter] and—when the sauce has come to a boil—cook it rapidly until all of the water has evaporated and the sauce turns a rich amber color. As soon as this happens, place the pan in a bowl of water and ice to keep the sauce from burning.

## Custard Sauce

*To make about 3 cups [¾ liter]*

| 6 | egg yolks | 6 |
|---|---|---|
| ¼ to ½ cup | superfine sugar | 50 to 125 ml. |
| 3 cups | milk, scalded | ¾ liter |

In a bowl, beat the egg yolks and sugar together with a whisk until the mixture turns pale and forms a ribbon when dribbled on the surface—about 10 minutes. Gradually add the hot milk, stirring all the time.

Transfer the mixture to a heavy saucepan. Cook the custard over very low heat, stirring it constantly with a wooden spoon in a figure-8 motion. Do not let the custard boil. When the custard is thick enough to coat the back of the spoon, remove the pan from the heat; arrest the cooking by standing the pan briefly in a bowl of ice cubes. Stir the custard gently so that a skin does not form on the surface.

To serve the sauce warm, strain it into a warmed serving bowl or sauceboat. To serve the sauce cold, keep the pan on ice—stirring the custard occasionally—until it is chilled; cover the sauce and refrigerate it.

*Caramel custard.* Whisk ⅓ cup [75 ml.] of caramel sauce *(recipe, left)* into the prepared hot custard before serving it.

## Sweet Sabayon Sauce

For a lighter sauce, beat an egg white until it is stiff and fold it into the prepared sabayon while the sauce is hot. Or cool the sauce and fold in 1 cup [¼ liter] of heavy cream that has been whipped. If a simple dry white wine is used for the sauce, a little grated lemon peel or vanilla extract may be added. If a fine wine is used, no other flavoring is needed.

*To make about 2 ½ cups [625 ml.]*

| 1 cup | superfine sugar | ¼ liter |
|---|---|---|
| 6 | egg yolks | 6 |
| 1 cup | dry white wine, Sauternes, Champagne, Marsala or sherry | ¼ liter |

Pour the sugar into a large, heavy saucepan and add the egg yolks. Place the pan in a larger pan of water heated to just below the simmering point; the smaller pan's bottom should not touch the water. Whisk the egg yolks and sugar together until the sugar has completely dissolved and the mixture is pale and creamy. Add the wine, whisking it all the time. The mixture will slowly froth up into an abundant mousse, doubling its volume after about five minutes. Continue to whisk for another five to 10 minutes, or until the sauce is very light and foamy. It is now ready to be served hot. To serve the sauce cold, set the pan in a bowl of ice cubes and continue to whisk the sauce until it is sufficiently chilled.

## Chocolate Cream Sauce

*To make about 2 cups [½ liter]*

| 8 oz. | semisweet chocolate, broken into small pieces | ¼ kg. |
|---|---|---|
| 1 cup | heavy cream | ¼ liter |

Combine the chocolate and the cream in a heavy saucepan and set the pan over medium heat. Stirring constantly, cook until the mixture begins to boil. Remove the pan from the heat and serve the sauce immediately.

# Recipe Index

*All recipes in the index that follows are listed by their English titles except in cases where a food of foreign origin, such as aioli, is universally recognized by its source name. Foreign recipes are listed by country or region of origin. Recipe credits are on pages 174-176.*

# General Index/ Glossary

Included in this index to the cooking demonstrations are definitions, in italics, of special culinary terms not explained elsewhere in this volume. The Recipe index begins on page 168.

# Recipe Credits

The sources for the recipes in this volume are shown below. Page references in parentheses indicate where the recipes appear in the anthology.

**Agulló, Ferran,** Llibre de la Cuina Catalana. Published by Alta Fulla, Barcelona. Translated by permission of Alta Fulla(101, 104).
**Albert, B.,** Le Cuisinier Parisien. Published in Paris by Louis Tenré, Libraire, 1833(91, 122).
**Allen, Ida Bailey,** Best Loved Recipes of the American People. Copyright © 1973 by Ruth Allen Castelli. Published by Doubleday & Company, Inc. Reprinted by permission of Doubleday & Company, Inc.(92).
**Alperi, Magdalena,** Tratado Completo de Comidas y Bebidas. © Magdalena Alperi. First edition June 1977. Second edition December 1978. Translated by permission of the author, Gijon (Asturias)(94).
**Barberousse, Michel,** Cuisine Provençale. Published by Librairie de la Presse, Biarritz. Translated by permission of Librairie de la Presse(133, 138).
**Barthélemy, F.,** Les Menus Expliqués de Cuisine Pratique. Copyright by Le Cordon Bleu. Published by Bibliotheque du Journal "Le Cordon-Bleu," Paris. Translated by permission of Le Cordon Bleu(91, 93, 123).
**Beck, Simone,** New Menus from Simca's Cuisine. Copyright © 1979, 1978 by Simone Beck and Michael James. Published by Harcourt Brace Jovanovich, Inc. Reprinted by permission of Harcourt Brace Jovanovich, Inc.(146).
**Beckwith, Lady Muriel,** Sauces, Sweet and Savoury—How to Make Them. Copyright Lady Muriel Beckwith. Published by Herbert Jenkins Limited, London, 1953. By permission of The Hutchinson Publishing Group, London(113, 153).
**Bertholle, Louisette,** La Cuisine des Saisons. © Opera Mundi, Paris, 1980. Copublished by Albin Michel—Opera Mundi, Paris. Translated by permission of Éditions Albin Michel(131).
**Boni, Ada,** Italian Regional Cooking. Copyright © 1969 by Thomas Nelson & Sons, Ltd. and E. P. Dutton & Co., Inc. Published by Bonanza Books, a division of Crown Publishers, Inc. Reprinted by permission of Crown Publishers, Inc.(102).
**Bontou, Aloïde,** Traité de Cuisine Bourgeoise Bordelaise. Third edition. Published by Féret et Fils, Éditeurs, Bordeaux 1910. Translated by permission of Éditions Féret et Fils(123, 124, 126).
**Böttiger, Theodor,** Schalen und Krustentiere. © 1972 by Wilhelm Heyne Verlag, München. Published by Wilhelm Heyne Verlag. Translated by permission of Wilhelm Heyne Verlag(117, 128).

**Bouillard, Paul,** La Gourmandise à Bon Marché. © 1925 by Albin Michel. Published by Éditions Albin Michel, Paris. Translated by permission of Éditions Albin Michel(94, 97, 131, 138).
**Bradley, Richard,** The Country Housewife and Lady's Director (Parts 1 and 2). Published in 1727 and 1732 respectively. © Prospect Books 1980. Published by Prospect Books, London. By permission of the publisher(95).
**Brazier, Eugenie,** Les Secrets de la Mère Brazier. © Solar, 1977. Published by Solar, Paris. Translated by permission of Solar(89, 96, 112, 116).
**Brennan, Jennifer,** Thai Cooking. © Jennifer Brennan 1981. Originally published as The Original Thai Cookbook by Richard Marek Publishers, New York. First published by Jill Norman & Hobhouse Ltd., London 1981. By permission of Jill Norman & Hobhouse Ltd.(93).
**Brown, Cora, Rose and Bob,** Soups, Sauces and Gravies. Copyright 1939 by Cora, Rose and Robert Carlton Brown. Published by J. B. Lippincott Company. Reprinted by permission of Harper & Row, Publishers, Inc.(99, 149).
**Brown, Dorothy** (Editor), Symposium Fare. © Prospect Books 1981. Published by Prospect Books, London. By permission of the publisher(145).
**Brown, Helen,** Helen Brown's West Coast Cook Book. Copyright 1952, by Helen Evans Brown. Published by Little, Brown and Company, Boston. By permission of Little, Brown and Company(89, 90).
**Brunetti, Gino,** Cucina Mantovana di Principi e di Popolo. Published by the Istituto Carlo d'Arco per la Storia di Mantova, Mantova. Translated by permission of Don Costante Berselli, Mantova(99, 102).
**Butel, Jane,** Chili Madness. Copyright © 1980 by Jane Butel. Published by the Workman Publishing Company, Inc. Reprinted by permission of the Workman Publishing Company, New York(141).
**Calera, Ana Maria,** Cocina Andaluza. © Ana Maria Calera. © Editorial Everest S.A., León-España. Published by Editorial Everest, S.A. Translated by permission of Editorial Everest S.A.(97, 101). 365 Recetas de Cocina Vasca. © Ana Maria Calera. © Editorial Everest, S.A., León-España. Published by Editorial Everest, S.A. Translated by permission of Editorial Everest S.A.(117).
**Cardona, Maria Dolores Camps,** Cocina Catalana. © Editorial Ramos Majos, 1979. Published by Editorial Ramos Majos, Barcelona. Translated by permission of Editorial Ramos Majos S.A.(100).
**Carlton, Jan McBride,** The Old-Fashioned Cookbook. Copyright © 1975 by Jan McBride Carlton. Published by Weathervane Books. Reprinted by permission of Holt, Rinehart and Winston, Publishers(134, 138, 154).
**Carter, Susannah,** The Frugal Colonial Housewife. © 1976 by Jean McKibbin. Published by Dolphin Books, an imprint of Doubleday & Company, Inc., New York. By permission of Doubleday & Company, Inc.(94, 110, 119).
**Catlin, Joan and Joy Law** (Editors), Royal College of Art Cook Book. © 1980 Royal College of Art. Published by

the Royal College of Art, London. By permission of the Royal College of Art(106).
**Ciurana, Jaume and Llorenç Torrado,** Els Olis de Catalunya i la Seva Cuina. © Jaume Ciurana i Calceran per la primera part. Published by Servei Central de Publicacions de la Generalitat, Departament de la Presidència Barcelona 1981. Translated by permission of Jaume Ciurana, Barcelona(107).
**Cocina Regional Española.** Published by Editorial Almena, Madrid 1963. Translated by permission of Editorial Doncel, Madrid(148).
**Contour, Alfred,** Le Cuisinier Bourguignon. Published by Laffitte Reprints, Marseille, 1978. Translated by permission of Éditions Jeanne Laffitte(154, 156).
**Craig, Elizabeth,** Court Favourites. First published 1953 by André Deutsch Limited, London. By permission of André Deutsch Limited(130).
**Il Cuciniere All'Uso Moderne.** Published by Presso Guglielmo Piatti, Firenze, 1825(115).
**La Cuisine Lyonnaise.** Published by Éditions Gutenberg, Lyon, 1947(132).
**La Cuisine Naturelle à l'Huile d'Olive.** © 1978 Éditions De Vecchi S.A., Paris. Published by Éditions De Vecchi S.A., Paris. Translated by permission of Éditions De Vecchi S.A.(135).
**Cùnsolo, Felice,** La Cucina del Piemonte. © by Novedit Milano. Published by Novedit Milano, 1964(129).
**Cutler, Carol,** Haute Cuisine for Your Heart's Delight. Copyright © 1973 by Carol Cutler. Published by Clarkson N. Potter, Inc. Reprinted by permission of Clarkson N. Potter, Inc.(98). The Six-Minute Soufflé and Other Culinary Delights. Copyright © Carol Cutler. Published by Clarkson N. Potter, Inc. Reprinted by permission of Clarkson N. Potter Inc.(88). The Woman's Day Low-Calorie Dessert Cookbook. Copyright © 1980 by CBS Consumer Publications, a Division of CBS, Inc. Published by Houghton Mifflin Company. Reprinted by permission of Houghton Mifflin Company(155).
**Daguin, André,** Le Nouveau Cuisinier Gascon. © 1981, Éditions Stock. Published by Éditions Stock, Paris. Translated by permission of Éditions Stock(104, 114, 124, 135).
**Davidis, Henriette,** Praktisches Kochbuch. Newly revised by Luise Holle. Published in Bielefeld and Leipzig, 1898(152).
**Davidson, Alan,** North Atlantic Seafood. Copyright © 1979 by Alan Davidson. Published by The Viking Press. Reprinted by permission of Viking Penguin Inc.(138).
**de Bourbon, Louis Auguste,** Le Cuisinier Gascon. Published by Les Amis du Tricastin. Reprinted by Éditions Daniel Morcrette, Luzarches, 1976. Translated by permission of Éditions Daniel Morcrette(105, 118, 125).
**de Croze, Austin,** Les Plats Régionaux de France. Published by Éditions Daniel Morcrette, Luzarches, France. Translated by permission of Éditions Daniel Morcrette(96, 122).
**Dege, Hroar,** Fra Neptuns Gaffel. Published by

H. Aschehoug & Co., Oslo, 1966. Translated by permission of H. Aschehoug & Co. (W. Nygaard) A/S.(148).

**de Gouy, Louis P.,** *The Gold Cook Book.* © 1947, 1948, by Louis P. de Gouy. Published by Greenberg Publisher, New York. By permission of Chilton Book Company, Rador, Pennsylvania(152).

**de Lazarque, E. Auricoste,** *Cuisine Messine.* Published by Sidot Frères, Libraires-Éditeurs, Nancy, 1927(137).

**de Pomiane, Édouard,** *Le Code de la Bonne Chère.* © Albin Michel, Paris. Published by Éditions Albin Michel, 1948. Translated by permission of Éditions Albin Michel(109, 136).

**Dickson, Paul,** *The Great American Ice Cream Book.* Copyright © 1972 by Paul Dickson. Published by Atheneum, New York. Reprinted by permission of Atheneum Publishers(154).

**Dinnage, Paul,** *The Book of Fruit and Fruit Cookery.* © 1981 Paul Dinnage. Published by Sidgwick and Jackson Limited, London, 1981. By permission of Sidgwick and Jackson Ltd.(105, 106, 108).

**Dubois, Urbain and Émile Bernard,** *La Cuisine Classique.* Volume 1, ninth edition, 1881. Published by E. Dentu, Éditeur, Palais-Royal, Paris(91, 126, 130). *La Cuisine Classique.* Volume 2, 10th edition, 1882. Published by E. Dentu, Éditeur, Palais-Royal, Paris(156).

**Dumas, Alexandre,** *Le Grand Dictionnaire de Cuisine.* Published by Henri Veyrier, Paris, 1973. Translated by permission of Éditions Henri Veyrier(122, 136).

**Dumont, Émile,** *La Bonne Cuisine Française.* Originally published in 1873. Thirtieth edition published by Victorion Frères et Cie, Éditeurs, Paris 1889(91).

**Enciclopedia Salvat De La Cocina: Tomo 8.** © 1972. Salvat, S.A. de Ediciones, Pamplona, y S.A., Femmes d'Aujourd'hui—Ediper, S.A. Published by Salvat S.A. de Ediciones. Translated by permission of Salvat Editores S.A., Barcelona(131).

**Ets-Hokin, Judith,** *The San Francisco Dinner Party Cookbook.* Copyright © 1975, 1982 by Judith Ets-Hokin. Published by Celestial Arts, Millbrae, Calif. Reprinted by permission of the publisher(139, 140).

**Favre, Joseph,** *Dictionnaire Universel de Cuisine Pratique.* Published by Laffitte Reprints, Marseille, 1978. Translated by permission of Éditions Jeanne Laffitte, Marseille(101, 105, 152, 154).

**Ferrandini, Armido,** *Onestà in Cucina.* © 1976 Vallecchi Editore Firenze. Published by Vallecchi Editore. Translated by permission of Vallecchi Editore(102, 132).

**Feslikenian, Franca,** *Cucina e Vini del Lazio.* © 1973 Ugo Mursia Editore, Milan. Published by Ugo Mursia Editore, Milan. Translated by permission of Ugo Mursia Editore, Milan(98).

**Foods of the World,** *Middle Eastern Cooking.* Copyright © 1969 Time Inc. Published by Time-Life Books, Alexandria(103).

**Francatelli, Charles Elmé,** *The Modern Cook.* Published by Richard Bentley, London 1862(110, 122, 127).

**Franey, Pierre,** *The New York Times 60-Minute Gourmet.* © 1979 by The New York Times Company. Published by Times Books, a division of Quadrangle/The New York Times Book Co. Inc., New York. By permission of Times Books, a division of Quadrangle/The New York Times Book Co. Inc.(144).

**Frank, Dorothy C.,** *The Peanut Cookbook.* Copyright © 1976 by Dorothy C. Frank. Published by Clarkson N. Potter, Inc. Reprinted by permission of Clarkson N. Potter, Inc.(154).

**Grigson, Jane,** *Jane Grigson's Vegetable Book.* Copyright © 1978 by Jane Grigson. Published by Atheneum, New York. Reprinted by permission of Atheneum Publishers and David Higham Associates Ltd.(95, 109, 112).

**Guasch, Juan Castelló,** *¡Bon Profit! (El Libro de la Cocina Ibicenca).* Published by the author. Published by Imprenta ALFA, Palma de Mallorca, 1971. Translated by permission of the author(88).

**Holleman, Ria,** *Uit Grootmoeders Keuken.* © 1972 Unieboek n. v. Bussum—Holland. Published by Van Dishoeck, Bussum. Translated by permission of Unieboek B.V.(92, 97, 126, 129).

**Horvath, Maria,** *Balkan-Küche.* © 1963 Wilhelm Heyne

Verlag, München. Published by Wilhelm Heyne Verlag. Translated by permission of Wilhelm Heyne Verlag(121).

**Ignotus,** *Culina Famulatrix Medicinae: or, Receipts in Cookery.* Published in York in 1804(110, 134).

**Kennedy, Diana,** *The Cuisines of Mexico.* Copyright © 1972 by Diana Kennedy. Published by Harper & Row, Publishers, Inc. Reprinted by permission of Harper & Row, Publishers, Inc.(100).

**Kernmayr, Hans Gustl,** *So Kochte meine Mutter.* © 1976 by Mary Hahns Kochbuchverlag, Berlin-München. Published by Wilhelm Heyne Verlag, Munich. Translated by permission of Mary Hahns Kochbuchverlag, München(88, 105, 106, 140).

**Kitchiner, Dr.,** *The Cook's Oracle.* Published by A. Constable & Co., Edinburgh, 1822(93, 96, 98, 136).

**Kramarz, Inge,** *The Balkan Cookbook.* © 1972 by Crown Publishers, Inc. Published by Crown Publishers, Inc., New York. By permission of Crown Publishers, Inc.(89, 121, 126).

**Labarre, Irène,** *La Cuisine des Trois B.* © Éditions Solar, 1976. Published by Solar, Paris. Translated by permission of Solar(136).

**Lassalle, George,** *The Adventurous Fish Cook.* © Caroline Lassalle 1976. Published by Macmillan London Limited, London and Basingstoke in association with Pan Books Limited. By permission of Macmillan Accounts and Administration Ltd.(133).

**Lenôtre, Gaston,** *Lenôtre's Ice Creams and Candies.* © Copyright 1979, Barron's Educational Series, Inc., solely with respect to the English language edition. Reprinted by permission of Barron's Educational Series, Inc.(153).

**Leyel, Mrs. C. F. and Olga Hartley,** *The Gentle Art of Cookery.* © The Executors of Mrs. C. F. Leyel, 1925. Published by Chatto and Windus, London. By permission of Chatto and Windus Ltd.(108, 111).

**Lujan, Nestor and Juan Perucho,** *El Libro de la Cocina Española.* © Ediciones Danae, S.A. 1970. Published by Ediciones Danae, S.A., Barcelona. Translated by permission of Editorial Baber, S.A., Barcelona(103).

**Marie, Annick,** *Le Grand Livre de la Cuisine Bourguignonne.* © Jean-Pierre Delarge, Éditions Universitaires, 1977. Published by Jean-Pierre Delarge, Éditeur, Paris. Translated by permission of Chantel Galtier Roussel, Literary Agent, Paris(155).

**Massey and Son's Comprehensive Pudding Book.** Published by Massey and Son's, London, 1865(151, 153, 156).

**Megnin, Paul,** *250 Manieres de Cuire et Accommoder Le Gibier.* © Albin Michel 1922. Published by Éditions Albin Michel, Paris. Translated by permission of Éditions Albin Michel(147).

**Menon,** *La Cuisinière Bourgeoise.* Paris, 1803(125).

**Minchelli, Jean and Paul,** *Crustacés, Poissons et Coquillages.* © 1977 Éditions Jean-Claude Lattès. Published by Éditions Jean-Claude Lattès. Translated by permission of Éditions Jean-Claude Lattès(90, 103, 129).

**Mosimann, Anton,** *Cuisine à la Carte.* © Anton Mosimann 1981. Published by Northwood Books, London. By permission of Northwood Books(117, 119, 155).

**Neuber, Wolf,** *Die K.u.k. Wiener Küche.* © 1975 by Verlag Fritz Molden, Wien-München, Zürich. Published by Wilhelm Goldmann Verlag. Translated by permission of Goldmann Verlag(128, 130).

**Neuner-Duttenhofer, Bernd.** *Die Neue Deutsche Küche.* © 1978 by Wilhelm Heyne Verlag, München. Published by Wilhelm Heyne Verlag, Munich. Translated by permission of Wilhelm Heyne Verlag(100, 115).

**Nignon, E.,** *Éloges de la Cuisine Française.* Copyright 1933 by H. Piazza, Paris. Published by L'Édition d'Art H. Piazza. Translated by permission of Éditions Daniel Morcrette, Luzarches, France(111, 121).

**Nilson, Bee** (Editor), *The WI Diamond Jubilee Cookbook.* © A. R. Nilson and National Federation of Women's Institutes 1975. Published by William Heinemann Ltd., London. By permission of William Heinemann Ltd.(88).

**Nolot, Pierre,** *À la Recherche des Cuisines Oubliées.* © Berger-Levrault, 1977. Published by Éditions Berger-Levrault, Paris. Translated by permission of Éditions Berger-Levrault(109).

**Norwak, Mary,** *The Farmhouse Kitchen.* © Mary Norwak, 1975. Published by Penguin Books Ltd., London. By permission of Penguin Books Ltd.(92).

**Oberosler, Giuseppe,** *Il Tesoretto della Cucina Italiana.* Published by Editore Ulrico Hoepli, Milano, 1948. Translated by permission of Ulrico Hoepli S.p.A.(111, 113, 114, 141).

**Ochorowicz-Monatowa, Marja,** *Polish Cookery.* (Translated and adapted by Jean Karsavina.) Copyright © 1958 by Crown Publishers, Inc. Published by Crown Publishers, Inc. By permission of Crown Publishers, Inc., New York(120, 125).

**Ojakangas, Beatrice A.,** *The Finnish Cookbook.* © 1964 by Beatrice A. Ojakangas. Published by Crown Publishers, Inc., New York. By permission of Crown Publishers, Inc.(89, 116, 128).

**Oliver, Michel,** *Mes Recettes à la Télé.* © Librairie Plon, 1980. Published by Librairie Plon, Paris. Translated by permission of Librairie Plon(90, 150).

**Olney, Richard,** *Simple French Food.* Copyright © 1974 by Richard Olney. Published by Atheneum, New York. Reprinted by permission of Atheneum Publishers(132). *The French Menu Cookbook* © 1975 by Richard Olney. Published by William Collins Sons & Co., Ltd., Glasgow and London. By permission of the author, Sollies-Pont(151).

**Ortiz, Elisabeth Lambert,** *The Complete Book of Mexican Cooking.* Copyright © 1967 by Elisabeth Lambert Ortiz. Published by M. Evans and Co., Inc., New York, N.Y. 10017. Reprinted by permission of the publisher(96, 99).

**Patil, Vimla** (Editor), *Kashmir to Kanyakumari.* Published by Rekha Sapru for Enar Advertisers Pvt Ltd., Bombay. By permission of Enar Advertisers Pvt Ltd.(142, 145).

**Philpot, Rosl,** *Viennese Cookery.* © 1965 by Rosl Philpot. Published by Hodder and Stoughton Limited, London. By permission of Hodder and Stoughton Limited(108, 128, 130).

**Platt, June,** *June Platt's New England Cook Book.* © 1971 by June Platt. Published by Atheneum Publishers, Inc., New York. By permission of Atheneum Publishers, Inc.(153).

**Puck, Wolfgang,** *Wolfgang Puck's Modern French Cooking for the American Kitchen.* © 1981 by Wolfgang Puck. Published by Houghton Mifflin Company, Boston. By permission of Houghton Mifflin Company(118).

**Quillet, Aristide,** *La Cuisine Moderne.* Published by Librairie Aristide Quillet, Paris, 1930. Translated by permission of Librairie Aristide Quillet S.A.(115).

**Ramella, Lucetto,** *Ricette Tradizionali Della Liguria.* Published by Collana Tradizioni Liguri, A. Dominici Editore, Oneglia, 1978. Translated by permission of the author, Imperia(141).

**Ratto, G. B.,** *La Cuciniera Genovese.* Published by Tipografia Pagano, Genova. Translated by permission of Industrie Grafiche Editoriali Fratelli Pagano S.p.A.(95, 100, 107, 108).

**Rey-Billeton, Lucette,** *Les Bonnes Recettes du Soleil.* © Éditions Aubanel 1980. Published by Éditions Aubanel, Avignon. Translated by permission of Éditions Aubanel(101, 104, 139).

**Richter, Louise and Sophie Charlotte Hommer,** *Illustrirtes Hamburger Kochbuch.* Published by B.S. Berendsohn, Hamburg, 1879(155).

**Roden, Claudia,** *Picnic: The Complete Guide to Outdoor Food.* © Claudia Roden, 1981. Published by Jill Norman & Hobhouse Ltd., London. By permission of the publisher(89, 108).

**Romagnoli, Margaret and G. Franco,** *The New Italian Cooking.* Copyright © 1980 by Margaret and G. Franco Romagnoli. Reprinted by permission of Little, Brown and Company in association with the Atlantic Monthly Press(90).

**Rundell, Mrs.,** *Modern Domestic Cookery.* Published by Milner and Company, Limited, London, 1837(92, 113, 134).

**Sahni, Julie,** *Classic Indian Cooking.* Text copyright © 1980 by Julie Sahni. Published by William Morrow & Company, Inc. Reprinted by permission of William Morrow & Company, Inc.(142, 144).

**Sastre Rayó, Gabriel and Antonia Ordinas Mari** (Editors), *Llibre de Cuina de Ca'n Cames Seques. (Cocina*

*Mallorquina de Siempre)*. Published by Antigua Imprenta Soler, Palma de Mallorca, 1977. Translated by permission of Antonia Ordinas Marí, Mallorca(127).
**Schlosser, Frau Rath,** *Urgrossmutters Kochbuch.* © Insel Verlag Frankfurt am Main, 1980. Published by Insel Verlag, Frankfurt am Main. Translated by permission of Insel Verlag(120, 129, 130).
**Senderens, Alain and Eventhia,** *La Cuisine Réussie.* © 1981, Éditions Jean-Claude Lattès, Paris. Translated by permission of Éditions Jean-Claude Lattès(137, 143, 147, 148).
**Stamm, Sara B. B. and the Lady Editors of Yankee Magazine,** *Favorite New England Recipes.* Copyright © 1972 by Sara B. B. Stamm and Yankee, Inc. Published by Yankee, Inc., Dublin, New Hampshire. Reprinted by permission of Sara B. B. Stamm(111,

140—Muriel Arbeton).
**Stan, Anisoara,** *The Romanian Cook Book.* Copyright 1951 by Anisoara Stan. Published by The Citadel Press, New York. By permission of Lyle Stuart Inc., New Jersey(120, 135).
**Suzanne, Alfred,** *A Book of Salads.* Published by Ward, Lock & Co., Limited, London and Melbourne(106).
**Theoharous, Anne,** *Cooking and Baking the Greek Way.* Copyright © 1977 by Anne Theoharous. Published by Holt, Rinehart and Winston, Publishers. Reprinted by Holt, Rinehart and Winston, Publishers(104, 107).
**Troisgros, Jean and Pierre,** *The Nouvelle Cuisine of Jean & Pierre Troisgros.* Translation copyright © 1978 by William Morrow & Company, Inc. Originally published in French, under the title *Cuisiniers à Roanne.* Copyright © 1977 by Éditions Robert Laffont, S.A. Reprinted by permis-

sion of William Morrow & Company, Inc.(112, 133).
**Viard and Fouret,** *Le Cuisinier Royal.* Published in Paris, 1828(118, 123, 124, 134).
**Watt, Alexander,** *Paris Bistro Cookery.* Published by Macgibbon & Kee, London, 1957. By permission of Granada Publishing Ltd., St. Albans(149, 150).
**White, Patricia Holden,** *Food as Presents.* © 1975, 1982 by Patricia Holden White. Published by Penguin Books Ltd., London. By permission of Deborah Rogers Ltd Literary Agency, London(151).
**Woman's Auxiliary of Olivet Episcopal Church,** *Virginia Cookery—Past and Present.* Copyright 1957 by the Woman's Auxiliary of Olivet Episcopal Church, Franconia, Virginia. Published by the Woman's Auxiliary of Olivet Episcopal Church. Reprinted by permission of the publisher(153).

## Acknowledgments

The indexes for this book were prepared by Karla J. Knight. The editors are particularly indebted to Gail Duff, Kent, England, and Ann O'Sullivan, Majorca, Spain.

The editors also wish to thank: Danielle Adkinson, London; Alison Attenborough, Essex, England; Josephine Bacon, Los Angeles; Markie Benet, London; Beverly Bernstein, London; Paul Bifulco, Bifulco's Stores, Ltd., London; Nicola Blount, London; Robert Bruce, London; Helen Duprey Bullock, Washington, D.C.; Josephine Christian, Somerset, England; Lesley Coates, Essex, England; Emma Codrington, Surrey, England; Mimi Errington, Nottinghamshire, England; Sarah Jane Evans, London; Jay Ferguson, London; Dr. George J. Flick, Department of Food Science and Technology, Virginia Polytechnic Institute and State University, Blacksburg; Neyla Freeman, London; Dr. Robert Gibbs, Division of Fishes, National Museum of Natural History, Smithsonian Institution, Washington, D.C.; Maggi Heinz, London; Hilary Hockman, London; Lotte Keeble, Middlesex, England; Pippa Millard, London; Wendy Morris, London; Dilys Naylor, Surrey, England; Rosemary Oates, London; Winona O'Connor, Essex, England; Neil Philip, Oxford, England; Sylvia Robertson, Surrey, England; Vicky Robinson, London; Adrian Saunders, London; Nicole Segre, London; Stephanie Thompson, London; Derek Walker, Port City Seafood, Alexandria, Virginia; Tina Walker, London; Rita Walters, Essex, England.

## Picture Credits

*The sources for the pictures in this book are listed below. Credits for each of the photographers and illustrators are listed by page number in sequence with successive pages indicated by hyphens; where necessary, the locations of pictures within pages are also indicated—separated from page numbers by dashes.*

Photographs by Tom Belshaw: cover, 4, 7, 8—bottom, 9—bottom, 10—except top, 11-12, 23—bottom, 25—top left, 41—bottom, 44-57, 60, 61—except bottom right, 70—bottom, 71—bottom right, 76-77—bottom, 79-81, 82-83—bottom.
Other photographs (alphabetically): John Cook, 9—top and center right, 18—bottom, 28, 32-33, 36-37—top, 38-39—bottom, 40—top, 41—top right, 68-69—top, 82-83—top, 86. Alan Duns, 9—top center and center left, 13, 20—top, 21, 22—bottom, 27—bottom, 39—top right, 41—top left and center, 58, 62, 63—bottom, 65—bottom, 66-67. John Elliott, 26—bottom left and center. Louis Klein, 2. Bob Komar, 8—top and center, 9—top left and center middle, 14-17, 18-19—top, 20—bottom, 22-23—top, 24, 25—except top left, 26-27—top, 30-31, 34-35, 36-37—bottom, 38—top, 39—top left and center, 40—bottom, 42-43—bottom, 63—top, 64, 65—top, 68-69—bottom, 70—top, 71—except bottom right, 72-75, 76-77—top, 84-85. Aldo Tutino, 10—top, 19—bottom, 26—bottom right, 42-43—top, 61—bottom right, 78.
Illustrations: Anna Pugh, 6. From the Mary Evans Picture Library and private sources and *Food & Drink: A Pictorial Archive from Nineteenth Century Sources* by Jim Harter, published by Dover Publications, Inc., 1979, 90-166.

*Library of Congress Cataloguing in Publication Data*
Main entry under title:
Sauces.
  (The Good cook, techniques & recipes)
  Includes index.
  1. Sauces. I. Time-Life Books. II. Series.
TX819.A1S28    1983    641.8'14         82-19701
ISBN 0-8094-2972-1 (lib. bdg.)
ISBN 0-8094-2971-3 (retail ed.)